W9-AOD-041

Faulkner and the Southern Renaissance
Faulkner and Yoknapatawpha
1981

WITHDRAWN

WITHDRAWN

PS
3511
.A86
Z7832113
1981

Faulkner and the Southern Renaissance

FAULKNER AND YOKNAPATAWPHA, 1981

EDITED BY
DOREEN FOWLER
AND
ANN J. ABADIE

UNIVERSITY PRESS OF MISSISSIPPI

JACKSON

Salem Academy and College
Gramley Library
Winston-Salem, N.C. 27108

Copyright © 1982 by the University Press of Mississippi
All Rights Reserved
Manufactured in the United States of America

*This volume is sponsored by
the University of Mississippi*

Library of Congress Cataloging in Publication Data

Faulkner and Yoknapatawpha Conference (8th : 1981 :
   University of Mississippi.
   Faulkner and the Southern Renaissance.

   1. Faulkner, William, 1897–1962—Criticism and inter-
pretation—Congresses.   2. American literature—Southern
States—History and criticism—Congresses.   3. American
literature—20th century—History and criticism—
Congresses.   4. Southern States—Intellectual life—
Congresses.   I. Abadie, Ann J.   II. Fowler, Doreen.
III. Title.
PS3511.A86Z7832113   1981   813'.52   82-6982
ISBN 0-87805-163-5   AACR2
ISBN 0-87805-164-3 (pbk.)

Contents

Introduction

The history of the Southern Renaissance has not yet been written. At the 1981 annual Faulkner and Yoknapatawpha Conference, a group of invited speakers gathered at the University of Mississippi in Oxford to begin the process of formulating that history. Although the questions posed and the answers offered ranged widely, the central theme of the conference remained constant—What is the Southern Renaissance? Why did it happen? And what role did William Faulkner play in its inception?

Among those who contributed to this discussion were such established authorities on Southern literature as Cleanth Brooks, Louis Rubin, and Floyd Watkins, as well as a group of scholars whose recently published works have attracted much attention—Richard King, David Minter, and Patrick Samway. To provide greater diversity of thought, two Southern authors, Elizabeth Spencer and Alexander Blackburn, contributed reflections on the Southern Renaissance from the point of view of those who carry on the tradition of Southern letters. While two lecturers in particular, Louis Rubin and Richard King, defined and delineated the Southern Renaissance, the other speakers focused more specifically on Faulkner's relationship to this literary phenomenon.

Numerous and diverse impressions were voiced, but all agreed on a single working definition of the Renaissance in the South—the upsurge of Southern literature which began after the First World War and which has continued, possibly somewhat abated, to the present day. The historical and sociological causes of this literary flowering were perhaps most directly addressed by Louis Rubin. According to Rubin, who credits Allen Tate with having originally formulated this theory, the Southern

Renaissance was the result of a long overdue, head-on collision of cultures. In the 1920s the Southern states—rural, agricultural, religiously orthodox, and closely allied by a shared history and mythology—attempted to rejoin a modern, industrial nation. This reentry changed the face of the South and gave rise to a dislocated sensibility—a dislocation which was articulated by Southern writers. Rubin speculates further that the more frontier-like the Southern state the more violent the confrontation and the greater the likelihood of eliciting a literary response. Thus, Mississippi, that most "threadbare and quixotic of Southern states," produced not only a seemingly inordinately large share of Southern writers but also the giant of Southern literature—William Faulkner.

Why is the Southern Renaissance called a renaissance? The term "renaissance" means, of course, rebirth or reawakening. If the Southern Renaissance is a rebirth, when was the original birth? Richard King addresses these questions in his essay, "Framework of a Renaissance," and finds that the term "renaissance" is honorific; or, if it does refer to an earlier cultural movement, the reference is to modern western culture's "ur"-renaissance—the revival of interest in classical thought which spread through Europe during the fourteenth, fifteenth, and sixteenth centuries. In order to bring the Southern Renaissance into focus, King compares it to another renaissance—the flowering of letters and thought in New England which began in the 1830s. This comparative method reveals that the Southern Renaissance was somewhat limited—defining itself almost exclusively in terms of literature. King speculates that the impoverished state of the South accounts for the literary nature of the Renaissance, for, while the other arts require money, patronage, and a base to work from, literature is able to flourish in the absence of such support.

Two simultaneous literary events in the 1930s first gave notice to the nation that something important was happening in the

South. The two events are, of course, the advent on the literary scene of William Faulkner and the Fugitives. In his essay, "Faulkner and the Fugitive-Agrarians," Cleanth Brooks attempts to explore the relationship between these two manifestations of the new Southern literature. Brooks finds that, despite their physical and temporal proximity, Faulkner, for his part, seems to have taken little notice of the Agrarians, and the Agrarians, although well aware of Faulkner's presence, seem to have been uninfluenced by his work. Brooks attributes this absence of interaction to Faulkner's greatness—"Faulkner was too big to be attracted into anybody else's orbit." A "literary loner," Faulkner neither asked for nor needed advice.

If Faulkner did not mingle with the Fugitives, was he perhaps closely, or even not so closely, associated with any other Southern authors? In "The Hound Under the Wagon: Faulkner and the Southern Literati," Floyd Watkins looks to see what, if any, connections existed between Faulkner and the other Southern writers whose works, during the '20s, '30s, and '40s, were calling the attention of the nation to the South. In pursuing this subject, Watkins extends the perimeters of Brooks's findings. Just as Faulkner and the Fugitives seem to have flourished independently of one another, so also does Faulkner seem to have worked in isolation from the other exponents of the new Southern literature. According to Watkins, though Faulkner did form friendships, there were no "dialectic literary friendships"—no writers on whom Faulkner exerted a clear formative influence— no mutually fruitful literary interactions. Watkins concludes: "As a literary man, Faulkner stayed by himself"; by his own choice, Faulkner was "a writer without a circle."

Even though Faulkner and the other writers of the Southern Renaissance did not meet for literary talk, they did, however, share and expound a common body of values. Brooks, Watkins, Rubin, King, and Blackburn all agree that the works of Southern writers are informed by a fairly consistent code of beliefs and ideas. If sometimes isolated from one another, Southern writers are nevertheless of one mind. King describes this distinctively Southern cast of mind as religious, suspicious of abstraction, and firmly rooted in place and community. (On this subject of community, Louis Rubin writes that "it is virtually impossible to overstate the importance [to the Southern writer] of the relationship with the Southern community.") Southern writers know what defeat, poverty, and guilt are; they characteristically respect history and tradition, cherish individualism, and distrust industrialism, big government, and bureaucracy. Above all, they share a passionate, if critical, attachment to the South—its history, culture, and people; or, as Alexander Blackburn more poetically puts it, all Southern writers are inescapably marked by a "marrow-deep experience of land and blood."

In discussing the distinguishing characteristics of Southern literature, the speakers continually acknowledged the key importance of one element—an intense preoccupation with memory and history. Two scholars, David Minter and Richard King, taking widely divergent approaches, analyze this dimension of the Southern consciousness. While Minter closely examines how cultural memory operates in the fiction of one Southern writer, William Faulkner, King attempts to look at historical consciousness not as a regional or even as an American phenomenon but as an obsession of modern culture. According to King, the modern world lacks a compelling cultural tradition. Contemporary man lives "between times"—the old order has passed, but no new order of binding authority has emerged. There is, then, no tradition within which the self can find meaning. This, says King, is the crisis which Quentin Compson and Ike McCaslin face; it is also the crisis of every modern man. Minter's thoughts on this same subject are somewhat less dramatic, but also less despairing. According to Minter, the past in Faulkner's work is not a burden, but a legacy; Faulkner is not obsessed with history, only preoccupied with it; characters like

Introduction

Miss Rosa Coldfield are not trapped by tradition, rather they keep traditions alive. "The past is never dead," says Gavin Stevens in *Requiem for a Nun*. "It's not even past."

History and memory are also Elizabeth Spencer's subjects. Addressing a highly specialized area of history, her own past as it overlaps with William Faulkner's, Spencer recalls the attitude of Faulkner's fellow Southerners toward this genius who, during the golden years of the Southern Renaissance, scribbled away at their very doorstep. According to Spencer, like most prophets, Faulkner was not well received by his own people. There were, of course, exceptions, but, as a general rule, during the years of Faulkner's greatest achievement, Mississippians tended either to dismiss Faulkner or, worse, to regard him as a traitor who, for profit, had invaded the South's own private skeleton closet.

Like Spencer, Patrick Samway focuses specifically on the major figure of the Southern Renaissance—William Faulkner. In "Faulkner's Poetic Vision," Samway attempts to rescue Faulkner's early poetry from the dark recesses of critical neglect. Did Faulkner's poetry play a part in the Southern Renaissance? Although inclined to sentimentality and romantic extravagance, the poetry nevertheless seems to have anticipated and paved the way for Faulkner's greatest work; through his poems, Faulkner seems to have located his true subject—his own native soil; and, in the poetry, we find the same themes, although certainly pale renditions of them, which inform Faulkner's enduring masterpieces.

Is the Southern Renaissance over? This question is addressed briefly by Richard King and at length by Alexander Blackburn. While both men agree that the Southern Renaissance continues into the present, although in a new and altered form, King's view is somewhat less sanguine than Blackburn's. King's contention might be summed up this way: Although others have risen to take his place, we will not soon see Faulkner's like again. According to King, the growth stage of the Renaissance ended with the publication of Faulkner's last acknowledged master-piece—*Go Down, Moses*. Since that time the tradition which has engaged the imagination of Southern authors is not the memory of the Civil War or the Reconstruction, but, to quote Lewis Simpson, "the memory of a memory." In other words, contemporary Southern authors are inspired not by Sutpen or Sartoris but by William Faulkner himself. On this point, Blackburn differs. Blackburn sees change, but no diminution of power or possibility. According to Blackburn, the Southern literary tradition is still vigorous—as writers like Eudora Welty, William Styron, Reynolds Price, Walker Percy, Elizabeth Spencer, and a host of others attest. Such authors have not been, Blackburn argues, cowed by Faulkner's stature, nor have they "been lying down on the tracks waiting for the Dixie Special to come helling along." Holding up William Styron's *The Confessions of Nat Turner* and *Sophie's Choice* as Exhibits A and B, Blackburn makes a convincing case for a continuity in Southern letters that is in no way derivative, diluted, or redundant. The modern Southern author, Blackburn contends, is confronted by the same inheritance of guilt and loss that inspired his predecessors, but he makes of this confrontation a new and different fiction—as great writers have always done. The Southern Renaissance is not dead; it may, in fact, be only just beginning.

Doreen Fowler
University of Mississippi
Oxford, Mississippi

Faulkner and the Southern Renaissance
Faulkner and Yoknapatawpha
1981

Framework
of a
Renaissance

RICHARD H. KING

To name something is to claim it, to call it into existence. This is especially true when we study something historically, when we assemble disparate phenomena and give them coherence. One does not presumably write as a "modernist" or a "romantic." These are categories imposed by later interpreters. Was it the "War Between the States" or "The Civil War"? This dispute over naming was a fighting issue at one time. Did it matter that "Falkner" became "Faulkner"? Obviously it did for the writer in question, at least early in his career.

A consideration of the act of naming suggests that the matter of the "Southern Renaissance" is a tricky business. Since all thinking is metaphorical, we should be clear on the trope employed and the connotational range evoked by the term "renaissance." It means, of course, "rebirth." When, we might ask, was the initial birth? The answer is scarcely forthcoming. There was no earlier upsurge of literary achievement in the South. At best one might advert to the "Virginia Renaissance" of Jefferson, Madison, John Taylor, and, a bit later, Poe as did Vernon Parrington in his *Main Currents of American Thought* (1927). But the more likely source for the term derives from the rubric applied to the revival of interest in classical thought and literature in Italy which then spread throughout Europe. That was modern western culture's "Ur"-renaissance. Moreover, the term is an honorific one. Overall, historical labels generally originate as highly charged, value-laden terms. They are examples of intellectual public relations.

More to the point, "rebirth" is an organic metaphor which suggests a starting-over, creation and growth, but also, more soberly, decline and death. For, to be on the up and up metaphorically, we must allow that if there was a rebirth, then there was or will be decline and death. And there will also be a stage of maturity. But how do we recognize maturity? Who decides that there was a rebirth in the first place? What writers and writing are we talking about?—And who decides that?

If such questions sound vaguely conspiratorial, they shouldn't be taken as such. They do, however, force us to recognize that to name something a "renaissance" is an act located in and shaped by historical forces and one which intends certain effects transcending the intellectual or the aesthetic. All this is to say that we must think historically about the Southern Renaissance by first locating it in its historical context. And this implies that our naming this cluster of writers and intellectuals the "Southern Renaissance" must also be understood historically. We should concern ourselves with what Faulkner or Tate or Welty has written, but also with what has been made of their writings, how they have been located in a larger framework and related to one another, and how this in turn works back upon our perceptions of these writers and others of the same historical time and place. In sum, a rubric such as the "Southern Renaissance" does not settle matters, but raises questions. It is a problem, not a solution; a goad to thought, not a way of avoiding it.

What I would like to do now is address several areas of concern that bear on the topic of "Framework for Renaissance." First, I want to suggest some different ways of looking at the Southern Renaissance, putting it into a certain comparative per-

4

spective. Then I would like to trace the process by which the term "Southern Renaissance" became common currency and the way in which the standard canon of writers and writings was established. Finally, I would like to mention certain ways in which our view of the Renaissance, particularly its leading writer, William Faulkner, has changed over the years, what new areas of concern have emerged, and finally whether we can still talk of a Southern Renaissance at all.

CONTEXT AND COMPARISONS

All renaissances seem inexplicable, uncaused, abruptly surprising. They are Sutpens not Sartorises: ruthless, peremptory, heedless of the past and reckless of the future. This is particularly true of a certain type of modern cultural awakening, of which the Russian, the Irish, and the Southern cases are prime examples. They are what might be called regional renaissances.[1] Their context of occurrence is generally one in which the region is making the difficult transition from traditional to modern forms of life: that is, they are the cultural expression of and reaction to modernization. It was of course Allen Tate who most clearly identified this particular sort of historical juncture as crucial in explaining the origin of the Southern Renaissance when he spoke of the South's facing in two directions as janus-faced.

What are the general characteristics of such cultural movements? First, they are usually elite phenomena rather than deeply rooted or widely resonant social movements. Within the regional elite, there is typically a crucial division between the

---

1. In "Faulkner and the Avant-Garde," *Faulkner, Modernism, and Film*, ed. Evans Harrington and Ann J. Abadie (Jackson: University Press of Mississippi, 1980), Hugh Kenner suggests that the English language has divided into three regional literatures—English, American, and Irish—and one international one (193). I have taken this notion of a "regional" literature and applied it to cultural awakenings which I call "regional."

party of the future and the party of the past, between cosmopolitans and nativists. In nineteenth-century Russia there was such an intellectual face-off between westerners, who looked to modern Europe for salvation, and the slavophils. They saw traditional Russia as the source of national rejuvenation and felt that Russia would be selling its soul if it imitated European modes of thought and action. Many figures of the Irish Renaissance were deeply concerned with the revival of Gaelic language and literature, while others looked to London and the modern spirit for their cues. In the South such a debate was carried on between the Vanderbilt Agrarians and the Chapel Hill Regionalists. There was no peculiarly Southern idiom to revive, but there was allegedly a style of life and set of values connected with the antebellum ethos which deserved preservation in the face of modern trends; or at least the older values should serve as a kind of measuring rod against which the inadequacies of the modern world could be more clearly seen.

In addition, these regional renaissances have been primarily, or at least most successfully, literary movements. I have objected elsewhere to the almost exclusively literary focus of students of the Southern Renaissance. But there is no gainsaying the fact that it was most obviously a literary flowering. As far as I know, Ireland offers us few thinkers of any consequence outside its literary culture. Russia, however, presents a harder case since, besides the literary achievements of Turgenev, Gogol, Tolstoy, Dostoevsky, and Chekhov, there was also a consequential and mature debate there about the proper direction of political and social change. The Agrarians and the Regionalists, various sociologists and academics such as V. O. Key and C. Vann Woodward dealt with similar issues in the 1930s and 1940s, but then only in muted and rather safe terms.

Why these renaissances take on a predominately literary coloration is another matter. In the case of the South, it may have something to do with the underdeveloped nature of Southern institutional and intellectual life. The enlightenment tradition in the South had long since played out; political progressivism had grown tame, while Populism had all but disappeared by the 1920s. Unlike the New England Renaissance, another point of comparison to which I will return, the South had neither a "culture city"[2] such as Boston-Cambridge nor a dominant university such as Harvard to serve as magnets for talents and generators of intellectual energies. Moreover, as Perry Miller has emphasized, Transcendentalism was an heir to much in Puritanism, despite the fact that Emerson *et al* had rejected its theology. Whatever its exact form of articulation, the life of the mind carried prestige in New England in a way that was foreign to the South. And, whatever its other virtues, Southern Protestantism has never been accused of promoting intellectual analysis. One thinks here of the way in which the Fugitive-Agrarians backed into, as it were, a defense of intellectual obscurantism in the 1920s.

One wonders, in fact, if literary renaissances don't flourish in cultural contexts which lack an institutional base for the other arts and the intellect. One seems to need other minds around, whether literally or as embodied in a tradition of thought, to do philosophy or sociology. Money, patronage, and schools of instruction are required for a flowering of the visual arts, architecture, dance, drama, or music. But writers seem to need only pen and paper, some books, and plenty of imagination. Even then, as several students of the Renaissance have noted, most of its main figures left the South for a time to sample the intellectual and cosmopolitan and urban pleasures of Oxford or New York or Paris before returning South to defend their province or at least to write about it.

Put another way, the Southern Renaissance was a quite different and frankly more limited sort of renaissance than others we

2. Van Wyck Brooks takes this term from Spengler and uses it in *The Flowering of New England* (New York: E. P. Dutton, 1952), 539.

might think of. Its energies empowered little abstract thought. In fact, hostility to abstract thought was an Agrarian point of pride. The New Criticism demonstrated quite clearly that Southerners had minds as well as memories, but it was a very specific kind of thought, always closely pinned to a text and rarely daring flights into the realm of high theory. The sociological theory of regionalism developed at Chapel Hill by Vance and Odum involved little more than head-counting and indexing of regional resources and should never be mistaken for sociological theory in the grand manner. The modern South has had more than its share of first-rate historians, but Clio's discipline is notoriously resistant, at least in this country, to theoretical speculation. Unlike, for instance, fin-de-siecle Vienna there was no Freud or Wittgenstein, no Schoenberg or Mahler, no Klimt or Schiele. Germany around the turn of the nineteenth century was a political and social backwater, yet produced Kant and Hegel, Goethe and Schiller. Closer to home, the Southern Renaissance saw no Emerson or Thoreau, those strange figures who worked in the interstices between imaginative literature, philosophy, and the personal essay. Nor did it see the emergence of any political thinker who begins to approach the stature of Jefferson, Madison, or even Calhoun and Fitzhugh. Its one undeniably great writer—William Faulkner—was one of the most creative, imaginative, and fertile literary minds of this or any century. Indeed one feels at times that Faulkner had more imaginative capacity than he knew what to do with. But Faulkner's attempts to create believable characters who could handle ideas, ones who could bring intellection to life and dramatize it, would have to be called failures.

At this point you may be muttering that I am engaging in intellectual overkill. This does bring into focus another matter which is crucial for establishing a framework for understanding the Southern Renaissance—what is the proper context of comparison? At times I suspect we have developed and hung on so doggedly to the label "Southern Renaissance" because it still seems so highly improbable. Who would have thought it? Who would have thought it, in particular, coming not only from the poorest, least developed region of the nation, but also from one which had been something of a national whipping-boy for its various sins against democratic ideals and national unity? Czarist Russia stood in a somewhat similar relationship to liberal Europe and was considered hopelessly benighted, hag-ridden by Orthodoxy and tyrannized by reactionary czars. But Russia certainly disposed over a tremendous potential and was more institutionally developed than the South. The comparison with Ireland is more apposite, for it stood to England and London as the South did to the North and, say, New York. (Here it seems to me that the South can stand up to the comparison quite well.) But when we come to this country, the obvious point of comparison is the New England Renaissance.

Interestingly enough, the New England Renaissance seems to have been named, i.e., discovered/invented, during the first decade or so of what later came to be called the Southern Renaissance. Lewis Mumford's *Golden Day* (1926) focussed on five major writers between 1830 and 1860—Emerson, Thoreau, Melville, Whitman, and Hawthorne. His thesis sounded much like the one later advanced by Tate. These figures, Mumford argued, "stood betweeen two worlds"—the Protestant and the natural, Europe and the New York, the utilitarian and the romantic visions.[3] In his coda, Mumford spoke of a loss of energy and vision by the end of the century and for evidence evoked the James brothers and Henry Adams. (With decline like that, who needs a renaissance?) Ten years later, Van Wyck Brooks retraced much of the same ground in his *The Flowering of New England* (1936), though he widened his purview to include historical writing and some of the other arts. Brooks claimed that

3. Lewis Mumford, *The Golden Day* (New York: Dover Press, 1968), 44.

the New England Renaissance was rooted in the soil of the region, but what followed was a gradual over-refinement and "cosmopolitan deracination," exemplified by the shift from Boston to New York and on to Henry James's Europe.[4] Finally in 1941 F. O. Matthiessen published his materpiece, *The American Renaissance*. (The cultural imperialism involved in the shift in titles should not go unnoticed.) In approaching his subject with New Critical tools, Matthiessen rejected both the literary-historical approach and the economic-social approach and instead chose to engage in a close reading of several major texts of the five major writers. As he said, he was concerned primarily with "what these books were as works of art."[5]

How then do these two renaissances on native ground compare? Both were examples of a kind of literary nationalism, one directed against the courtly muses of Europe, the other against the industrial vision of the North. Neither had much use for the empiricist vision of the natural world or human nature nor was either enthusiastic about the commerical obsessions of the modern world. And yet the world-view of the New England Renaissance was more optimistic and expansive and took its bearings from the spirit at work in nature, while the Southern Renaissance was concerned much more with the past and with historical consciousness. The New England spirit inclined toward the anti-institutional, even the utopian; but many of the central figures in the Southern Renaissance yearned for a more stable, institutionally textured, hierarchical society.

It is safe to say that the Southern Renaissance can claim no poet of Whitman's range or influence, but the general level of poetic output from poets such as Tate, Ransom, and Warren exceeds that of its predecessdor. As mentioned, Dixie had no Emerson or Thoreau, but one might mention James Agee's *Let*

4. Brooks, *Flowering*, 540.
5. F. O. Matthiessen, *The American Renaissance* (New York: Oxford University Press, 1941), vii.

Us Now Praise Famous Men as the kind of highly personal, even confessional, work of mixed modes and stunning observation that can bear comparison with *Walden*. Of the New England figures only Hawthorne might have felt at home in the South. Faulkner can more than match Hawthorne and does match Melville in range, energy, and power. The South lacks two novelists of such sustained achievement, but, as is the case with poetry, its general level of fictional production—one thinks here of *The Fathers* or *All the King's Men* or the shorter fiction of Porter, O'Connor, and Welty—stands higher than that of New England.

What are we to make of all this? My purpose in skipping here and there across a couple of centuries and several continents is simply to point to the range of questions and problems we need to begin confronting if we are to take the measure, all regional pride and chauvinism aside, of the Southern Renaissance.

DEFINITION AND CANON FORMATION

As I have already mentioned, it is not accidental that the idea of the Southern Renaissance began taking shape in the same years which saw the formulation of the notion of the New England Renaissance. The 1930s was a decade of regional self-consciousness in America; and that decade abounded in discussions of the new Southern writing in literary journals in the South and elsewhere. These discussions were full of assessment and prediction—and not a little self-congratulation. Indeed the notion of a regional renaissance was a brainchild of one of its seminal figures, Allen Tate. Highly self-conscious as publicists as well as poets and critics, Tate and company combined a defense of traditional Southern society and culture with a counter-offensive assertiveness concerning Southern literary achievement.

It is not clear (and probably less than crucial) who first used the term "Southern Renaissance" to describe what was happen-

11

Salem Academy and College
Gramley Library
Winston-Salem, N.C. 27108

ing in Southern literary and cultural life. Howard Mumford Jones asked "Is There a Southern Renaissance?" in *The Virginia Quarterly Review* in 1930, but gave a distinctly unclear answer, a "yes, but not yet." Tate used the term in 1936 and again in 1945 when he declared that the Renaissance was over. More important for our purposes was the growing sense after World War II that something important had happened and that it was time to set about announcing the fact to the literary world. Minerva's owl had apparently taken wing.

What took place in the years between the mid-1940s and the early 1960s was a process of defining the Southern Renaissance and establishing its canonical texts and writers. The first and most important stage in the process, it now appears in retrospect, was the resurrection of the literary standing of William Faulkner. Even then there was a general acceptance among Southerners and non-Southerners alike that Faulkner was the "main man" among Southern writers. The story of Faulkner's neglect as of 1945 and his rehabilitation by Malcolm Cowley and Robert Penn Warren with assists from Tate and earlier George Marion O'Donnell is well-known, if a bit overdrawn. It is important to note here that Faulkner was initially read as a kind of honorary Agrarian who wrote marvellous fiction in defense of the Sartoris ethic and community of spirit against the Snopesian anarchy of avarice. More generally he was seen as a writer with universal and not just regional scope and implication. In both incarnations Faulkner became a spokesman for modern humanism, the South's mouthpiece for teaching the world what had been lost.

Then in 1947 Allen Tate edited a set of essays, fiction, and poetry entitled *A Southern Vanguard*. The process of canon formation was underway. Besides Cowley on Faulkner, it included essays on the New Criticism, Thomas Wolfe, Eudora Welty, and Robert Penn Warren as well as general essays by Marshall McLuhan and Robert Heilman that attempted to define what was distinctive about the South and hence about Southern literature. This latter sort of effort was to become a favorite exercise in the ensuing years which saw worthy successors to Tate's volume compiled by Louis Rubin and Robert Jacobs—*The Southern Renascence* (1953) and *The South: Modern Southern Literature and Its Cultural Setting* (1961). From these works, along with C. Vann Woodward's highly influential essays in *The Burden of Southern History* (1960) and Cleanth Brooks's "Southern Literature: The Wellsprings of Its Vitality" (1962), emerged an initial but comprehensive sketch of the Southern Renaissance.

One important matter to settle was the connection between the Southern experience and the Southern Renaissance, regional history and regional self-expression. The emerging consensus might be called the Tate-Woodward-Brooks thesis. (Here it is important to note that the figures who forged this initial definition of the Renaissance were often participants in or closely linked with the initial generation of Renaissance writers.) Very briefly the standard account went as follows. The Renaissance, according to Tate, had resulted from the historical position of the South after World War I when it had faced the unavoidable disparity between traditional attitudes and the modern world. This was Tate's "backward glance" or "past in the present" thesis.

But if this established the historical context for the Renaissance, there were also specific characteristics which set off the South and hence Southern literature from the rest of American life and literature. Here the emphasis fell upon a Southern cast of mind which suspected abstraction and utopian schemes, was fundamentally religious, and had a sense of life's tragic conflicts, and which was firmly rooted in place and community. This Southern mentality had arisen from the region's experience of occupation and defeat, of poverty, and of racial oppression and guilt. The result was an ironic view of the overweening ambi-

13

tions and dangerous innocence of those who would change society and human nature. Unlike most Americans, Southerners allegedly possessed an active sense of history and historical consciousness. When Tate's historical dynamic was combined with these specific experiences and characteristics, one has the conditions necessary for the Southern Renaissance.[6]

There are several things to be observed regarding this initial explanation-sketch of the Southern Renaissance. First, the period in which it emerged saw the South decidedly on the defensive in its efforts to stave off challenges to segregation. Though there was considerable general talk of sin and guilt, tragedy and irony (these after all were favorites in literary and cultural discourse in the 1950s), the South's particular racial agonies in the past or the immediate present (of the 1950s and early 1960s) received little specific attention. This is *not* to maintain that the consensus view of the Renaissance sought to defend segregation or constituted an ideological defense of Southern racism. Louis Rubin wrote insightfully of Ralph Ellison and Richard Wright as Southern writers in the introduction to his anthology of 1961. And, in his *The Strange Career of Jim Crow*, Woodward provided invaluable support to critics of segregation on both sides of the Mason-Dixon line. But for all that, race did not seem to occupy center stage in modern Southern literature nor did it seem central to the Southern experience.

Second, if the explanation of the Southern Renaissance was not exactly a restatement of the Agrarian vision, it came close to it in certain essentials. It was a kind of distillation of Agrarianism, shorn of its specific commitment, such as it was, to an agricultural economy and absent its blatant hostility to the North and its decorous racism. Still, by emphasizing the sense of place and past, the importance of religion, a distrust of abstraction,

6. See C. Vann Woodward, "Why the Southern Renaissance?" *Virginia Quarterly Review*, 51, No. 2 (Spring 1975), 227–39 for a clear statement, along with crucial questions, about the description and explanation of the Renaissance.

and a kind of cultural conservatism, the new view partook strongly of the Agrarian spirit. Third, and most general, the consensus view of the Renaissance quite shrewdly turned what had been taken to be regional weaknesses and faults into definite advantages. Poverty, defeat, and occupation, curses though they were, had taught the South an essential wisdom. Anti-intellectualism became a healthy fear of ideologies, particularly those emanating from beyond the Urals. And so on.

Finally, as one might expect in these years of national and, particularly, regional conservatism, even reaction, there were few recognizably liberal or radical literary critics found among the contributors to the anthologies. The literature about the Southern Renaissance was a kind of home industry. Edmund Wilson's name was absent; and neither Alfred Kazin nor Irving Howe, both of whom had written insightfully though not uncritically of Faulkner, contributed. On the other hand, except for one contribution by Andrew Lytle to *Southern Renascence,* none of the Agrarian fire-eaters or more militantly Southern spirits graced the pages of the anthologies either. Thus the standard account of the Southern Renaissance was established in a mood, not of celebration or belligerence, but of sober, measured appreciation.

This framework for understanding the Renaissance was accompanied by a canon of essential writers and texts. At the center of course stood Faulkner, lately a Nobel Prize winner and spokesman of humanist pieties. Then came the major Fugitive-Agrarians—Ransom, Tate, Warren, and Donald Davidson (the poet not the polemicist). Ellen Glasgow and James Branch Cabell were viewed warily, though respectfully as forerunners, while Erskine Caldwell was treated a bit nervously. Professors Rubin and Hugh Holman spoke bravely and persistently for the virtues of Thomas Wolfe. Besides Welty, Katherine Anne Porter, Caroline Gordon, and Carson McCullers had articles devoted to them, while younger writers such as Peter Taylor,

Flannery O'Connor, James Agee, and William Styron were held to bear watching. The 1961 anthology included an essay on Southern dramatists, Tennessee Williams and Lillian Hellman, but recognizable Southern poetry, asserted Louise Cowan, was a thing of the past.[7] With this canon established, it might be said that the Renaissance had become a tradition. It had entered into its maturity. A general agnosticism prevailed as to whether the Renaissance was still going strong. Both Rubin and Walter Sullivan spoke of the loss of community and historical immediacy in (then) recent Southern fiction, but the novelists and short story writers, circa 1960, seemed as prolific as ever.

III. THE VIEW FROM THE PRESENT

How does it all look from here? Exact generalizations and judgments are certainly risky at such close quarters, but we can point to several problem areas in the original formulation of a framework for the Southern Renaissance. For instance, the problem with the Tate thesis was its high degree of generality. In the modern world, and throughout much of human history, change has been a constant. Even in the context of Southern history, the changes in the South as a result of the Civil War and Reconstruction were more profound than those after World War I. Why was there no cultural revolution in the later part of the nineteenth century? In general, except for Marxism, we have no general theory connecting changes in the social and economic "base" with transformations in the realm of culture. Even then, sophisticated Marxists make no easy, one-to-one correlations between changes in the base and changes in the superstructure of society. The realm of culture has a certain autonomy, and

7. Louise Cowan, "The Pietas of Southern Poetry," in *South: Modern Southern Literature in Its Cultural setting*, ed. Louis Rubin and Robert Jacobs (Garden City, N.Y.: Doubleday Dolphin, 1961), 94. Cowan also suggests that the South, Ireland, and Russia should be seen as examples of cultures responding to the tension between tradition and change.

what literary and cultural historians need to do is focus more closely on what Raymond Williams calls the "structures of feeling and experience" of a society.[8]

In this cultural sphere, it is hard to quarrel with much of the framework established by Woodward, Brooks, and Rubin. Their work was pioneering and invaluable. And yet several recent studies of Southern literature and culture emphasize the region's tendency toward phantasy, its historical inability to engage reality. Here Cash's *The Mind of the South* deserves new attention, since Cash stressed the negative, not positive, qualities of Southern tradition. The tradition was, according to the North Carolina journalist, marked not by a fear of abstraction but by a refusal of reality, not by a sense of community but by rampant individualism and divisive racism, not by a sense of the tragic and the ironic but by a love of the melodramatic and the chauvinistic, not by sobriety but by violence, not by tolerance but by devotion to the "savage ideal." Indeed, for a generation that has lived through and participated in the Civil Rights struggles of the 1950s and 1960s, the virtues that Brooks and Woodward saw as inherent in the Southern experience have seemed remarkably fragile, hollow, even non-existent. At least among white Southerners.

Further, we can wonder why the Southern Renaissance was defined in exclusively literary terms, a strange delimitation given the emphasis upon historical consciousness as a central characteristic of the Southern mind and a central theme in the literature of the Renaissance. Though Howard Odum and the Chapel Hill Regionalists could never be accused of literary grace or felicity, the issues they raised were certainly crucial to the question of the fate of the modern South and thus an important Renaissance theme. Pioneering work in the formation of modern Southern political culture was done by Woodward in his *Tom*

8. See Raymond Williams, *Marxism and Literature* (Oxford, England: Oxford University Press, 1977).

17

Watson, Origins of the New South, and *The Strange Career of Jim Crow* and by V. O. Key in *Southern Politics.* These were major contributions to Southern intellectual and cultural discourse. Just as glaring was the neglect by nearly all the contributors to the anthologies of Cash's *Mind of the South,* a work of consummate literary and historical imagination. One would have hardly known that Cash had even put pen to paper.

There were other omissions as well. If Lillian Smith's novel, *Strange Fruit,* was allegedly a bit of liberal agitprop (and I think that judgment too harsh), then certainly her memoir, *Killers of the Dream,* was one of the few works outside of Faulkner's corpus to confront the South's racial agonies head-on and in a very specific way. Sin and guilt were personal, not literary, in her writings; they were experiences, not postures. James Agee's *A Death in the Family* received notice, but the anthologies were silent about his *Let Us Now Praise Famous Men,* which contains some of the most powerful and experimental writing from a Southerner in the Renaissance period. One might see all this as reflecting the conservative or "apolitical" orientation of the consensus view of the Renaissance. But though there is something to that, it does not explain the relative neglect of Tate's *The Fathers* or Will Percy's *Lanterns on the Levee,* neither of which was exactly representative of the liberal imagination.

Moreover, after the experience of the Civil Rights movement and the way it forced matters of race upon us all, black and white, North and South, it is difficult to understand the relative neglect of racial themes and concerns by Renaissance writers and chroniclers of the Renaissance. It is again a measure of Faulkner's greatness that he faced up to the necessity of dealing with race from early on. But for many Southern writers, race (like sex in other contexts) was approached obliquely. More to the point, we have yet to see an adequate treatment of the fiction of Richard Wright, Ralph Ellison, or even Jean Toomer in

18

the context of Renaissance themes and concerns. To shift our focus away from the strictly literary, the future may judge Martin Luther King's theory and practice of non-violent social action as the most important combination of social analysis and political action since *The Federalist Papers* and it may also judge Alabama's Hugo Black as one of the major reshapers of constitutional law in this century. They surely belong in any study of the mature stages of the Renaissance as an intellectual as well as literary movement.

What about William Faulkner, the South's star witness in its argument for having had a literary renaissance? As far as I can tell, there has been no slackening in enthusiasm for his work, and there is general agreement that Faulkner's great period from 1929 to 1942 stands unmatched in Southern or American literature. I do think, however, that, though Faulkner's post World War II fiction is seen as a falling-off, his general pronouncements on the human condition and his glosses of his own work have been taken too seriously. We should trust the tale and not the teller, for the real Faulkner, the display of his energies and full commitment of his talent, is found in his lacerated, agonized, nihilistic, even psychotic characters and wildly impossible situations of the earlier fiction. Some have wanted to make him a latter-day Agrarian, while others have seen him as a liberal *malgré lui*. The real Faulkner is both better and worse: he is dangerous. There *is*, as Alfred Kazin claimed in *On Native Grounds*, often a kind of void at the center of the rhetorical storms Faulkner unleashes in his writing. In sum, Faulkner cannot be tied up and neatly claimed for any one position, however much we academics may try.

This view of Faulkner has been reenforced by the publication of several perceptive biographical studies of Faulkner recently. What emerges from them is an all-too-human Faulkner, one who was neither a sonorous stoic, a writing machine, nor a

19

Mississippi rustic with an inexplicable way with words.[9] David Minter's skillful interweaving of Faulkner's life and work shows us a quite moving and heroic as well as quite ruthless and cruel man who transformed himself from a shiftless dandy into a writer of genius. We see Faulkner dogged by familial and sexual problems, a Faulkner who created an imaginary world so as to reduce or assuage the pain of the real. We can now see the costs to himself and to his family of these acts of literary and self-creation. Finally, such psychological explorations of Faulkner's life and art reduce neither to triviality or pathology, but rather serve to augment them and lend them the poignancy of human existence.

Is the Renaissance over? Somehow, the more one thinks about this question, the less important it becomes. Still, provisionally, I would say that the seminal or "growth" stage was over around 1942, the year in which Faulkner published his last great work, *Go Down, Moses*. The debate between the Regionalists and the Agrarians was silent; the issue was moot. The period from the end of the war until the early 1960s marks a levelling off, the maturation of the new Southern literature. The work of major Southern writers shifted in a very general way from a concern with the South as a theme and problem to a concern with the South as a setting, a recognizable and unmistakable one, but still a backdrop rather than an object of explicit exploration. As Lewis Simpson has written, there was in these years "an increasing depletion of the Southern memory." "The memory of a memory" became central.[10] The tradition which Southern writers now engaged was no longer that of the fathers and grandfathers who had lived through the heroic days of the War and

9. See David Minter, *William Faulkner: His Life and His Work* (Baltimore: John Hopkins University Press, 1980) and Judith Bryant Wittenberg, *Faulkner: The Transfiguration of Biography* (Lincoln: University of Nebraska Press, 1979).

10. Lewis Simpson, "The Southern Recovery of Memory and History," *Sewanee Review*, 82 (1974), 20.

Reconstruction, but of the first generation of the Renaissance itself. It was not Sartoris or Sutpen or Colonel W. C. Falkner but William Faulkner himself who presided over the tradition and had to be submitted to or faced down. The Renaissance had become a tradition. But this is not to say that the Renaissance is dead; only, to repeat, that it has matured. Now we might even say that Faulkner and Tate and Warren and Welty and Cash and Woodward and all the others are names which have taken on, like Sartoris, a "glamorous fatality."

I would like to think that there is another tremendously important historical experience, peculiar to the South, which awaits its literary and intellectual articulation: the Civil Rights revolution of the 1950s and 1960s. The time, the place, the opposing forces were full of high hopes and wild fears. One saw unbelievable heroism and unutterable cowardice, examples of the highest courage and the meanest, sorriest avoidance. Some kept faith and some wilted under pressure. Many asked too much of the Civil Rights movement, that it serve as a symbol of everything which was good and important about the country and about the South. Others saw it as the final blow to the only culture and society worth having. In truth, the Civil Rights movement and the changes it unleashed were neither, but the South and the nation would be immensely enriched if somebody began getting it down on paper and trying to make sense of it.

Faulkner
and the
Fugitive-Agrarians

CLEANTH BROOKS

The two most brilliant manifestations of the great upsurge of
letters in the twentieth-century South were the advent of William Faulkner, of Oxford, Mississippi, and of the Fugitive poets
of Nashville, Tennessee, These events were not interconnected,
but they did occur at about the same time. Faulkner's first
volume, *The Marble Faun*, a long poem, was published in 1924.
Several of his novels rapidly followed: *Soldiers' Pay* in 1926;
Mosquitoes, in 1927; and *Sartoris* and *The Sound and the Fury*,
both in 1929. It was *The Sound the Fury* that made a resounding
impact. It is, of course, as a powerful novelist, not as a poet, that
Faulkner is known today. The Fugitives also began as poets, and
though some of them were to become novelists, they are still
best known for their poetry, which appeared in their own publication, *The Fugitive* (1922–25) and elsewhere. But in 1930 a
number of these poets joined other friends in publishing *I'll
Take my Stand*. This Agrarian manifesto was a collection of
twelve essays on Southern culture in its various aspects. It was
praised as a defense of Southern values, or, and more usually,
condemned as the work of a group of unreconstructed Confeder-
ates. So the Fugitive-Agrarians made their impact in a dual
capacity—as writers of a rather quirky intellectual poetry and as

conservative critics of the culture. But one notes that the dates of their appearance on the literary scene and of Faulkner's almost exactly coincide.

There is little evidence that the Fugitives took any notice of Faulkner's poetry or he of theirs. Actually they had on this level almost nothing in common. The Fugitives were in conscious rebellion against Swinburne, Dowson, and the early Yeats. They were defiantly experimental. On the other hand, Faulkner's poetry was redolent of the Victorians and of the British decadents of the 1890s. But when it came to Faulkner's novels, the Fugitive camp was quick to notice and to respond.

This latter point is one worth making and fully developing in view of the fact that the relations between these two manifestations of the new Southern literature have heretofore been so little explored as to give rise to misconceptions. Hints of rivalry have got about, particularly the notion that the Nashville poets were reluctant to recognize talent outside their own snug little circle, and that only after the acclaim of Faulkner's achievement had become a tidal wave did they join in praise for him. What had amounted to no more than a hint or suspicion of such jealous coolness was put quite clearly and emphatically in 1973 by Daniel Aaron in his book entitled *The Unwritten War: American Writers and the Civil War*. Aaron begins his chapter on William Faulkner as follows:

> Only after the flurry of Agrarianism petered out did the Neo-Confederates come to a proper appreciation of William Faulkner. Some of them knew him, of course, in the 1930s as one of the talented representatives of the Southern literary "renaissance," but a decade passed before they canonized him belatedly as "the most powerful and original novelist in the United States" and as "one of the best in the modern world," and inadvertently made his achievement ancillary to their own social and aesthetic dicta. The exegesis of Warren and especially of Cleanth Brooks influenced Faulkner scholarship so profoundly, in fact, that the differences between him

and the Nashville group have become obscured. Yet Faulkner remained outside the Agrarian orbit.

In being mentioned in such terms, I do not consider that I am
paid much of a compliment in these extraordinary remarks.
Aaron's reference to my alleged influence is not even a left-
handed compliment but a left hook to the solar plexus, and
perhaps a little below the belt. At the least, the whole paragraph
from which I have just quoted is a very slippery piece of ques-
tion-begging rhetoric. What is more important, it is just not
grounded in fact. Professor Aaron's so-called Neo-Confederates
were not an organized agit-prop group, a kind of Chinese tong
equipped with hatchet men. They were a group of friends who
shared some common views, but had their own firmly maintained opinions. A glance through the letters of Davidson and
Tate, for example, will make abuntantly clear how frequently
they disagreed with each other.

A further fact needs clearing up. They did not write *I'll Take
My Stand* in the hope of becoming a force in political affairs and
then, when the ploy failed to catch on, proceed to take up *belles
lettres* as a means to fame and fortune. Yet is this not what Aaron
suggests? If not, his first sentence involves a complete non-
sequitur. For what otherwise is the logical connection between a
failure at effective sectional polemic and a belated proper "appreciation" of William Faulkner? Actually, the most overtly
polemical of all the Agrarians, Donald Davidson, was very quick
to appreciate Faulkner and give his work high praise.

Consider once more the passage quoted by Aaron, that in
which some one refers to Faulkner as the most powerful and
original novelist in the United States and one of the best in the
modern world. The person who wrote that was Allen Tate.
Aaron quotes it from an essay that Tate published in 1945. Now
in 1945 Faulkner still had no nationwide popularity. I can testify
to that personally, for when I first began to teach Faulkner at
Yale in the autumn of 1947 there were only two volumes by
Faulkner in print and both were cheap Modern Library edi-

tions. I searched the second-hand bookshops for copies of such masterpieces as *Light in August, Absalom, Absalom!, The Hamlet,* and *Go Down, Moses* in order to find extra texts. Faulkner became known nationally only after he had been awarded the Nobel Prize in 1950. There were individual critics who praised him before that date, and the Fugitive-Agrarians were among that band of critics. Let us examine the facts.

In 1926 Donald Davidson promptly reviewed *Soldiers' Pay* on his book page in the Nashville *Tennessean*. It was a favorable notice, and he declared that Faulkner wrote better than either Dos Passos or Sinclair Lewis. In the next year, 1927, Davidson reviewed *Mosquitoes*. He had some reservations about this work, which most of us consider Faulkner's weakest, but he was "full of admiration" for what he called Faulkner's performance in it and observed that Faulkner had by now happily assimilated Joyce. In 1929 Davidson reviewed *Sartoris*, Faulkner's third novel and wrote that "as a stylist and as an acute observer of human behavior . . . Mr. Faulkner is the equal of any except three or four American novelists who stand at the very top." Further on in his review Davidson remarked that Faulkner "needs only to find a theme worthy of his talent and perception." This prophecy was, of course, soon to be fulfilled, for Faulkner's masterpieces began to appear almost at once. In 1935, when *Publisher's Weekly* asked Davidson as a Southerner and as a by-this-time well known book reviewer, to name the best Southern novels of the past and the present, he included two by Faulkner: *The Sound and the Fury* (1929) and *As I Lay Dying* (1930).

R. P. Warren has told me that he read Faulkner's first novel in 1929. This was the year in which the English edition first appeared. (Warren was then in his second year at Oxford. I was also at Oxford at the time, and read the English edition.) In 1931 Warren was praising Faulkner to his faculty associates, as Blotner has recorded, and in that same year Warren reviewed, and favorably, Faulkner's first collection of short stories, *These Thirteen*. Warren has gone on through his own literary career to write intelligently and sensitively about Faulkner's work. But for the moment I am concerned to establish a more immediate point: that the Fugitive-Agrarians, from a very early date, were aware of, and on record about, Faulkner's promise and his genius.

With John Crowe Ransom, the response to Faulkner's work was somewhat mixed. When Ransom reviewed *Pylon* in March of 1935 the title of the review read: "Faulkner: South's Most Brilliant But Wayward Talent, Is Spent." Yet a month later, in an essay in *The Virginia Quarterly Review*, Ransom called Faulkner "the most exciting figure in our contemporary literature." And Warren has told me of a conversation that he and Ransom had about Faulkner in the spring of that same year in which Ransom explained that, though he didn't like *Pylon*, he admired most of Faulkner's work immensely. Later, in 1945, while Ransom was editing *The Kenyon Review*, he joined enthusiastically in plans for a number of *The Kenyon* to be given over exclusively to Faulkner criticism. Unfortunately, the plans fell through when a sufficient number of articles on Faulkner were not forthcoming. (How changed this situation is today: we have, I expect, too many people writing about Faulkner. An editor who planned a Faulkner number today would have to beat off the would-be contributors with a stick.)

A fourth Fugitive, Allen Tate, apparently did not review any of Faulkner's early novels, though there is no reason to suppose that he was not aware of a man whom his friends had been praising for some years. The *Davidson-Tate Correspondence* makes reference to Faulkner as early as 1932.

The best refutation to the implication that people such as Allen Tate did not climb aboard the Faulkner bandwagon until it had got up momentum lies in the character and personality of Allen Tate. He was all his life scornful of such intellectual acrobatics. He held himself aloof from literary self-promotion of every sort. As a critic, he was the least impressionistic, the least

26

impulsive, of all that this country has produced. He took a pride in informed and reasoned judgments. One may disagree on occasion with his judgments, or with the reasons adduced for proposing them, but one could be sure that they were never thoughtless or self-serving in their motivation.

Tate's final appraisal of Faulkner (in 1963) as one of the best writers in the modern world went hand in hand with a personal dislike for Faulkner, a dislike which he freely acknowledged. I shall not try to justify Tate's personal dislike for Faulkner, though I can understand it. Faulkner was essentially a shy man, and his modesty in part accounts for his being uncomfortable with university professors, writers of national renown, and representatives of the press. Part of his self-deprecation was his unwillingness to call himself a literary man. He was, he said, simply a teller of tales or even more simply, just a farmer. Such downplaying of the role of the artist irritated Tate, who set great store by the vocation of poet and novelist, and liked to point to the veneration in which the French, for example, held their men of letters, compared to the disparagement offered them in the United States in the thirties and forties.

In any case, Faulkner was not easy to get to know. I remember a story that the late Thornton Wilder told me. He admired Faulkner's work very much and looked forward to meeting him in Boston and talking to him about his play, *Requiem for a Nun*, which was just opening there. Had I, at that time, known Wilder much better, I would have told him: don't try to get him into literary conversation right off. You'll scare him to death. He probably is already overawed by your reputation. A highly successful dramatist who is also a learned man will cause him to shrink into a corner. But I could not tell Wilder this—at that time we barely knew each other—and sure enough, as Wilder ruefully told me later, the worst had happened. Faulkner had withdrawn into himself. No rapport was established. Wilder was disappointed and perhaps his feelings were hurt. But the story has a happy ending, for later the two men met again. Somehow this time they did hit it off and Faulkner became warm and friendly.

I mention Tate's personal dislike for Faulkner—and there was, I would assume, an answering dislike in Faulkner for him—simply to make an important point. Tate's high praise of Faulkner's work was in the best sense disinterested. In proclaiming Faulkner one of the great writers of the century, he was neither climbing onto a bandwagon nor influenced by his regard for a friend. His praise reflected his considered opinion.

To make the tally complete, I ought to say a word here about Andrew Lytle, the novelist and Agrarian. On the subject of Faulkner I find nothing by him in print in the early period, but he has published three fine essays on Faulkner, generous in praise and highly perceptive, particularly in regard to Faulkner's account of the individual in his relation to society and specifically to the older Southern society.

Now we must return once more to Professor Aaron's account of the relation between the Fugitive Agrarians and Faulkner. Aaron's reason for praising Faulkner and disparaging the Nashville group amounts to this: The latter group were extremist Neo-Confederates, indulging in special pleading for their section, intransigent secessionists still, whereas Faulkner was able to stand back from the more emotional issues, regard the faults of the older Southern culture with a critical eye, and thus achieve a mature fiction, one that accorded with the facts of history and with universal humanistic values. In the interests of brevity, I have paraphrased and condensed Aaron's full argument, but I believe that I am giving a fair account of what it is. Without arguing the matter of whether or not the South had real grievances that ought to have been redressed, and that, in spite of black chattel slavery, the old South posessed certain virtues, I think that I can meet Aaron on his chosen ground.

What Aaron does is to measure Faulkner's later and more

detached work against the most intemperate and intransigent writings—mostly early—of the Nashville group. Had he taken account of Faulkner's early novels he would have found Faulkner about as unreconstructed as anybody, with at least a measure of glorification of romantic Confederate cavalrymen, and even with some stereotypes of the contented slave. Irving Howe, for example, has reproached him for such. Similar indictments by Northern critics were made right on down to *Intruder in the Dust* (1949). On the other hand, one can find plenty of detachment, soul-searching, and critical self-examination in the writings of Ransom, Warren, and Tate. Only Davidson and Lytle might be deemed partial exceptions.

In *The Fathers* (1938), for example, Tate provides an account of the Virginia patriarch whose life is thoroughly ordered by tradition. As Tate describes it, the tradition is out of touch with reality, and Major Buchan, the patriarch, acts so rigidly in accordance with it that he actually disowns his son. Tate's attitude is "mature" indeed: if the older order has virtues, it also has major deficiencies and defects. Aaron acknowledges as much in his specific discussion of *The Fathers*, but in his summary of the Fugitive-Agraians, relationship to Faulkner he scarely takes it into account. In fact, as I look back over the writings of the Fugitive-Agrarians I find very little that simplistically defends the Old South. The poetry of Ransom, Tate, and Warren is very mature indeed—some will call it almost sternly intellectual. The same can be said of Warren's fiction. It reflects no idyllic legend of the Old South, though one ought also to point out that neither are Warren and Tate taken in by the American Dream. That dream is indeed present in their various writings, but only as a promise yet to be fulfilled.

In short, it would be a fair procedure to compare the myth of the Old South with the myth of the New America, or to compare the realities of the Old Southern culture with the realities of the civilization of the North. But to demolish one myth by pointing

29

out that it was mythical—not literally fulfilled and real—while at the same time asserting that the other dream was no dream but a matter of fact, is neither fair reporting nor good history. Specifically, "American the Beautiful," one has ruefully to admit, is still mostly a dream. America's "Alabaster Cities" *have* been "dimmed by human tears," Her purple mountain majesties overshadow an Appalachia with a population which have lived for centuries in dire poverty. The American Dream is a noble one, but it is not to be taken as an accurate reflection of our lived experience.

Aaron's special praise for Faulkner was that he grew out of a defensive parochialism into a detached and rather dispassionate judgment of his native region. Such a view seems to me substantially correct and represents a fair appraisal of Faulkner's achievement. But ironically for Aaron's estimate of the essential difference between Faulkner and, say, Tate or Warren or Ransom—the very best single statement of the necessity for Southern self-criticism was penned by Allen Tate. In his fine 1959 essay, "A Southern Mode of the Imagination," Tate provided the very basis for Aaron's own 1973 approval of Faulkner: that is to say, Tate pointed out that Faulkner and even lesser members of the Southern Renaissance were at last able to look at their native region from a distance—to move from defensiveness to intelligent criticism, to come to realize that everything wrong with the South, as Tate puts it in a memorable phrase, "could not be blamed on the Yankees." Nevertheless, Tate continued to think that the Yankees were blameworthy in some important regards. Or to put matters more positively, he found certain virtues in the Southern tradition that he regarded as worth defending and preserving. And so did Faulkner.

I've spent a considerable time in talking about what the Nashville group thought about Faulkner. What did he think about them? I simply don't know. There seems to be very little in print on the subject. Among his *Selected Letters* (1977) there is a passage of high praise of the Cass Mastern episode in Warren's *All the King's Men,* though he wrote rather disparagingly of the novel as a whole. Perhaps someone will come to tell us from memory what Faulkner said about this or that one of the group. But in print thus far I have found only one further scrap of evidence and it comes not from a Faulkner letter or interview but from a speech that Faulkner puts into the mouth of one of his characters. In "Knight's Gambit" (1940) Charles Mallison observes to himself that "Huey Long in Louisiana had made himself founder owner and supporter of what his uncle Gavin said was one of the best literary magazines anywhere, without ever once looking inside it." I would like to think that Gavin Stevens was here speaking for Faulkner himself. In 1935 we had invited Faulkner to a writers' conference that was to be held in Baton Rouge that spring, the conference at which the foundation of *The Southern Review* was announced. We got from Faulkner a polite refusal couched in the most modest terms possible. For he wrote that he would have liked to come but had nothing to contribute. Later, Warren and I tried to get a story from him for the *Review,* but we were aware that such a catch was unlikely. We could pay only one and a half cents a word, and Faulkner needed the best payment he could get—the rate paid by *The Saturday Evening Post* and such—to meet his household expenses during the years when his great novels were being written but did not sell. Whether or not Gavin Stevens's high opinion of *The Southern Review* was shared by Faulkner himself, his guess that Long never looked inside its covers is a shrewd one. I myself doubt that Long ever knew the *Review* existed. He was dead before the second issue appeared.

If the relation of Faulkner to the Fugitive Agrarians has now been cleared up—and I would hope that you present would agree that the available evidence seems to support my conclusion—what remains to be said on this general subject? Two things in particular, I should think. First, what did Faulkner lose—or perhaps gain—by being a kind of literary "loner"? And second, what interests, beliefs, and attitudes did Faulkner and the Fugitives have in common? I am going to deny, of course, that the exegeses of his work done by Warren and by me were designed to make it appear that he shared our views. In any case, Faulkner was too big to be attracted into anybody else's orbit. Warren and I would have been fools to think so.

With regard to the first question, I think that I can be rather brief. Many writers have found that a fairly close-knit literary fellowship is a positive aid toward producing good literature. There was such a literary group in the golden age of the literature of New England, for example, but even at that time and in that place there was a Melville, who seems not to have had or needed close literary affiliations. The truth is that almost any literary situation might conceivably provide sufficient nourishment for the production of good and even great literary art. Some personalities seem to prefer relative solitude, others a congenial group of friends. In any case, the presence of a literary community will not make up for à lack of talent. As someone observed long ago, good poems are not written by committees, nor are good novels. In an important sense, every writer is self-taught—has to find his own mode of utterance and devise his own language. The Fugitive poets, for example, showed no standard pattern—did not conform in the least to a house style. In fact, the major poets of this group are so diverse in the ways of saying something that one could never for a moment confuse a poem by Davidson with one by Tate, or a poem by Warren with one by Ransom.

Of course, to have the association of a group of friendly critics who know you well and share your literary interests does confer great benefits. In some comments published in *The Harvard Advocate* (1951) Ransom draws upon his experience with his fellow Fugitives as he comments on Faulkner. He observes that Faulkner had "not had the advantage of the society of his literary

peers" nor that of "intellectuals with their formidable dialectic."
I agree. Every careful reader of Faulkner can see that this lack
shows up in numerous small ways. Like Humpty-Dumpty,
Faulkner sometimes made particular words mean what he
wanted them to mean—the dictionary be hanged. Yet in the
same passage Ransom sets out some of the advantages of Faulkner's relative isolation—which was, of course, never absolute:
from the beginning there were Phil Stone and Ben Wasson to
talk matters over with. Ransom remarks that for Faulkner there
was no acquaintance with the literary "academy [to] adulterate
the natural directness of his style." Ransom sums up with a
resounding compliment. He writes that Faulkner's "perfections
are wonderful and well sustained, and without exact precedent
anywhere." In short, the leader of the Fugitives could see certain advantages that Faulkner had in not being a member of any
literary group.

The second point—and the more important one, of course—is
this: What did Faulkner and the Fugitives have in common, if
anything? Did they see their native region in much the same
way? I've earlier indicated that they did, but we need some
illustrations. In spite of their rather different approaches to
poetry, they were equally concerned to explore what was good
in the Southern tradition and to fortify and preserve it. They did
not oppose change, but they saw that change was not in itself
necessarily good and that sudden drastic changes could be disastrous for a culture. Neither, by the way, looked uncritically at
the plantation system too often tied to a one-crop economy. The
Fugitive-Agrarians stressed a mixed economy, including mixed
farming conducted basically by yeoman farmers. This bias in
part reflected the situation in the upper South, the subregion
from which most of the Agrarians came. But since Faulkner also
was well aware of the perils of the slave system on which the
great plantations depended, he hardly differed on this point
from the Fugitives. In what high regard Faulkner held the

yeoman farmers of his own state comes clear in his fiction. Though he wrote some of his most powerful novels about the founding of the great plantations and about the later generations of such planter stock, he had a genuine respect for the small farmer, and his characters like the McCallums or V. K. Ratliff possess backbone and determination and also moral force. We make a grave mistake if we take as representative of this class of yeoman farmer the despicable Anse Bundren or the ridiculous I. O. Snopes.

To turn to the Fugitives once more. In Donald Davidson's fine essay "Still Rebels, Still Yankees," the heroes are small farmers from Georgia who live what Davidson sees as a good life, unpretentious and quiet though it be. They are still rebels against the soulless secularism of modern industrial civilization. But so are the Yankees depicted in his essay, the yeoman farmers of Vermont who have character and the richness and tang of their native background to match that of their Georgia counterparts. Davidson exults in them both. He is delighted with their local differences, which do not for him constitute any denial of their essentially common values. Those who want to convict Davidson of a narrow and intransigent Southern nationalism and of itching to fight the Civil War over again ought to read this essay.

To assess the parallels that exist between Faulkner and the Fugitive-Agrarians, let us have some concrete examples. Audiences such as this tend to be skittish of high-flown generalizations, for literature is incorrigibly concrete. Generalizations are important, but they need to be defined, illustrated, and generally nailed down by specific illustrations from the poetry and fiction being discussed.

Yet, let me begin with a fairly obvious generalization. With Faulkner, the Fugitives shared a passionate devotion to the land in which they lived and which had brought them forth. For them the various bits of American landscape were not interchangeable parts, each asking for as much or as little love as any other. For Faulkner and the Fugitives, their native landscape was alive with the deeds of men, a region literally steeped in history. One of the closing paragraphs of *Sartoris* (1929) reads in part: "The dusk was peopled with ghosts of glamorous and old disastrous things. And if they were just glamorous enough, there would be a Sartoris in them. . . . For there is death in the sound of [this name], and a glamorous fatality, like silver pennons down rushing at sunset, in a dying fall of horns along the road to Ronsevaux." This is Faulkner's final salute to the family of the Sartorises who gave their name to his third to-be-published novel. They are a romantic and daredevil breed, and the young Bayard Sartoris whose actions bring this novel to a close is clearly a hero built on the old Byronic model, a hero who is imprudent to the point of sheer folly, but to whom women are powerfully attracted and whose career is indeed glamorous. Faulkner's prose poetry in this passage retains the tonality of romantic verse, filled with echoes of Housman and Swinburne. But Faulkner sees the Sartoris breed, with some warrant, as specifically Southern. The Old South was the kind of world that could produce this kind of man, and the South itself—"peopled with ghosts of glamorous and old disastrous things"—partakes of their quality.

If one turns to John Crowe Ransom on the subject of the South, the tonality of the poetry is clearly different. There are no echoes of the British poetry of the nineties. The verse is invincibly modern. Yet notice the resemblances. The land described in the poem from which I shall quote is like Faulkner's land, impoverished. Some would even call it too worn out to yield a decent crop. Its great crop is memory and history. As the poet puts it:

> We pluck the spindling ears and gather the corn.
> One spot has special yield? "On this spot stood
> Heroes and drenched it with their only blood."

35

> And talk meets talk, as echoes from the horn
> Of the hunter—echoes are the old man's arts,
> Ample are the chambers of their hearts.

In the next stanza the hunters come into sight in this autumn landscape. But if this foxhunt reminds us of chivalry—a cavalry charge, say—it is itself little more than a far-away echo. It is play—not a practical activity—for what is pursued is in itself of no value: one doesn't eat foxes—doesn't really want to catch them. The chase is its own reward.

> Here come the hunters, keepers of a rite:
> The horn, the hounds, the lank mares coursing by
> Straddled with archetypes of chivalry;
> And the fox, lovely ritualist in flight
> Offering his unearthly ghost to quarry
> And the fields, themselves to harry.

If such a stanza rather undercuts the value of chivalric glory, the love of the land itself is strongly asserted in the closing stanzas of the poem. Granted that this land is unprosperous, no place for a young man to make his fortune, the young are exhorted not to leave it—for they have a deep emotional allegiance to it. If someone tells them "that easily will your hands / More prosper in other lands,"

> Angry as wasp-music be your cry then:
> "Forsake the Proud Lady, of the heart of fire,
> The look of snow, to the praise of a dwindled choir,
> Song of degenerate specters that were men?
> The sons of the fathers shall keep her, worthy of
> What those have done in love."

The mystique of the South as a kind of sacred land is as unmistakeably here as in Faulkner's patch of purple prose. In spite of the taut angularity of Ransom's verse, the attitude is fully as romantic. The South is the Proud Lady, a kind of patron goddess.

The relation of all these writers to their native soil went very deep. I could give you dozens of instances from Faulkner and dozens from the poetry and prose of the Fugitive-Agrarians if time permitted. But for all their depth of emotion, they keep their eyes on the object. They rarely if ever drift into mawkish local patriotism. Faulkner's realism and his sense of humor also tend to keep him free of it, while the Fugitives' tart sense of irony is their special safeguard. Moreover, as I have already suggested, the South is for neither party just a landscape. The scene is so closely related to its history and to the character of its people that the celebration of a landscape for its merely pictorial qualities is rare. This means that one's emotion has to do with a whole complex of relations and one's sense of affiliation is also complex. Several times an author went so far as to speak of his relation to the South as a love-hate relation.

There are many parallels, though considerations of time will allow me to note only one more. One particularly exact parallel occurs in Faulkner's *Light in August* and Warren's *All The King's Men*. In Warren's novel, the Cass Mastern episode, to which as you remember Faulkner gave high praise, tells of the young Mastern's betrayal of his best friend. Mastern had seduced his friend's beautiful wife, or, as the novel makes plain, it was really the other way around: she had seduced him. Now Mastern was a sensitive and idealistic young man, and when he discovered that his friend's sudden death was not accidental as was first thought, but an act of suicide at having discovered his double betrayal by friend and wife, Mastern feels a terrible remorse. An attractive slave girl in the friend's household, the wife's personal maid, had made the same discovery as Mastern. The unfaithful woman, suspecting this, sells the girl down the river, probably to end up in a New Orleans brothel. When Mastern learns that the slave girl has been sold, he makes frantic efforts to find the new buyer, intending to buy her back and give her her freedom. But this search is fruitless, though his desire to make amends or at least to do penance remains unabated. The

Civil War had just broken out, and Mastern found a solution in joining the Confederate Army, but as an act of expiation, for he makes a vow to himself that he will never fire a shot at the enemy. In fact, he longs for the enemy bullet that will end his own life. The narrator writes that if Mastern "had put on the gray jacket in anguish of spirit and in hope of expiation, he came to wear it in pride, for it was a jacket like those worn by the men with whom he marched. 'I have seen men do brave things,' Mastern wrote, 'And they ask for nothing.' And he added, 'It is not hard to love men for the things they endure.'" Finally, in the battles around Atlanta, Mastern receives the bullet he had longed for and dies in reconciliation with his God. He writes "I have lived to do no man good, and have seen others suffer for my sin. I do not question the Justice of God, that others have suffered for my sin, for it may be that only by the suffering of the innocent does God affirm that men are brothers."

No wonder Faulkner admired this tale: it developed a dramatic situation dear to his own heart. But Faulkner's use of the instance of a Confederate soldier's taking part in the defense of his country but refusing to fire at the enemy is only incidental to the two main stories that he narrates in *Light in August*. Near the end of that novel Faulkner tells us about the family background of the Reverend Gail Hightower. His grandfather had been a profane, hard-driving, utterly reckless Confederate cavalryman, but his son, Gail Hightower's father, was a man of entirely different stripe: a home-made abolitionist, something of a Puritan who practised the restrictive virtues; yet also a brave man who, "during the four years" of the war "had never fired a gun."

Did such Southerners exist? Are Faulkner and Warren simply inventing such characters for their own fictional purposes? I think not. We have plenty of proof that Southerners existed who disliked slavery and who opposed secession to the very end, but loyally went into the Southern armies when hostilities commenced. *Mrs. Chestnut's Civil War*, so superbly edited recently by Vann Woodward, will provide numerous examples. Both Faulkner and Warren, though they did not claim to be historians, actually knew their Southern history very well.

My time is up. I cannot deal with further parallels between the fiction of Faulkner and the poetry and fiction of the Nashville group. But perhaps I have adduced enough to drive home my point: namely, that for all their differences in forms, tonalities, and specific subject matters, these writers differed very little in their devotion of their native region and what they have to say about it in praise and in reproof. I shall not undertake to compare the worth of their various achievements. In any case, I have no wish to revise the Fugitive Allen Tate's own praise of Faulkner as the "most powerful and original novelist in the United States."

What Stand Did Faulkner Take?

FLOYD C. WATKINS

Place, Eudora Welty has said many times, is where the author "has his roots, place is where he stands."[1] The Nashville Agrarians who wrote that fundamental document of faith in the South, *I'll Take My Stand*, were thinking like Miss Welty—of a place where they would stand. They were trying to say also what principles they would stand on. They chose a difficult task, but I suppose that no Southern writer of accomplishment has been so far removed from place that he did not in some way try to describe where he stood. The several essays on place written by Miss Welty suggest that the happenings and the people who become a significant part of that spot remain there at least in spirit for as long as the place endures. This is a different way of putting Faulkner's statement that "the past is never dead. It's not even past."[2] So Faulkner had a lot to stand on in Oxford, Mississippi (or call it Yoknapatawpha, if you will), and he and his family knew almost all about it. That place provided what he had to stand on in his beliefs, whatever he thought: "It is both natural and sensible," Miss Welty has written, "that the place where we have our roots should become the setting, the first and primary proving ground of our fiction."[3]

1. Eudora Welty, *The Eye of the Story: Selected Essays and Reviews* (New York: Random House, 1977), 117.
2. Faulkner, *Requiem for a Nun* (New York: Random House, 1951), 92.
3. Welty, 129.

What Stand Did Faulkner Take?

Writers are not remarkably consistent in their beliefs. Faulkner probably rose every morning believing something just a little bit different about the South from what he had thought before. From that variability of the mind and the heart comes some confusion. Many of Faulkner's readers and critics do not know where he stood, have not been able to understand what he thought on one single morning, much less them all. Many there are who lived near to the places where Faulkner stood all his life, and some of them never came close to sharing his larger views. Few know his stand well.

Criticism, we need not be reminded, is an exercise of the ego. One who talks or merely puts pen to paper to interpret assumes that the critic has something to say that the hearer or reader does not know. Criticism, then, tends to be arrogant. Many critics of Faulkner seem to believe that they know almost all. But given that Faulkner is fairly constant, even with all his ambivalence, the discrepancies in the criticisms of his work prove necessarily that the truth is not in much of the writing about Faulkner. Too many interpreters contradict others. It is the pleasure of the critics to prove themselves right, and the first step in that pleasant task usually is to prove others wrong. One of the great delights for a Faulkner critic is that there is already so much interpretation to refute. So, early in a lecture or paper a critic wishes to show where Faulkner did not stand. Race, perhaps the most frequent point of contention, will not be much discussed here. There are enough other disputes and stands to make fools of us all.

Points at issue by the oversimplifiers, the allegorists, the polemicists, the radicals with a blinding cause, the misreaders run to all astronomical depths and directions. In brief form, the following is a miscellany of some of the points of view:

Faulkner was so bigoted as a Southerner, according to Sherwood

41

Anderson, that he was "poisoned with pernicious Southern attitudes."[4]

The regional theme is so strong that a character's "life and career mirror the history and heritage of the South, moral as well as social and political."[5]

Faulkner regarded himself as "a social historian, who hopes that by recording the minute changes in Oxford's life he can suggest the changes that are transforming the whole South."[6]

In the South and in Faulkner's fiction "concepts of social classes and castes prevent the South from recognizing and admitting the moral guilt underlying present social and economic problems."[7]

Marxism is the "most relevant" model in "dealing with the social and historical disposition of literature," including Faulkner's fiction. "Faulkner's class bias was thus directly involved in the formal, most purely 'artistic' aspects of his writing."[8]

Faulkner's "basic Southern subject is the defeat of the homeland, . . . the ordeal and collapse of the homeland."[9]

The major event of Faulkner's world is the Civil War, "in which the accumulated tensions and moral crises read a catastrophic and a significant violent expression."[10]

Faulkner's novels are "concerned mainly with the lowest strata of Southern society and hardly imply, even, the presence of a middle class."[11]

Faulkner's "characters are too inescapably oppressed by sadism and impotence."[12]

4. Joseph Blotner, *Faulkner: A Biography* (New York: Random House, 1974), 498.

5. Melvin Backman, "Sutpen and the South: A Study of *Absalom, Absalom!*," *PMLA*, 80 (December 1965), 597.

6. Quoted in Blotner, 1016.

7. Elizabeth M. Kerr, *Yoknapatawpha: Faulkner's "Little Postage Stamp of Native Soil"* (New York: Fordham University Press, 1969), 22.

8. Myra Jehlen, *Class and Character in Faulkner's South* (New York: Columbia University Press, 1976), viii, 25.

9. Irving Howe, *William Faulkner: A Critical Study* (New York: Vintage Books, 1952, 1962), Vintage Books, second edition, 24, 46.

10. Frederick J. Hoffman, *William Faulkner* (New Haven: College and University Press, 1961), Twayne's United States Authors Series, 25.

11. H. Arlin Turner, "The Southern Novel," *Southwest Review*, 25 (January 1940), 211.

12. Harry Thornton Moore, "The American Novel To-day," *The London Mercury*, 31 (March 1935), 463.

What Stand Did Faulkner Take?

Faulkner's fictions are *"fleurs du mal."*[13] He and some other Southern writers are "merchants of death, hell, and the grave, these are the horror-mongers-in-chief."[14]

"The creatures of Faulkner's world are completely phony, but even if we believe in them, they are so insensitive and stupid that their actions have no meaning for us. . . ."[15]

These general comments about Faulkner's world, I believe, represent many of the enemies of true reading.

The comments on particular novels seem to be worse than the general views. The closer a false criticism is pinned to a fact, a person, or a condition, the more erroneous the statement seems to become, the more ridiculous. All of the novels are sometimes misread. No matter how one reads Faulkner, there are statements which have to seem like nonsense. Years ago I wrote an article on purely factual errors in Faulkner; I dealt with nothing which was not as obviously wrong as a mouse in the cheese pantry. At the time I did not trespass on the territory of the errors of interpretation. I collected over four thousand provable factual errors before I quit any systematic attempts to add to the list ten years or more ago. The errors of interpretations, I firmly believe, are almost as apparent and are of more consequence. I avoided them at first because an error of interpretation may not be demonstrably wrong. Exactly opposite angry opinions about the same passages of fiction, however, prove that many errors of interpretation do exist.

The great novels of the late twenties, the thirties, or the early forties seem to have suffered most at the hands of absurd criticism. The early critics of Faulkner as we can see them now were more mistaken about him than those of recent years. Now, the theorists who march in named platoons of criticism wander so far

13. Louis B. Wright, "Myth-Makers and the South's Dilemma," *The Sewanee Review*, 53 (1945), 544.

14. Gerald W. Johnson, "The Horrible South," *The Virginia Quarterly Review*, 11 (April 1935), 211.

15. Don Stanford, *"The Beloved Returns* and Other Fiction," *The Southern Review*, 6 (1941), 619.

from the materials of the novel that often one does not know what they are saying and thus can make only poor judgments of their views.

One of the greatest novels, *Absalom, Absalom!*, is a good testing ground for the critics. The most significant of the errors (except perhaps for those about sex and religion) are the misapprehensions of history and sociology.

"The story of Sutpen—like the story of the South—becomes for Faulkner an image of social oppression."[16] (This statement was written after I thought that the common sense of Cleanth Brooks had set the issues straight.)

"A central quest in the novel" is "the quest to discover the truth about the rise and fall of . . . [the] South."[17] (Good fiction cannot be so limited. It does not care for the South, one must be reminded, except as it provides images of the concrete world and of the heart of mankind. Artistically and religiously, one may care very much for Adam and Eve, but geographically they matter very little at all. Fictionally, one is deeply concerned for the characters of *Absalom, Absalom!*, but to a reader not limited by time they are as relevant in one place as another.)

Quentin is said to hate the South. He ardently declares that he does not. Faulkner has said that Quentin hates "the bad qualities in the country he loves."[18]

"The deeds of violence in *Absalom, Absalom!* are based on class and caste hostility."[19]

"Race and even slavery were issues within the white class conflict and perhaps more destructive because of that context than they would have been otherwise."[20] (Class as this critic uses it is a meaningful term only to radical or academic intellectuals.)

There are broader opinions, still strictly regional. "*Absalom* is a

16. Donald M. Kartiganer, "Faulkner's *Absalom, Absalom!*: The Discovery of Values," *American Literature*, 37 (November 1965), 292.

17. Backman, 596.

18. *Faulkner in the University: Class Conferences at the University of Virginia 1957–1958*, ed. Frederick L. Gwynn and Joseph L. Blotner (Charlottesville: University Press of Virginia, 1959), 71.

19. Kerr, 215.

20. Jehlen, 68.

full review of the South as a representative kind of experience."[21] It is "Faulkner's most comprehensive view of the South's history."[22] "Sutpen himself is a mirror image of the South."[23]

One of the falsest views of *Absalom, Absalom!* ever created is that elaborate design on the jacket of the Modern Library edition of the book. The driveway is wide as a highway, arched over by long and beautiful drooping limbs of liveoaks and by Spanish moss. Underneath the large trees on the jacket is a luxurious and well-manicured lawn. (Faulkner's Rowan Oak has a one-lane driveway between the two rows of cedars that are typical in the area.) The road curves into the distance and up to an enormous three-storied mansion with tall portentous columns and a long balustrade. Whoever drew that picture never saw any of the antebellum homes in Lafayette County and possibly none of the old homes in the entire area of the South. A tall and ghostly woman in black stands lonely and vaguely in the foreground. Without a word, the jacket has misled generations of readers of the novel. The terrain, the house, the landscape, the whole picture is wrong.

So many narrow views of *Absalom, Absalom!* by a wide range of critics, early and late, amply document the case. Some miscellaneous opinions of other novels are also extraordinary enough to merit at least passing attention. When all the humanity of the poor characters in their terrible plights is omitted, *The Sound and the Fury* becomes a provincial consideration of the fall of the South. It is also Christian allegory. Benjy is "the parable of Jesus reborn in the Deep South at the time of its fall."[24] Now that one would surprise both Oxford and Faulkner—and Jesus. *Light in August* for some readers is a racist

21. Hoffman, 78.
22. Warren Beck, *Faulkner* (Madison: The University of Wisconsin Press, 1976), 24.
23. Olga W. Vickery, *The Novels of William Faulkner: A Critical Interpretation* (Baton Rouge: Louisiana State University Press, 1961), 93.
24. Joachim Seyppel, *William Faulkner* (New York: Frederick Ungar Publishing Company, 1971), 45.

tract. If Percy Grimm is a Ku Klux lyncher, if Doc Hines is a prime example of a Southern Calvinist bigot, what shall we say of the loves of Lena and Mrs. Hines? Are they regional generalizations too? Faulkner's country whites are misinterpreted as much as his Sutpens and Compsons. Some criticism of *As I Lay Dying* mistakes a Southern farm family in terrible adversity for the worst of contemptible rednecks. "It does sort of amuse me," Faulkner once chuckled, "when I hear 'em talking about the sociological picture that I present in something like *As I Lay Dying.*"[25]

One piece of criticism of *Light in August* illustrates the major problems in the allegorical interpretations and equal-sign criticism of the novel. Every single one of these glaring revelations makes a misstatement about the South. The Reverend Hightower is said to represent the "enchanted soul of the South in its shanty castle-keep" as well as "the historical American South in its most tenuous mythic form." Joe Christmas's life is the story "in which the South is revealed as a psychological battleground on which is waged a racial civil war." His struggle is "an analogue of the South that Faulkner saw as present actuality." For this sort of critic, race cannot be disentangled from sex; so "this aspect of the South," "hating the self, . . . fastens on the sexual act as a form of self-debasement." Joe, then, is an "avatar of that South." Hightower, himself more Southern than human in these terms, is "the exemplar of tradition that has failed the South." And finally, adding it all up, the critic asserts that *Light in August* is a "parable of Southern culture."[26]

Some interpretations are beyond confrontation, presumably arrived at by sophisticated students of literature who write with positive certainty about human and regional conditions which

25. Carvel Collins, "Faulkner and Mississippi," *The University of Mississippi Studies in English*, 15 (1978), 159.

26. R. G. Collins, *"Light in August:* Faulkner's Stained Glass Triptych," *Mosaic,* 7 (Fall, 1973), 100, 101, 102.

they have never observed. They have few questions as they have little knowledge. Judging by their critical statements, they know little more of the South than they know of the lost Atlantis. They cannot read Faulkner, and they apparently have no comprehension of the ways of the human heart, whether or not it is Southern. Presumably intelligent editors have accepted their work, readers listen to and believe their errors, and conferences of amateurs and professionals listen and sometimes approve what they cannot rationally believe. Considering the breadth of the chasm that separates the culture of Faulkner and the South from the modern world, I see little cause for change or improvement. Much of the criticism is certainly becoming more abstract, and abstraction is more difficult to combat than error. Future criticism may remove us further and further from Faulkner's stand about the South and mankind.

Fortunately, however, there are good critics, many of them. They have made the works of Faulkner available to the sensitive mind. The best of all his interpreters, I believe, is Faulkner. A single sentence sometimes cuts to the heart of the truth. Often he spoke with his tongue in his cheek; sometimes he teased his listeners; sometimes out of shyness or forgetfulness he plainly did not tell the truth. But in all of his statements about his fiction, I believe, he provided very little basis for absurd interpretations of his writing or of his homeland. He took a stand in his statements about himself, his region, and his writing, in his statements ouside of fiction. Rarely indeed did he take a stand *in* his fiction, and when he did it was usually in his worst fiction.

He took his stand all by himself. He could not have collaborated with any group, not even with one other man. It was a lonely stand, devout and independent, but one by which he stood alone, wrote his fiction, and lived his life. Faulkner clearly stated beliefs which make his fiction non-sociological and non-regional. If he had written a single book with the same purpose

for him that *I'll Take My Stand* had for the Agrarians, an assembled statement of principles like the one Ransom wrote for
the Agrarians would contain some of the following:

As a writer, Faulkner found the South necessary because it was
the place he knew. "I just happen to know it, and don't have time in
life to learn another one and write it at the same time."[27]

The South "is probably as good [a place] as another, life is a
phenomenon but not a novelty. . . ." "Man stinks the same stink no
matter where in time."[28]

Editorial criticisms "deriving from ignorance of Southern ways"
are irritating.[29]

In April, 1939, Faulkner said, "The South . . . was the only part of
the country that currently seemed interested in art."[30]

"Art is no part of Southern life."[31]

"The rest of the United States knows next to nothing about the
South. The present idea and picture which they hold of a people
decadent and even obsolete through inbreeding and illiteracy—the
inbreeding a result of the illiteracy and the isolation so that there is
nothing else to do at night— . . . is as baseless and illusory as that
one a generation ago of (oh, yes, we subscribed to it too) columned
porticoes and magnolias."[32]

"I love my country [here he means the South] enough to want to
cure its faults and the only way that I can cure its faults within my
capacity, within my own vocation, is to shame it, to criticize, to try
to show the difference between its evils, its good, its moments of
baseness, and its moments . . . when it was glorious."[33]

The South is "the only really authentic region in the United
States, because a deep indestructible bond still exists between man
and his environment. In the South, above all, there is still a common

27. Blotner, 1172.
28. *Ibid.*
29. *Ibid.*, 937.
30. *Ibid.*, 1022.
31. *Ibid.*, 810.
32. *Essays, Speeches and Public Letters*, ed. James B. Meriwether (New York: Random House, 1965), 88.
33. *Faulkner at Nagano*, ed. Robert A. Jelliffe (Tokyo: Kenkyusha Ltd., 1956), 125–26.

acceptance of the world, a common view of life, and a common morality."[34]

"I think that no writer's got time to be drawing a picture of a region, or preaching anything—if he's trying to preach you a sermon, then he's not really a writer, he's a propagandist."[35]

"The sociological qualities are only, in my opinion, coincidental to the story—the story is still the story of the human being, the human heart struggling."[36]

There are contradictions as well as paradoxes and complexities in these bare assembled statements. Overall, the supreme and singular statement is that the individual, the person, transcends any single system or pattern. Faulkner's beliefs are not comparable in schematized thinking to the Declaration of Independence, a communist manifesto, a diplomatic white paper, or the ninety-five theses nailed on the church door. Faulkner was not a man of lesser integrity than the authors of these proclamations; rather, he was an artist. It is the duty of an artist to see in terms of contradictions and complexities. Indeed, those of Faulkner's time who thought most like him, the Nashville Agrarians, shared similar bewilderments and inconsistencies. It is not remarkable that in later years they spoke of their *I'll Take My Stand* in philosophical more than in programmatic terms.

Those who have read Faulkner correctly are usually Southern or rural or extraordinarily empathetic. In reading about Faulkner's people they have St. Paul's faith, hope, and charity as well as the anger of an Old Testament prophet. The statements of principles which may be derived from the good critics about Faulkner are basic and almost plain. Some of the most important things that have been said are these:

---

34. *Lion in the Garden: Interviews with William Faulkner 1926–1962*, ed. James B. Meriwether and Michael Millgate (Lincoln: University of Nebraska Press, 1968), 72.
35. *Faulkner at West Point*, ed. Joseph L. Fant and Robert Ashley (New York: Random House, 1964), 50–51.
36. *Ibid*.

"We jump to conclusions if we assume, as some people have, that Faulkner sees the Southern community as constituted of bigoted ruffians."[37]

"We have no grounds for assuming that any detail of the fiction is present for historical, sociological, geographical, or political reasons."[38]

"The drama that engrosses Faulkner concerns a state of being, a conflict involving, to some degree at least, the spiritual integrity of a character."[39]

"The novels of William Faulkner . . . show in elaborate profusion . . . concern for 'blood' "—that is in the sense of family, tradition.[40]

"To forge the conscience of his race, he stayed in his native spot and, in his soul, in images of vice and of virtue, reenacted the history of that race."[41]

The "emphasis" is "not in terms of South and North, but in terms of issues common to our modern world."[42]

"Many of our critics . . . refuse . . . to extend any sympathy or recognition to the grief of the white redneck."[43] "The book most fully about the poor white, As I Lay Dying, is full of sympathy and poetry."[44]

"Faulkner is not concerned ultimately with the South."[45]

Some generalizations of particular critics about Southern writers are so directly applicable to Faulkner that they deserve

37. Cleanth Brooks, "The Sense of Community in Yoknapatawpha Fiction," *The University of Mississippi Studies in English*, 15 (1978), 12.

38. Michael Millgate, "Faulkner and the South: Some Reflections," *The South and Faulkner's Yoknapatawpha*, ed. Evans Harrington and Ann J. Abadie (Jackson: University Press of Mississippi, 1977), 205.

39. Robert Penn Warren, "T. S. Stribling: A Paragraph in the History of Critical Realism," *The American Review*, 2 (February 1934), 484.

40. Keith F. McKean, "Southern Patriarch: A Portrait," *The Virginia Quarterly Review*, 36 (Summer 1960), 379–80.

41. Robert Penn Warren, "Faulkner: The South and the Negro," *The Southern Review*, 1 n. s. (Summer 1965), 529.

42. Robert Penn Warren, *Selected Essays* (New York: Random House, 1958), 65.

43. Calvin S. Brown, "Faulkner's Universality," *The Maker and the Myth: Faulkner and Yoknapatawpha, 1977*, ed. Evans Harrington and Ann J. Abadie (Jackson: University Press of Mississippi, 1978), 161.

44. Robert Penn Warren, "Cowley's Faulkner," *The New Republic*, 115 (August 26, 1946), 234.

45. Warren, *Selected Essays*, 68.

to be included in any statement of principles to which he would subscribe.

"In their social criticism the Southerners are led, by their sense of the concrete, to suspect the fashionable abstraction, the clichés and slogans, which to the unperceiving may seem the very embodiment of truth but which on inspection are found to ignore many realities of the actual human being."[46]

For the Southerner "the point of the story is the story, and he is stopped and confused when a single statement is extracted from it for sociological or political analysis."[47]

"Southern piety is basically an acceptance of the inscrutability of nature."[48] "The right attitude toward nature and man is love. And love is the opposite of the lust for power over nature or over other men."[49]

"The South could remain simple-minded because it had no use for the intellectual agility required to define its position. Its position was self-sufficient and self-evident. . . . The Southern mind was simple, not top-heavy with learning it had no need of, unintellectual and composed; it was personal and dramatic, rather than abstract and metaphysical; it was sensuous."[50]

No one may summarize fully and well the aesthetic, philosophical, and cultural views of a man of profound mind. Faulkner and all of his critics cannot codify his fiction and its meaning.

Just as the quantity of publications on religion or Christianity is beyond the comprehension of the mind while the Bible (despite some textual disagreements) is accepted as the Word, so the quantities of writings about the South are enormous; but two books seem to summarize for many the opposing classical views

46. Robert B. Heilman, "The Southern Temper," in Louis D. Rubin, Jr., and Robert D. Jacobs, *Southern Renascence: The Literature of the Modern South* (Baltimore: The Johns Hopkins Press, 1953), 6.

47. Richard M. Weaver, "Aspects of the Southern Philosophy," in Rubin and Jacobs, 16.

48. *Ibid.*, 20.

49. Warren, *Selected Essays*, 71.

50. Allen Tate, "Remarks on the Southern Religion," in *I'll Take My Stand* (New York: Harper and Brothers Publishers, 1930), 171–72.

of Southern culture and Southern life: the twelve Nashville Agrarians' *I'll Take My Stand* and W. J. Cash's *The Mind of the South*. Of those who were Fugitives and Agrarians, Davidson, Tate, and Warren liked Faulkner's work exceedingly; Ransom sometimes demurred. Cash was a member of the not always loyal opposition. So far as I know, Faulkner, characteristically, never spoke of either book. He would have regarded *The Mind of the South* with utter contempt except for an occasional and perhaps accidental or casual agreement. The comparison between Faulkner and *I'll Take My Stand* is a different matter. If it were not for the personality of Faulkner, it would be amazing that good minds who were so much alike in so many ways and who lived geographically so close together during the same time span could have had so little to do with each other personally and intellectually. I do not know of any serious conflicts in the thinking of Faulkner and that of the Agrarians. The nearest thing I can find to opposition is the willingness to enlist active political aid from non-Southern allies. Faulkner would have scorned even loose political and social alignments.

The similar principles and beliefs between Faulkner and his contemporaries in Tennessee are surprising because of certain irreconcilable differences in temperament. The Agrarians were bookish and intellectual; they were academic; they earned academic degrees and graduate degrees; their personal gatherings sometimes resembled classroom meetings; they knew the current literary fads; they studied the critical schools and thinking; they even created schools of critical thinking (if indeed there ever was much reality to the associations among the New Critics, as they were called); they corresponded on literary matters; they founded little magazines; they delighted in terminologies; they read and criticized each other's works.

Faulkner read a lot; he talked some (though seldom with high-toned literary groups); he listened more; he ignored many literary fads; he was not at all academic; he did not finish high school

or attend universities except as a special student; he never pro-
fessed to teach in a university except when he agreed to talk to
students in his office at the University of Virginia and when he
would answer questions (but never lecture) before a class in that
institution. Faulkner was a writer, and he at least claimed to be a
farmer.

Strangely, Faulkner and the Fugitive-Agrarians all preached
anti-intellectualism even though they were themselves intellectuals. Quentin Compson and Gail Hightower are to be loved and
ardently to be pitied, but the life of their minds greatly out-
weighed the love of their hearts and the activities of their
bodies. So also with Allen Tate's thinker at the gate of the Confederate cemetery; so with Ransom's friar contemplating the
dead warriors and with the unfilled lovers in Ransom's poems; so
with Warren's Jack Burden for most of the years of his life and
with Jed Tewksbury in Warren's last novel.

Without exchanges except through the public media, Faulkner and the Agrarians opposed what Davidson called
"megalopolitan agglomerations," sociology and its methods and
attitudes and conclusions, modernism (see the old General's
view of the future world in *A Fable*), industrialism and mass
production (see the description of the Northern use of black
labor in "The Bear"), massive populations and organizations,
mechanization, science and its products (note Mrs. Ab Snopes's
cream separator in *The Hamlet* and Faulkner's statement about
automatic piloting devices for airplanes in a letter to a New York
newspaper), the belief that labor *per se* is evil, big government
and bureaucracy, the lack of reverence and religion in industrial
societies, ardent social idealism, the lack of a place for the arts
and the artist in an industrial society, progress, advertising, and
the mass media (neither Robert Penn Warren nor William
Faulkner ever allowed a television set in his home).

The Agrarians and Faulkner philosophically like the same
things: a close relationship to the land and nature, the historical

and the traditional, farming, the rural, the South, individualism and small communities, labor (especially that of a craftsman such as the carpenter Cash Bundren), and a simple religion (such as that of Faulkner's Brother Fortinbride in *The Unvanquished*). Of course this is not to say that the Mississippi author and the Nashville group lived in the same way, practiced the same customs, or followed their doctrines religiously and without deviation from their own principles or from the beliefs of their literary confreres. But all were Southern, they thought alike, and in many ways a great deal of the time they did the same sort of thing. Between 1929 and the early forties, Faulkner wrote fiction which, in Frost's terms, did not "state its sting." In his later, lesser works, Faulkner paraded forth his meanings, and some of his art verged on or became explicit, doctrinaire, hortatory, proclamatory. The great years of Faulkner's fiction lasted an extraordinarily long time, however, compared to the Roman candle flameouts in the careers of many authors. But the evangelical Faulkner also wrote for a period of many years after the great time was past. As critics, we can arbitrarily omit the Faulkner of obstrusive meanings which had become dominant by *Intruder in the Dust* and the late 1940s. His art did not cease. It just diminished as the preachments inflated. But given the facts of the beliefs of Faulkner the man, how much are they present in the great period, what are they, and where do they appear? First, still mostly excluding race, what are some of the evangelical preachments of the Faulkner who intended first to *mean* and only second to *be* in his art? Faulkner usually is an artist, not a polemicist, but within and without his fiction there are some statements which suggest he was a politician, a radical, or an idealist for a cause. Sometimes these statements ignore the fiction, suspend his usual principles, and make him sound unlike the novelist from Oxford.

Especially when Faulkner spoke extemporaneously and especially when the subject was race, he became doctrinaire. He said at West Point "that basically what the people in the South are afraid of is the Negro vote."[51] He told a Japanese audience that "the whole trouble between the black and the white is not in anything racial or [ethnic]. It's an economic fear that if the white man allows the Negro any sort of advancement whatever, the Negro will take his economy away from him."[52] I can only believe that Faulkner was caught offguard and that in this instance he overstated because of the whim of the moment.

Even the staunchest defenders of Faulkner admit that there are degrees of polemical explicitness in the later works: *Intruder in the Dust,* in the long parts spoken by Gavin Stevens for himself or for Faulkner, contains extended argument on the race question; *Requiem for a Nun* speaks to the issues of modernism and bureaucracy; *A Fable* moralizes on the issues of the meaning of humanity, freedom, modernism, and warfare; passages in the Snopes trilogy proclaim as much as they enact and create; a few of the short stories are sentimentally patriotic about World War II; and even in *Go Down, Moses,* especially in the fourth book, there are too many preachments for the book to be, as some have described it, Faulkner's finest work. Some of the best writing appears occasionally toward the end of his career, but most of it is not there. Not only did the late Faulkner sometimes nod—he almost entirely went to sleep.

In the great period of his writing and in some of the great works, Faulkner also occasionally nodded. That is, he took a stronger stand on controversial and regional questions than a writer of fiction should take. In two of the great novels, *Light in August* and *The Hamlet* especially, there are caricatures of the South in the manner of cartoonists. These oversimplifications of the characters are superficial and even stereotyped representations; they do not probe the profundities of the human heart as

---

51. *Faulkner at West Point,* 53.
52. *Faulkner at Nagano,* 77.

Faulkner did at his best. If the wonder of Darl Bundren is that so much sensitivity and poetry could exist in the heart of a man seen as a stranger even in his own country community as well as in the minds of non-Southern critics, such wonder is not apparent in the family of Lena Grove. Her relatives resemble cartoons of bearded and overalled Southerners sitting around whiskey stills, holding shotguns, and uttering funny one-liners.

On the one hand, consider the complexities of the emotions and tensions at work around the deathbed of Addie Bundren. On the other, consider the deaths of Lena's parents. The setting is two dimensional, a representation of all that the hostile ones could gleefully find in the depraved backwoods of Mississippi:

> When she was twelve years old her father and mother died in the same summer, in a log house of three rooms and a hall, without screens, in a room lighted by a bug-swirled kerosene lamp. . . . Her mother died first. She said, "Take care of paw." Lena did so. Then one day her father said, "You go to Doane's Mill with McKinley. You get ready to go, be ready when he comes." Then he died. McKinley, the brother, arrived in a wagon. They buried the father in a grove behind a country church one afternoon, with a pine headstone. The next morning she departed forever.

The love one expects to find regularly in Faulkner is here. The mother thinks of the father, and the father thinks of the daughter as Caddy did of Benjy and her father. But the love is not *revealed* as it is in *As I Lay Dying* or *The Sound and the Fury*. Lena's origins are depicted in thin penciled drawings unusual in the best of Faulkner.

Lena's brother works in a sawmill. "It was cutting pine. It had been there seven years and in seven years more it would destroy all the timber within its reach. Then . . . it would be loaded onto freight cars and moved away. . . . The machinery . . . left . . . [would be] gaunt, staring, motionless wheels . . . [in] a stumppocked scene of profound and peaceful desolation." It does not matter whether the exploiters were capitalists from the

North or the South. This desolate waste land is drawn in stick figures and wisps of smoke with a pencil mark or two trailing off into the blank sky. For the moment Faulkner has lapsed into the falseness of simplistic cartoons. Lena becomes one of the most remarkable women of his fiction, but she begins in a more barren place artistically than any other scene in Yoknapatawpha. By way of contrast, there is the depth and the complexity and even the humanity of the wilderness in *Go Down, Moses*. Here too the machinery comes and the forest is destroyed, but the fall of the wilderness is the decline of a world depicted in fullness rather than in sparse haste and barren art.

The Hamlet (the first book of the Snopes trilogy) also begins in all the externality of social conditions and poverty and inhumanity rather than the internality and the humanity of fiction. The materials resemble the studies of the North Carolina sociologists like Howard Odum and Arthur Raper. Faulkner writes of "the gutted shell" of the Old Frenchman's place, of jungles, "small shiftless mortgaged farms," squabbling directors of banks, "home-made whiskey stills and Protestant psalm-books," illiteracy, immigrant frontiersmen who brought with them only what "they could carry in their hands," of cotton and corn used for making whiskey, "frequent homicides," and other materials of a socially caricatured South. These whites, most of them poor, were not the Snopeses. They were the good country people of Frenchman's Bend.

The beginning of the book, however, is only a small part of the story of the community. Even though the Snopes trilogy is one of the works in which Faulkner paints many human beings as despicable, the poor farmers of the community ultimately do endure. True, they seem to lose in the horse trades of "Spotted Horses." They lose their money and they wind up without horses, but those with humanity in the beginning preserve it to the end. Flem Snopes outsmarts them in a horse trade, but their loss in trading is not the ultimate value of their character. It's a "good sign," Faulkner says, when a man "can still be taken off by the chance to buy a horse for three dollars."[53] They lose hard-earned money, and the wrong-headed Armstid even loses his sanity. But they have their fun. So Faulkner begins with a stereotyped sociological picture of the Southern country white at the first of the trilogy; and he probes deeper. But it must be admitted that the Snopes trilogy never does reach the poetry of *As I Lay Dying*. *The Hamlet* is a book as much about the rural South, perhaps, as any work ever written, but it is not primarily a sociological study except in the beginning.

Some of the short stories written during the great years of Faulkner's career present in various degrees the Southern stereotypes much beloved in the prejudiced souls of those hostile to the region. "Pantaloon in Black," from *Go Down, Moses*, is a marvelous and sympathetic portrait of the soul of the black, but during the entire course of the story there is not a good white man or even a good word or a good action by one white man—or anything bad (without great provocation) in the black. To avoid writing propaganda, Faulkner would have had to omit altogether in some fashion his racist poor whites in the story. "Dry September" has the mood, the atmosphere, the characters, and the situation of Southern lynchings as they are depicted by the naturalistic and inferior writers of the South like T. S. Stribling and Erskine Caldwell. The conniving deputy sheriff in "Old Man" and the bureaucracy that gives the tall convict a ten-year sentence for ardently trying to carry out an assigned duty present comical and slouchy representations of Southern political demagoguery. The strength of the convict, however, is more than enough to offset the sheriff; so the book endures. The crime of Emily Grierson and her secluded loneliness without love in the admiring and somehow sympathetic

53. *Faulkner in the University*, 66.

community of Jefferson without Faulkner's art would have been a regional horror tale, but Emily remains strong and even noble despite her isolation. In "That Evening Sun" the whorehopper and deacon Mr. Stovall, who does not pay Nancy for her wares, could have been created as one kind of typical Southerner, one of the stereotyped leaders of the mercantile class in Cash's *The Mind of the South*, but he is offset by the extraordinary kindnesses of the caring Mr. Compson as he leads Nancy safely home through the perils of her fear of death from the knife of her violent and jealous husband.

The thorough prober and searcher for polemical politics and regional asburdities can find them in Faulkner's fiction, but they are rare. In the books where they do appear some other factor contradicts them. As a writer of fiction, Faulkner took no stand at all sociologically and regionally. Personally he believed in the South and he wrote about it, but he was not a student of its depravities. Whatever frailties of mankind appear in his fiction, they are the weaknesses of us all. His books, then, are works about mankind cast in a Southern vehicle. Faulkner did take a stand, but it was only human.

Those who speak for the universalism of Faulkner's fiction have understandably been forced into extreme positions and statements. One ultimate resort has been to say simply that Faulkner is not writing about the South and to leave it at that. But he did write about the South, and he *did* take a stand. Southerners are good and bad, usually unique unto themselves, sometimes stereotyped in the molds of national patterns or ideological forms. The lack of education and money and luxurious housing, the lack of chromium are characteristics of the South just as the sociologists say. The governments have been demagogic and folkish as well. But if anything these patterns have perhaps just possibly made the individual character a little more eccentric, a little more human, perhaps just slightly better than the modern individuals and the societies that surround the South.

The great themes of Faulkner's fictions are, I think, simply privacy and individualism and love. These beliefs are prevalent everywhere, but it is possible that they are more prevalent and even stronger in the South because of the nature of the Southern heart and the culture of the Southern community.

If Faulkner was not merely creating regional horrors, if he was writing about the universal human verities, what was his supreme theme and truth? The desire and effort of man to be immortal, the impossible yearning to establish a dynasty that will last forever in this world or any other. A character who loves but who does not think first of himself wishes for the sake of others to make an eternal imprint of love on the souls of some other beings. The great villains and demons of this earth struggle for self and for power. The lover of mankind who wishes to live forever by making his own eternal imprint will simultaneously and paradoxically maintain an inviolable privacy and integrity; he will do what he does rather than philosophizing about what ought to be done.

This struggle for an eternal identity—in some ways personal, Southern, human—is at the core of all the great works. Thus:

> Caddy Compson, the darling of Faulkner's heart, loves dearly and also, alas, loosely and promiscuously. She loves her lovers and Benjy and Quentin and her father, perhaps even a Nazi general after her good love becomes impossible. In a sense, she achieves her glory of immortality (I am aware of the contradiction) at least for a time. The idiot Benjy as he goes to sleep on his terribly confusing day told about in *The Sound and the Fury* thinks of Caddy still in the present tense although she has been gone for decades. In his last words on that day he talks of what Caddy "says" when he has been asleep. She still lives.

> Thomas Sutpen wishes to establish a dynasty that will live forever in the bloodlines of his descendants. Evil as he is, in the very title Faulkner links Sutpen's impossible and tragic desires with the eter-

nity of the line of David and, through the line of David, with the immortality of Christ.

With all his adversaries and with his limitations, Joe Christmas—directly linked with the details of the life of Christ—has aspirations. Before he could possibly yearn as Sutpen and Addie Bundren do, he would have to learn who he is. Before he can be like the others, he must first overcome the primordial and at the same time modern task of establishing his own identity.

Addie Bundren, one of the most ardent aspirers of them all, endures marriage, childbirth, adultery, and even death to attain an immortality which will make her unforgettable to her children and to any who know them in the times to come. And one cannot even deny that she aspires to a greater immortality even than that.

Ike McCaslin, prophet and failure, defines the wrongs of his own world and even of all time, and though he fails to correct them, he tries—at least for a long time.

One of the lesser novels, *A Fable* places man's hope for peace and immortality in the common grave of the human race, the tomb of the unknown soldier. He is a corporal, too obviously an image of the Christ. The old theme is there, but the novel is not great fiction at least in part because of its lack of a Southern vehicle to embody the meaning.

When Faulkner became didactic and used non-Southern vehicles, he created his weakest art. His fiction was best when he spoke softly in a Southern voice and carried no stick at all. His success as a Southern writer ultimately is an inexplicable mystery. He did not comprehend his stand himself. In 1953 he wrote to Joan Williams, "Now I realize for the first time what an amazing gift I had: uneducated in every formal sense, without even very literate, let alone literary, companions, yet to have made the things I made. I dont know where it came from. I dont know why God or gods, or whoever it was, selected me to be the vessel."[54]

54. Faulkner, *Selected Letters*, ed. Joseph Blotner (New York: Random House, 1977), 348.

He did have an amazing gift; it was Southern and also transcendent of such limitations; he *did* take a stand. But it must not be given the wrong definitions; and perhaps it is impossible to state very exactly outside Faulkner's own writing what it was.

The Dixie Special:
William Faulkner and the
Southern Literary Renascence

LOUIS D. RUBIN, JR.

"Because he's the head bear. He's
the man." FAULKNER, "THE BEAR"

On the grounds of the capitol of Ohio in Columbus is a large
statue in which that Midwestern state is represented, in classical
garb upon a granite pedestal, as Cornelia, mother of the Grac-
chi, holding forth her hands and declaring, "These are my
jewels!" The jewels, depicted in bronze statuary below, are
Ulysses S. Grant, Philip Sheridan, James A. Garfield, W. T.
Sherman, Edwin M. Stanton, Salmon P. Chase, and Rutherford
B. Hayes. Unfortunately William McKinley, Mark Hanna, and
Warren G. Harding came along too late to make the cluster.

I wish to propose, to anyone who has political influence, that a
similar statue be erected on the capitol grounds in Jackson. Let
the State of Mississippi be Cornelia. Let the gems in her tiara be
William Faulkner, Eudora Welty, Richard Wright, Elizabeth
Spencer, Shelby Foote, Tennessee Williams, and the late Major
Frederick Sullens. (Major Sullens's replica should have its eyes
averted from the others.) I leave it to the State Fine Arts Com-
mission to decide whether the Roman motif should be carried
out in all details. I cannot quite imagine William Faulkner clad
in a toga, though I daresay it would seem no more incongruous

upon him than the riding-habit in the famous Cofield photograph. One thing is certain, however: in any such cluster Faulkner should be placed in the center, with the others grouped around him.

The Southern Literary Renascence, as it is called, is now some sixty years old. It was the literary product and image of the belated and violent confrontation of the Southern states with modern, secular, industrial civilization. A closely-bound community, threadbare, traditional, agricultural, religiously orthodox, with a somewhat flexible system of class and a very rigid, inflexible caste system, infused with a powerful mythology and a commonly-shared history of pride and defeat, rejoined the American Union. The reunion had been long in coming. Slavery, the defeat of the war, Reconstruction, and then decades of social, political, and economic trauma had held off the impact of the industrial revolution and its technological, urban-centered society. When finally the change did begin to come to the Southern community, the social and moral drama of its advent, the dislocation of sensibility, was uncommonly intense.

Because the Southern community had always had a pervasive, if hitherto mostly ineffectual, literary tradition, and had for generations, in pulpit, hustings, editorial sanctum, and front porch, been given to defining itself in and through language, it was only to be expected that it would be in literature, through stories, novels, poems, that the transaction would be articulated. In short order the Southern literary imagination shook off its blinders of local color and apologia. As Allen Tate noted, with the war of 1917–1918 the young Southerners of his generation looked around them and began realizing, for the first time, that the Yankees were not to blame for everything that was unsatisfactory about Southern experience. From rhetoric—the defense of the community from fixed, preestablished premises, the quarrel with others—the literary South moved into dialectic—the quarrel with oneself, the effort to define oneself in relation to the community.[1] *Who am I in time and place? What is my history?*

The ideological headquarters for this investigative activity was Nashville, Tennessee. There, in and about Vanderbilt University, the question was articulated topically and programmatically. The publishing headquarters, alas, was New York City, which posed certain difficulties for the writers, and still does. The artistic headquarters was clearly Mississippi, though there were numerous additional branch offices from Texas to Virginia. The Renascence lasted, in its most intense phase, for something over thirty years. Though with diminished intensity it is still going on.

Why have so many of the very best writers of the Southern Literary Renascence come out of Mississippi? In part, perhaps, because of all the Southern states it was the most rural, the most threadbare and quixotic, the least removed from the conditions of a frontier. The two largest cities in Mississippi, it used to be said, were Memphis and New Orleans. In Mississippi the suddenness of social and cultural change was most violent, the contrasts it offered most dramatic. Mad Ireland hurt you into poetry, the poet Auden remarked of William Butler Yeats; one might also say the same for the sole owner and proprietor of Yoknapatawpha County.

But all this sounds rather more like sociology than literary analysis, and one feels uncomfortable making such generalizations. One might justly feel uncomfortable, indeed, talking about an entity known as "Southern Literature," instead of about the works of this particular writer or that. Yet what can one do? If there were only Faulkner, or only Eudora Welty—or only Thomas Wolfe, or the Nashville Fugitives, or whoever—the

1. See Tate's essays "A Southern Mode of the Imagination," in *Essays of Four Decades* (Chicago: The Swallow Press, 1959), 577–92, and "Faulkner's *Sanctuary* and the Southern Myth," in *Memories and Opinions, 1926–1974* (Chicago: The Swallow Press, 1975), 144–54.

matter could be ascribed simply to the workings of chance and the unaccountability of the incidence of genius. But there are so many of them, and all at the same time and in the same place. The economically-deprived, culturally-remote states of the onetime Confederacy, with a modest-sized population, a high illiteracy rate, and a substandard economy, produced, during the years when President Roosevelt called the South the nation's Number One economic problem, a disproportionate number of widely talented writers. Faulkner was perhaps the most distinguished of a galaxy of accomplished literary artists.

The resemblances, the common subjects, themes, attitudes toward human nature and history shared by most of the writers of the Southern Renascence have long since been documented, and I have nothing very new to add to that now. Suffice it to say that the adjectives "modern" and "Southern" modify the noun "literature" not merely geographically and temporally but artistically and culturally, in terms of history, politics, language, and even religion. However the lineaments of Yoknapatawpha County may differ from those of Altamont in Old Catawba, or from Morgana 150 miles or so to the south, or from Burden's Landing down on the Gulf Coast, however individual the imaginations of every one of the modern Southern writers, they are united by shared concerns and common attitudes that make their work, whether in verse or prose, indentifiable culturally and geographically. " 'The South,' " a young Canadian remarks to a young Mississippian in a Faulkner novel. " 'The South. Jesus. No wonder you folks all outlive yourselves by years and years and years.' "[2] And again, " 'What is it? something you live and breathe in like air?' "[3] Whatever it is, or was, it provided the Southern Renascence with a recognizable and distinctive literary flavor, one unlike that of any other notable body of American writing.

2. William Faulkner, *Absalom, Absalom!* (New York: Random House, 1936), 377.
3. *Ibid.*, 361.

Faulkner and the Southern Literary Renascence

Leslie Fiedler wrote that the "mythopoetic genius" of Faulkner has largely been responsible for the fact "that the South has remained through the last three decades our preferred literary arena of terror"; the regional confrontation with racial difference is also responsible for that, he says.[4] Yet even without Faulkner's work the output of the literary South in the twentieth century would have been considered quite remarkable indeed. Nor is it merely Fiedler's particular obsession—gothic terror, the angularities of violence and pain—that is its hallmark. The rituals of community experience, the complexities of social involvement, the celebration of idiosyncracy: these have also characterized a body of literature that has been unmistakably identifiable as growing out of a place and time.

Of course there can be little doubt that Faulkner is the giant of the Renascence—as Sam Fathers would put it, he is the Head Bear. A younger contemporary, Flannery O'Connor, was always ready to reply to the almost inevitable question of how she felt, as a Southern author, about working in the shadow of Faulkner, that nobody likes to get caught on the tracks when the Dixie Special comes through. As for Faulkner himself, he appeared to take little interest in the work of most of his Southern contemporaries. Allen Tate wrote that "it is a part of Mr. Faulkner's legend about himself that he did appear, like the sons of Cadmus, full grown, out of the unlettered soil of his native state, Mississippi. But we are under no obligation to take his word for it. Two other modern writers of prose-fiction, Mr. Stark Young and Miss Eudora Welty, quite as gifted as Mr. Faulkner, if somewhat below him in magnitude and power, are also natives of that backward state, where fewer people can read than in any other state in the Union."[5] I would say that Tate was right about Miss Welty, who to my mind is nearest to Faulkner's stature

---

4. Leslie A. Fieldler, *Love and Death in the American Novel* (New York: Criterion Books, 1960), 448.
5. Tate, "A Southern Mode of the Imagination," 577.

among all their contemporaries, and that about Stark Young he was betrayed by his own weakness for authentic plantation ancestry into elevating a talented local colorist into the company of two greater writers. No matter; the point is that as one of the better modern Southern authors, William Faulkner was not unique but exemplary: *primus inter pares*.

Faulkner's attitude toward his identity as a Southern writer was rather ambivalent. At times he readily accepted the identification, at other times he sought to deny it. We need pay little heed to his remarks of the latter sort. They were made mostly in interviews, and depending upon his mood at the time, how much he had had to drink, and his feeling toward the interviewer, Faulkner was prone to say almost anything, however outrageous, during the course of an interview. He is also not the only good Southern author of his day who felt compelled at times to deny the regional literary identification; they seem to fear that to be labeled in such fashion would rob them of some of their universality and make them into genteel local colorists who purvey the quaint surfaces of regional life. Joel Chandler Harris and Harry Stillwell Edwards were Southern writers; therefore, to be a Southern writer is to write like Joel Chandler Harris and Harry Stillwell Edwards—so the equation goes. Faulkner knew better, however, as when he told the youth of Japan in 1955 that "I believe it is war and disaster which remind man most that he needs a record of his endurance and toughness. I think that is why after our own disaster there rose in my country, the South, a resurgence of good writing, writing of a good enough quality that people in other lands began to talk of a 'regional' Southern literature until even I, a countryman, have become one of the first names in our literature which the Japanese people want to talk to and listen to."[6]

A characteristic aspect of Faulkner's public personality was his

6. Faulkner, "To the Youth of Japan," in *Essays, Speeches and Public Letters*, ed. James B. Meriwether (New York: Random House, 1965), 83.

dislike of being taken for an intellectual, a mere *litterateur*. It is this that accounts in large part for his notable reluctance to associate with other literary people or to admit to an interest in his fellow Southern authors. Joseph Blotner, in his splendid biography, tells us about the occasion in 1931 when Ellen Glasgow and Professor James Southall Wilson of the University of Virginia organized a conference of Southern writers. Faulkner was one of thirty-four authors invited to take part. He was obviously flattered at being asked to come to the University of Virginia, but he was also uneasy with the idea of being involved in such overt literary doings. In this letter of acceptance he replied that "you have seen a country wagon come into town, with a hound dog under the wagon. It stops on the square and the folks get out, but that hound never gets very far from that wagon. He might be cajoled or scared out for a short distance, but first thing you know he has scuttled back under the wagon; maybe he growls at you a little. Well, that's me."[7] He showed up well fortified for the literary occasion, and spent much of his time thereafter replenishing his armor. At the opening session, as Ellen Glasgow offered a series of authoritative pronouncements about "The Southern Writer and His Public," Faulkner would raise his head softly and murmur, "I agree, I agree." Obviously he wasn't very comfortable at being part of an intellectual and social event involving so many formidable men and women of letters. He also graciously informed a newspaper reporter that Southern writers of the day were only pioneers, and nothing "of any real value" was likely to emerge from the South for at least twenty-five years.[8]

The image of the hound dog, ostensibly so modest and self-

7. Joseph Blotner, *Faulkner: A Biography* (New York: Random House, 1974), I, 706.
8. Blotner's description of the conference at Charlottesville is in *Faulkner: A Biography*, I, 707–16. Dorothy Scura gives an account of the conference in "Glasgow and the Southern Renaissance," in M. Thomas Inge, ed., *Ellen Glasgow: Centennial Essays* (Charlottesville: University Press of Virginia, 1976), 46–61.

deprecatory, is really nothing of the sort. What Faulkner was suggesting to James Southall Wilson, and what he was doing when from time to time he described himself as just a plain old countryman, was that he was no intellectual with lean brow and hollow eye, given to unseasonable meditativeness, who went about attending literary teas and discoursing learnedly about the artist in the modern world; he was the real thing, a natural-born story teller, of the earth earthy, with nothing of the highbrow about him. If this fails fully to explain how *The Sound and the Fury* got written, never mind. The same stance, somewhat more skillfully camouflaged, is characteristic of almost all the Southern writers of his time (and, indeed, of many other American writers). It has been very important to the Southern writer of Faulkner's generation to insist that, for all his literary interests, he is still a working member of the general middle-class community. One must not be set apart from the hurly-burly of the practical, everyday, non-literary world. Ideas and the intellect are to be kept in their place.

Intellectually and temperamentally a distrust of abstract ideas has been a long-standing characteristic of Southern life. Perhaps in part it goes back to the time when the South was forced to defend the massive and complex reality of the Southern community, defaced as it was with the presence of human slavery, against the single-minded ideological assault of Abolitionist reformers. Whatever the origins, the Southern sensibility has long been marked by a suspicion of intellectual formulations, and the fear that too great a reliance upon theory will falsify the complexity of real life. Is it merely coincidence that the one important school of literary criticism that the Southerners have developed should be based upon the assumption that ideas alone will not do, that theories will of themselves never suffice to explain the poem?

Faulkner, of course, was no theorist. But the same distrust of the pure idea is very much a part of his aesthetic. His very style itself, with the long sentences, the liberal deployment of adjectives, the parentheses, and the parentheses within parentheses, proceeds from the conviction that reality can be represented only when presented in its full complexity, leaving out nothing that is important. His admiration for Thomas Wolfe, he said on several occasions, was for that novelist's attempt, however impossible of fulfillment, to put all experience on the head of a pin.

In any event, the suspicion of theory as leading to oversimplification is something that the Southern writers of Faulkner's generation came by naturally. There is more to it than this, however; it is not only a philosophical attitude that is involved, but a psychological need. For the writers of the Southern Renascence were not merely dubious about too much celebration; they were also zealous to avoid giving the *appearance* of being intellectuals. As I have already suggested, when Faulkner informs a reporter that he is no intellectual but only a countryman who writes stories, he does so because he feels uncomfortable at being thought of as an intellectual. To assume such a role, or to appear to be assuming it, would be to concede that one is no longer a working member of the general middle-class community.

Thus when Faulkner was informed by a Swedish newspaper correspondent that he had been awarded the Nobel Prize, his response was typical. Having expressed his gratitude, he said that he would be unable to come and accept the prize in person: "It's too far away. I am a farmer down here and I can't get away," he said.[9] (Later he changed his mind about not going.) Not long after the award was announced he went on the annual hunting trip to the Delta with his friends, and though he said nothing about it, one of his companions read about the prize in a newspaper someone had brought along. That evening it was Faulkner's turn to help wash the dishes, and Uncle Ike Roberts spoke up:

9. Blotner, *Faulkner: A Biography*, II, 1338.

"Bill," he said, "what would you do if that Swede ambassador came down here and handed you that money right now?"

With scarcely a pause, Faulkner answered, "I'd tell him just to put it on that table over there and grab a dryin' rag and help," he said, to the delight of his companions.[10]

He had passed the test. He was, in other words, still one of the boys.

Elsewhere I have suggested that an important part of the dynamics lying behind the art of William Faulkner is the creative tension between his ardent desire to write and be a writer, and the feeling, in the small Southern community in which he grew up as oldest son of one of the leading families, that there was something undignified and even unmanly in pursuing such an occupation rather than being a red-blooded, stalwart man of affairs.[11] Throughout his best work there is not just a division but a dichotomy between the man of sensibility and the man of action: Horace Benbow and Bayard Sartoris in *Flags in the Dust*, Quentin Compson and Dalton Ames in *The Sound and the Fury*, Quentin and Thomas Sutpen in *Absalom, Absalom!*, Darl and Jewel Bundren in *As I Lay Dying*, and so on.[12]

This kind of division, which Faulkner felt so strongly during his childhood and early manhood, is by no means peculiar to the South, as witness what was possible to another young man growing up in Oak Park, Illinois, at about the time. But it is certainly characteristic of the South, because the South was small town, middle class, with a long military heritage, given to outdoor pursuits, with little place within the doings of the community for the cultural and intellectual sophistication whereby artistic inclinations on the part of a young man might be understood. Writ-

10. *Ibid.*, 1347.

11. Louis D. Rubin, Jr., "William Faulkner: The Discovery of a Man's Vocation," in George H. Wolfe, ed., *Faulkner: Fifty Years After "The Marble Faun"* (University: University of Alabama Press, 1976), 43–68.

12. For an excellent discussion of this, see an unpublished dissertation by Daniel V. Gribbin, "Men of Thought, Men of Action in Faulkner's Novels" (Ph.D. Dissertation, University of North Carolina at Chapel Hill, 1973).

ing poetry or fiction, taking them seriously: that sort of thing was for women. Any young male who did so, and who had the sensibility to do so, must perforce be less than properly masculine: sicklied o'er with the pale cast of thought, so to speak (or perhaps, since literary and intellectual inclinations usually went along with heresy on racial issues, with the thought of pale caste). This is why Quentin Compson is made so to despise himself for his inability, as protector of the honor of the family females, to stand up to Dalton Ames; he faints dead away. And why he is both fascinated and horrified at the story of the ruthless, unfeeling, entirely masculine Thomas Sutpen. For though Quentin is not overtly a poet or a novelist, he is very obviously Faulkner's young man of sensibility, with the emotional resources of the artist. And this is clearly related to Faulkner's anti-intellectual, country-boy pose. No Quentin Compson he!

I have observed very much the same kind of assumption in the work, and the lives, of almost every one of the modern Southerners, from Cabell and Will Percy on to Wolfe, Tate, Caldwell, Warren, and on up through Walker Percy, Shelby Foote, James Agee, and James Dickey (and in a diminished mode, I do not except myself, either). All seem impelled to demonstrate their masculinity. The element of overkill in Cabell's repeated insistence upon his amatory propensities while young and unmarried is all too obvious. Tate's amusing insistence upon challenging his literary foes to duels was well known. Warren's use of four-letter words for his redneck characters seems highly self-conscious. Wolfe continually depicts his youthful autobiographical protagonists as ridiculed by a crass, unfeeling commercial community because of their artistic leanings. Dickey's novel *Deliverance* is full of it: the ultimate atrocity is to be forced by a redneck to engage in sodomy. And so on.

What I am getting at is that, along with all the other Southern authors of his time, Faulkner's relationship with the rank and file of the Southern community from childhood on was of profound significance, involving powerful tensions and ambiguities. It is not the situation commonly portrayed as that of the writer in modern industrial society—that of the alienated artist. There are elements of alienation, but also strong emotional and intellectual ties to the community. When Faulkner insists that he is no literary man but merely a plain dirt farmer, when he tells James Southall Wilson that he is like the old hound dog who is out of place and uneasy at being in town, he is protesting against an identity that his artistic talents and achievements have tended to force upon him: that of someone who is no longer part of the community. He is denying any such alienation.

And rightly so. For despite the obvious fact that the people who read and value his fiction were mostly not his fellow townsfolk at all, but outsiders who lived in big cities and taught in universities and were sophisticated moderns, nevertheless he wrote the fiction about the community, as a way of giving form and order to his experience as part of the community.

The more that I read and think about the work of the Southern writers, the more convinced I am that it is virtually impossible to overstate the importance of the relationship with the Southern community. The writers of the Southern Renascence grew up in a closely-knit community. The terms of membership were not merely economic but social, political, historical, cultural. It was not the cosmopolitan society of the urban metropolis, but a small town and small city community, mostly middle class, without vast extremes of wealth and station. The Faulkners may have been the local squirearchy, but the boys went to public school with the children of rich and poor, played with them, grew up with them. Though William Faulkner's nascent literary interests set him apart in certain respects from his fellow townsfolk, and though for a time in his very young manhood he made a point of appearing to be different in a small town, he shared, and continued to share, numerous interests and attitudes with his neighbors. Any change in condition or situation, any adult role that tended to remove him too far from his membership in the community made him uncomfortable, because a great deal of what he considered as real and important in his experience was bound in with the life of the community.

Thus the gestures that he made from time to time in the way of emphasizing his community identity constituted a means of assuring not only others but himself as well that he was still a part of the community. It was a way of remaining in close touch with much of what he continued to believe was in important ways *reality*. To do otherwise would be to deny vital aspects of his own identity. He was an artist, and he was a Mississippian; and they were not, so far as he was concerned, mutually irreconcilable roles. Moreover, to be the artist he *had* to remain a Mississippian, for otherwise his contact with reality would be imperilled. His best fiction was an exploration of the sometimes-tortured relationship.

This is true not only for Faulkner but for every one of the writers of the modern South, without regard for whether or not they actually lived and worked in their home communities or even in the South at all. It was there that their imagination had its origins and its links with actuality. Robert Penn Warren, for example, has lived in Connecticut for more than three decades, yet he has remarked that if he were to write a story about a Connecticut farmer, "I wouldn't know where to begin. But writing a story about such a family, rich or poor, grand or miserable, in the South, I wouldn't have any hesitation. It would be as natural as breathing to me. I'd know what they did, I'd know what they ate, I'd know what they'd say."[13] What is striking about the comment is the assumption that the story he would write would perforce be about a farmer, or a farming family: when he thinks about writing fiction he thinks in terms of the

13. "The South: Distance and Change. A Conversation with Robert Penn Warren, William Styron, and Louis D. Rubin, Jr.," in Rubin, ed., *The American South: Portrait of a Culture* (Baton Rouge: Louisiana State University Press, 1980), 305–306.

Southern community of his boyhood and youth. For the Southern novelist of Warren's generation there is where the stuff of fiction is to be found: in the middle-class, non-specialized community experience that he knew before he became an adult writer and man of letters. His fiction is a way of reasserting that identity, not as nostalgia but through the passionate examination of its meanings.

It is true that the very fact that the books are written is emblematic of the writer's distancing from the community. For one thing, the nature of writing poetry and fiction is such that no one would want to do it who was completely and creatively satisfied with the everyday actualities of his experience. For another, the intense exploration of the underlying dimensions of community experience within himself, the insistence upon discerning patterns and meanings, could only come as the result of a perspective, a removal far enough away in time and space to make possible their recognition. But that distancing did not customarily produce, for the men and women of the Southern Renascence, precisely the maimed artist described in Edmund Wilson's wound-and-bow theory of the writer. The Southerners did not flee the community, whether geographically or inwardly, to live in a place of solipsistic pain and isolation. Far from it; emotionally and intellectually they stayed within the thick of things, and sought to understand their time and place in the unique way that literature does: through the passionate rendition of the detailed specificities of that time and place.

The difference between Faulkner's generation of Southern writers, that of the Renascence, and those of an earlier day lay in just that combination of passionate involvement together with aesthetic and moral distancing. In Tate's formulation, the moderns did not view themselves as rhetoricians, charged with the promulgation and defense of Southern ideals. Here is Tate's description of the Southern literary situation before the coming of the modernists:

. . . the South was Uncle Sam's Other Province. This social situation produced a sentimental literature of Narcissism, in which the South tried to define itself by looking into a glass behind its back: not inward. It was thus not a literature of introspection, but a literature of romantic illusion; and its mode was what I have called elsewhere the Rhetorical Mode.

. . . rhetoric in the Reconstruction South was a good way of quarreling with the Yankees, who were to blame for everything. The quarrel raged with sòme cunning and versatility, for it elicited a good deal of fiction in which the Southern gentleman was a Chevalier Bayard *redivivus*, the Poor White a picturesque buffoon who spoke a quaint dialect, and the Negro Rousseau's Natural Man spoiled by having been deprived of the benefits of slavery.[14]

The local color writer was very much involved in the mythic delineation of what he already knew and felt about the community—about the experience of being a Southerner. I do not want to characterize the transaction as merely a patriotic rehearsal of Southern virtues; certainly it was undertaken lovingly and fervently, and it was not always uncritical. A writer such as Joel Chandler Harris, for example, not in his animal tales but his novels, sought to remedy what he saw as flaws in his community by appealing to its better instincts, thereby showing his fellow Southerners what could be while at the same time presenting to outside readers a depiction of Southern life that was both flattering and appealing. But just as it was only in the animal stories that Harris could look at *human* nature as it was, rather than as it ought to be, and describe, albeit as comedy, his own experience without making use of blinders or tinted glasses, so the fiction and poetry of the pre-1917–1918 South was for the most part a celebration of pleasant surfaces, one which has not outlived its occasion.

By contrast the writer of Faulkner's generation, rather than adumbrating what he already knew about his community, en-

14. Tate, "Faulkner's *Sanctuary* and the Southern Myth," *Memories and Opinions*, 146.

gaged in an intense exploraton of himself as a member of that community, writing about what he knew and felt about his community not to edify or encourage others but to understand himself. Faulkner has described the relationship vividly in the never-used introduction of a proposed new edition of *The Sound and the Fury*. The Southerner, he says, writes not about his environment but about himself. He has "figuratively speaking, taken the artist in him in one hand and his milieu in the other and thrust the one into the other like a clawing and spitting cat into a croker sack. And he writes. . . . That cold intellect which can write with calm and complete detachment and gusto of its contemporary scene is not among us. . . ."[15]

It is scarcely surprising that a literary art created in such a spirit would offend Southern partisans of the old school with its depiction of some of the less edifying traits of human nature as manifested in the Southern community. No wonder the late Major Sullens of the *Jackson Daily News* was outraged when a committee of Swedish academicians inexplicably decided to award the Nobel Prize to William Faulkner. The Major did not want literary explorations of the human heart in conflict with itself undertaken in Mississippi; he wanted a defense and reinforcement of contemporary Southern social and racial arrangements. And of course Faulkner was not alone in receiving such treatment. When Thomas Wolfe published *Look Homeward, Angel,* for example, his former classmate Jonathan Daniels declared in the *Raleigh News and Observer* that "here is a young man, hurt by something that he loved, turning in his sensitive fury and spitting on that thing. In *Look Homeward, Angel,* North Carolina and the South are spat upon."[16] And so on.

The onslaught also came from the other end of the spectrum sometimes—from Southern reformers who could not under-

15. Quoted in Blotner, *Faulkner: A Biography,* I, 811.
16. Quoted in Elizabeth Nowell, *Thomas Wolfe: A Biography* (Garden City, N.Y.: Doubleday and Co., 1960), 151.

stand the kind of literary imagination that seeks to explore inwardly instead of taking to the pulpit to preach, as witness Lillian Smith's frequent slaps at Faulkner because he wouldn't produce well-intentioned, easily-digested propaganda for racial justice such as her own *Strange Fruit*.

No doubt the speculation and theorizing on just why an outpouring of important literature in the South appeared when it did and in the forms it took will go on for some time to come. We are, after all, still arguing about just what was involved, culturally, historically, economically, theologically in the American Renaissance (to use the customary spelling for that event) of the 1840s and 1850s. Such interpretations are always bound in with the needs, interests, and fashions of the age doing the interpreting, and these are constantly changing. The tendency for dealing with the phenomenon of modern Southern literature in recent years has been to turn from social history and to adopt the methods and the terms of psychoanalysis, with much talk of incest, doubling, repetition, father figures, and the like. I rather admire some of it—psychoanalysis is something I find fascinating—but I confess that I am too much bound in with the historical ordering itself to be able to do much with so conceptualized an approach to what for me is still very much contemporary literature—which may be where the trouble lies. Moreover, psychoanalysis, especially when conducted by English scholars rather than by trained psychoanalysts, can be a rather glib affair sometimes. The basic assumption usually is that the writer is the neurotic patient, and the novel or poem that patient's daydream. The more imaginative the dream, the more neurotic the dreamer: thus a writer such as Faulkner becomes the South's all-time champion neurotic. What the assumption leaves out is that great art is distinguished by its powers of control and synthesis, of making the disparate and disjointed experience of life into that which is unified and whole: by its shaping form. This is precisely what the neurotic person is *unable* to do. Thus the analogy of writer with patient and work of art with the patient's dream-work is not enough; for if that is the kind of relationship involved, then the writer is also the psychoanalyst interpreting the dream, giving it coherence and pattern. Art is not neurosis; it is *wisdom*.

When, therefore, I encounter some of the Jungian, Freudian, and Lacanian readings of Southern literature, I tend to adopt the approach of Quentin Compson—in the historical, though not the geographical, sense. In *Absalom, Absalom!* Quentin keeps correcting the historical details of the Canadian Shreve McCannon's freely imaginative patterning, and finally he tells him that "you can't understand it. You would have to be born there."[17] I find myself in agreement.

No doubt the book that will offer a proper understanding of the relationship of Faulkner and his contemporaries to the South of the early decades of the twentieth century will ultimately emerge, but it would appear that the time is not yet. Yet in one very real sense, I think that William Faulkner himself may already have written that book for us. Each time I read *Absalom, Absalom!* I am more taken with the notion that, whatever his other concerns may have been in it, Faulkner was also writing about the Southern writer of his generation, and that this, in part at least, is what Quentin Compson is doing in that novel.

Faulkner was not an "autobiographical" novelist as the term is commonly used, but it has always seemed to me that Quentin occupied a special place in his imagination, one that went beyond the immediate demands of the stories in which he figures. In his own way Quentin is Faulkner's artist-figure, Southern-style, by which I mean that it is Quentin who most of all possesses the sensibility and the moral and psychological insight necessary to discern and pronounce the meanings of what happens.

17. *Absalom, Absalom!*, 361.

Clearly this is why Faulkner resurrected him from his watery fate in *The Sound and the Fury* midway in the process of writing *Absalom, Absalom!* To his editor in New York he wrote that he had decided to use Quentin "because it is just before he is to commit suicide because of his sister [in *The Sound and the Fury*], and I use his bitterness which he has projected on the South in the form of hatred of it and its people to get more out of the story than a historical novel would be. To keep the hoop skirts and plug hats out, you might say."[18] But if that was his intention it changed almost at once, for there seems little bitterness in Quentin's telling of the story. He is first bored, then fascinated, then appalled, and finally almost overwhelmed, but he is neither cynical nor bitter.

It seems likely that in venturing to write a novel about what goes on in *Absalom, Absalom!*, Faulkner himself felt that simply to do so involved an act of bitterness toward the community, so that he wanted Quentin for his persona. He was, after all, proposing to portray the Old South, the Lost Cause, the institution of antebellum slavery, the planter aristocracy and the like, in ways that were quite unlike, and highly subversive of, the Southern mythos. This was not going to be a treatment of the community's history along the order of *So Red the Rose* (1934) by his fellow Mississippian Stark Young; the evil in Faulkner's novel was not going to be composed entirely of what was imported from outside by the Yankees. It was one thing, perhaps, to write about unpleasant goings-on in the contemporary South, and another to expose the presence of warts and excrescences in the sacred Confederate tradition. The 1930s, after all, were years when Confederate reunions were still being held, when Southern legislators could furiously assail the United States Post Office Department for daring to portray the visage of General

18. Letter, William Faulkner to Harrison Smith, probably February 1934, in *Selected Letters of William Faulkner*, ed. Joseph Blotner (New York: Random House, 1977), 79.

William Tecumseh Sherman upon a stamp to be sold in Southern post offices, and the United Daughters of the Confederacy met regularly. The extent to which the treatment of race and racism in *Absalom, Absalom!* was heretical when it appeared is not often remembered today.

The bitterness that was being projected, therefore, and that needed Quentin Compson for its spokesman, consisted of looking at the legend of the Old South critically, and of daring to do so in print, in public. So Faulkner chose Quentin Compson, because Quentin embodied that aspect of his own imagination that could look at slavery, racism, *noblesse oblige*, the Confederate cause, the ambition of a poor white to become a planter, the class structure, openly and honestly. Yet at the same time it was not going to be an exposé, a naturalistic depiction of man at his least common denominator. He wanted the kind of sensibility that could recognize the heroism as well as the ruthless and callousness of a Thomas Sutpen, identify the pathos and agony of those caught in the toils of history, recoil at the violations of humanity, comprehend the historical plight of a Henry Sutpen.

We can get an idea of the process that led to Quentin's being chosen to tell the story if we look at the two short stories from which the novel evolved, "Evangeline," written in 1931 and published for the first time in Joseph Blotner's edition of the *Uncollected Stories*, and "Wash," written somewhat later and first published in *Harper's* in 1934.[19] "Evangeline" is built around the story of Charles Bon and Henry and Judith Sutpen; it is told by a newspaperman and an architect-painter. It has little or nothing of the resonance of *Absalom, Absalom!* Thomas Sutpen is barely involved at all. Henry acts to slay Bon entirely out of his fear of miscegenation. "Wash" involves Thomas Sutpen's

---

19. See Joseph Blotner, ed., *Uncollected Stories of William Faulkner* (New York: Random House, 1979), 583–609; also Note, 709. "Wash" is included in *The Faulkner Reader: Selections from the Work of William Faulkner* (New York: Random House, 1954), 603–14.

fathering of a child upon Wash Jones's granddaughter. The lowly Wash Jones's outrage at being used and then betrayed by the lordly Confederate colonel is what gives the story its direction and meaning. Unlike "Evangeline" it is told by an omniscient author.

To develop the story of Charles Bon and Henry and Judith Sutpen so that its full emotional and moral dimensions could be realized, however, Faulkner needed a narrator capable of exploring those dimensions and of articulating his findings. Moreover, he should be someone familiar with the local terrain and with a strong emotional stake in the history of the community over the generations. An outsider in search of a newspaper feature would hardly do. Otherwise the symbolic meanings of the racial theme for the history of the community and its people could not be developed; it would remain a melodramatic horror story about miscegenation. And to unite that theme with one involving the catastrophic impact of a strong-willed, ruthless man of lowly origins, ambitious to establish a plantation dynasty, upon the lives and fortunes of those who came into his orbit, the narrator must be someone who was very decidedly unlike that man, in no way selfish, or ruthless, or insensitive, but if anything hypersensitive to cruelty. What more appropriate choice for that narrator than Quentin Compson, bookish, of poetic temperament, vulnerable, of the fifth generation of a once distinguished family now fallen upon evil days, whose own ineffectiveness and inability to act boldly and decisively could contrast so strikingly with the arrogant, unthinking assertion of will that characterized the behavior of the story's central figure? A well-intentioned but weak young aristocrat to relate and to speculate upon the meaning of the story of a powerful, self-centered, supremely self-confident plebian striving for status: what better way to articulate the meaning of the story of Thomas Sutpen and his descendants?

But again, there is more to it than that. There would also be needed a voice, and a way of seeing, that was clearly modern and a bit cynical and hardboiled, to protect against the almost unbearable intensity of some of the material and for purposes of narrative counterpoint. The newspaperman had furnished that voice in the story "Evangeline," in order to save that story from becoming too melodramatic even to be believable. Now whatever the Quentin of *The Sound and the Fury* was, he was not hardboiled and cynical (melancholy, even when verging upon hopelessness, is not the same as cynicism).

What Faulkner did, therefore, was to divide Quentin's sensibility into two viewpoints, two ways of thinking and feeling. Sitting in the office of Miss Rosa Coldfield's home and listening to her telling her story, he became two Quentins—or rather, he identified *within himself* two different modes of response to his own experience:

> Then hearing would reconcile and he would seem to listen to two separate Quentins now—the Quentin Compson preparing for Harvard in the South, the deep South dead since 1865 and peopled with garrulous outraged baffled ghosts, listening, having to listen, to one of the ghosts who had refused to lie still even longer than most had, telling him about old ghost-times; and the Quentin Compson who was still too young to deserve yet to be a ghost, but nevertheless having to be one for all that, since he was born and bred in the deep South the same as she was—the two separate Quentins now talking to one another in the long silence of notpeople, in notlanguage . . .[20]

At this outset, therefore, as Quentin begins to tell his story, he becomes in effect the Southern writer, deeply involved in his material by virtue of his membership in the community, yet sufficiently detached from it to view it objectively, both as a story and in terms of its moral and historical meanings. He is the citizen who shares the pieties, loyalties, and concerns of the historical time and place, and he is the modern who distances himself from the rhetorical responses and unexamined assump-

20. *Absalom, Absalom!*, 9.

tions in order to explore and understand his own relationship to them. Obviously Faulkner recognized what he had arrived at, for the very next thing that Quentin hears Miss Rosa Coldfield saying makes the precise connection: "'Because you are going away to attend the college at Harvard they tell me,' Miss Coldfield said. 'So I don't imagine you will ever come back here and settle down as a country lawyer in a little town like Jefferson, since Northern people have already seen to it that there is little left in the South for a young man. So maybe you will enter the literary profession as so many Southern gentlemen and gentlewomen too are doing now and maybe some day you will remember this and write about it.'"[21]

Surely Lewis P. Simpson is correct when he declares of Faulkner that "once he looked through Quentin's eyes at Sam Fathers distanced in the mythic twilight [in the story entitled "A Justice"] and moved with Quentin's mind toward the day when he would pass from the *a*historical childhood vision of the old people into the knowledge of modernity, Faulkner discovered in Quentin the first profound portrayal of his own imagination—a fiction yet a symbol of a deep inner reality, a powerful apprehension of modern existence."[22] In being made to confront not merely the past but its impact upon and meaning for the present, Quentin is the Southern writer of Faulkner's generation. In Thadious Davis's words, "Quentin's major activity is imagining a world as real as his twentieth-century one."[23] His division into the two Quentins, Miss Davis declares, "symbolizes the unresolved tensions of his existence as Southerner."[24]

As he moves toward his perception of the full implications of what Thomas Sutpen and his quest for dynasty mean, he be-

21. *Ibid.*, 9–10.

22. Simpson, "Faulkner and the Legend of the Artist," in Wolfe, ed., *Faulkner: Fifty Years After "The Marble Faun,"* 96–97.

23. Thadious M. Davis, "'Be Sutpen's Hundred!': Imaginative Projection of Landscape in *Absalom, Absalom!,*" *Southern Literary Journal,* 13, 2 (Spring 1981), 7.

24. *Ibid.*, 8.

comes so deeply involved in the tale that someone else is needed to ask the questions and to collaborate with the answers. So Shreve McCannon comes into the narrative. Yet it is still, ultimately, Quentin's vision; it is the young Southerner who will someday enter the literary profession who hears what Shreve and himself are formulating, just as earlier on he recognized the modern and the ghost Quentins registering the significance of what Miss Rosa Coldfield's voice was saying. Throughout the narrative everything dissolves into Quentin's perceptions; even the language that the historical participants speak repeatedly keeps turning into the language of Quentin's consciousness.

How fitting it is, then, that at the very end, Faulkner has Shreve McCannon ask Quentin the questin he does: "'Why do you hate the South?'" It is not only a question that a disinterested outsider might ask, but also one that the Southern community itself would propose, in its puzzlement as to why this young man, of good family, brought up with all the proper schooling in the Southern mythos, should nevertheless insist upon telling a story so critical of that mythos. To which Quentin replies, quickly, at once, immediately, "'I dont hate it'":

> "I dont hate it," he said. *I dont hate it he thought,* panting in the cold air, the iron New England dark; *I dont. I dont! I dont hate it! I dont hate it!*[25]

As indeed he does not. What he hates is the injustice, the cruelty, the smugness, not because he is an outsider, and detached from it, but because he is *not*. It is *his* community, *his* country, and in denouncing its flaws and its sins he is simultaneously revealing the intensity of his affection, his love for it. As Faulkner himself wrote of his relationship to his native state: "Loving all of it even while he had to hate some of it because he knows now that you don't love because: you love despite; not for the virtues, but despite the faults."[26]

25. *Absalom, Absalom!,* 378.
26. Faulkner, "Mississippi," in *Essays, Speeches and Public Letters,* 42–43.

The love/hate relationship—hating because one loves, loving despite the faults—between Quentin Compson and Yoknapatawpha County comes deeply out of William Faulkner's situation, and it mirrors that of the modern Southern writer and the South. It is personal, inward, and it is given public literary form out of the need of the men and women of Faulkner's literary generation to understand themselves. Language art was for them a way of knowing. A writer *tells* in order to *know*. And what the writer knows is discovered from within. Perhaps another Mississippi writer has expressed it best. She is ostensibly writing about photographs: "We come to terms as well as we can with our lifelong exposure to the world, and we use whatever devices we may need to survive. But eventually, of course, our knowledge depends upon the living relationship between what we see going on and ourselves. If exposure is essential, still more so is the reflection."[27]

I want to close this discussion of Faulkner and the Southern Literary Renascence by making one other point, which I think needs to be made nowadays as much as ever.

Quentin Compson is Faulkner's premier artist-figure, perhaps, but he is not the only one. Another is Isaac McCaslin in *Go Down, Moses*. In "The Bear," as is well known, Ike McCaslin decides, on the basis of what he has learned about man, nature, and God from Sam Fathers, to decline his patrimony because only in that way can he end his complicity in the racial evil that made it possible. In the same episode, when asked by his cousin McCaslin Edmonds why he had failed to take a shot at the bear named Old Ben when he was very close to him, Ike hesitates, and McCaslin provides the answer by reading some lines from Keats's "Ode on a Grecian Urn":

> '*She cannot fade, though thou hast not thy bliss,*' *McCaslin said:*
> '*Forever wilt thou love, and she be fair.*'

27. Eudora Welty, "One Time, One Place," in *The Eye of the Story: Selected Essays and Reviews* (New York: Random House, 1977), 354.

'He's talking about a girl,' he said.

'He had to talk about something,' McCaslin said. Then he said,
'He was talking about truth. Truth is one. It doesn't change. It
covers all things which touch the heart—honor and pride and pity
and justice and courage and love. Do you see now?'[28]

The dubious wisdom of Ike McCaslin's renunciation of his
patrimony had been noted by numerous commentators, even as
McCaslin Edmonds himself doubted it, and Lucas Beauchamp
as well. In declining to own property tainted by his grandfather's
inhumanity, Ike gains the personal comfort of a clean conscience
in exchange for the ability to rectify future injustice, as we learn
in the story entitled "Delta Autumn." He also gives up his hope
for a family and posterity, for his wife will have none of a husband who declines to insure the material welfare of his family
within the community which she and any offspring will inhabit.
Ike McCaslin's decision may be seen as personally admirable,
and in motivation even heroic in its way, but it is also a retreat
from involvement in the world, an abnegation of responsibility,
and a refusal to take such part as he might in any continuing
effort for human betterment in a flawed time and place.

Not very much attention has been paid to the relationship
between Ike's decision to give up his patrimony and his disincli-
nation to shoot the bear, together with McCaslin's explanation
for it, even though the two episodes appear almost side by side
in the fourth section of "The Bear." Ike doesn't want Old Ben to
die because he doesn't want the wilderness that the huge bear
symbolizes to disappear. He wants the thrill of the chase without
the finality of the kill. He wants, in short, immunity from all
time and change. And this, as McCaslin Edmonds quite rightly
indicates by quoting from Keats's poem, is possible only in art,
not in life. The only way to arrest action in time and fix it so that
it is impervious to change is to convert it into artistic form,

28. Faulkner, "The Bear," *Go Down, Moses* (New York: Random House, 1942), 297.

whether in ceramics like the urn or in language, as Keats did in his poem and Faulkner also did in his story about the running and baying of Old Ben: "It fell just once. For an instant they almost resembled a piece of statuary: the clinging dog, the bear, the man stride its back, working and probing the buried blade. They they went down."[29] In sensibility and in wish Ike is not the hunter, but the artist. But a bear hunt is a human action in time, not a work of art. Ike may wish the chase to go on forever, but Sam Fathers knows better, and so do all those who have come to hunt the bear, and who are actively engaged in an event in time, not in an act of aesthetic contemplation. And if art is ultimately moral—"He was talking about truth"—then Isaac McCaslin's attempt to abdicate future responsibility for his patrimony, to get free of participation in history, is doomed to failure because of the fatal confusion, with Ike's sensibility, of what is possible to art and to life. The ideal exoneration from history for which he yearns can never be accomplished in life, though action, because it requires what is by definition *non*-life: freedom from involvement in time. Just as by its very nature the annual running of the bear cannot continue forever, so the escape from complicity in evil, past, present, and future, the attainment of a perfection of motive and action, is beyond the capacities even of a man named Isaac McCaslin.

The point is that Ike may be confused about what is possible in life and in art, but Faulkner is not confused. The sight of bear, man, and dog locked in the embrace of the kill *almost* resembles a statue for the young Ike McCaslin; it is not a statue. But to us, as readers of the episode, it *is* free of time and change, for we are not participating in a hunt but viewing a work of literary art.

I go into this because it is becoming fashionable to criticize William Faulkner, in common with many of his fellow Southern writers of the 1920s, 1930s, and 1940s, for the supposed failure

29. *Ibid.*, 241.

of his fiction to take a properly activist role in the struggle for racial equality in the South. Some very sophisticated and intelligent critics have made this charge, and among them must be numbered Richard King in his stimulating and informative study *A Southern Renaissance* (1980). King doesn't fault Faulkner's intentions, but he sees his actual performance as leaving much to be desired. Discussing Isaac McCaslin's renunciation of his property, King declares that Ike "lacks a way of translating this new mythos" of racial justice "into a collective historical tradition to replace that of his grandfather, that is, the South's." Identifying Ike's views with Faulkner's, he concludes that "it was the tragic fact of Faulkner's (and Ike's) world that historical consciousness and refusal to participate in the skein of injustice did not of itself lead to or suggest a way of translating moral gesture into political action."[30]

What King is doing, I am afraid, is to make precisely the same kind of error that Isaac McCaslin made, and which Faulkner portrayed him as making. In demanding that Faulkner's presentation of his community's heritage of racial injustice "lead to or suggest a way of translating moral gesture into political action," he is asking that literature become, in effect, the agency of action. But the novelist's responsibility to truth is through and in art; and the morality, racial or otherwise, of a work of fiction must lie not in a prescription for action but in its exploration, in language, of the human experience it recreates. To paraphrase something that Faulkner told Malcolm Cowley about *Absalom, Absalom!*, "I think [Isaac], not Faulkner, is the correct yardstick here. I am writing the story, but he not I was brooding over a situation."[31] Ike McCaslin's solution to the laying down of the racial burden, by way of renunciation, may have been personal

30. Richard H. King, *A Southern Renaissance: The Cultural Awakening of the American South, 1930–1955* (New York: Oxford University Press, 1980), 139.

31. Quoted in Malcolm Cowley, *The Faulkner-Cowley File: Letters and Memories, 1944–1962* (New York: Viking Press, 1966), 15.

and private, achieved at the price of its translation into future action, but William Faulkner's solution was artistic and public, and therefore capable of being read and its meanings understood by others.

For literature *is* "moral gesture," not "political action"—a way of seeing and knowing in language. Faulkner's responsibility to truth, his commitment to action, was to the act of seeing, and thus making it possible for us to see. As Eudora Welty put it, "What is written in the South from now on is going to be taken into account by Faulkner's work; I mean the remark literally. Once Faulkner had written, we could never unknow what he told us and showed us. And his work will do the same thing tomorrow. We inherit from him, while we can get fresh and firsthand news of ourselves from his work at any time."[32]

King declares that "aside from Lillian Smith and W. J. Cash, it would be difficult to find a Southern writer, sociologist, or historian of Faulkner's era who has clearly identified and critiqued the essential foundations of the Southern tradition."[33] But if Faulkner "identified and critiqued" Southern racial injustice, he did so in a crucially different way than the authors of *Strange Fruit* and *The Mind of the South* did: he made it into a magnificent work of art. In Miss Welty's words, "the novelist works neither to correct nor to condone, not at all to comfort, but to make what's told alive."[34] That is why Miss Smith's *Strange Fruit* is all but forgotten as a work of art, and survives only for its value as an already-outdated document in American social history, along with *The Clansman* and *Freedom Road*. But *Absalom, Absalom!* and *Go Down, Moses* speak to us as clearly nowadays as on the day they were first published. They remain more powerful, wiser, more effective indictments of racial inhumanity *because* they are achieved works of literary art.

---

32. Welty, "Must the Novelist Crusade?", *The Eye of the Story*, 158.
33. King, *A Southern Renaissance*, 139.
34. Welty, "Must the Novelist Crusade?", 152.

It is the accomplishment of William Faulkner and his fellow novelists and poets of the modern South to have given us an enduring set of artistic images of their time and place. Writing about themselves as human beings, they wrote about themselves as Southerners. Writing about men and women alive in history, they wrote about the community of people they knew and the history they shared with them. Because they wrote in order to know, we can know what they wrote. What we choose to make of it is none of their concern any longer. But we will ignore it at our own risk. In Flannery O'Connor's terms, nobody wants to get caught on the tracks when the Dixie Special comes through.

The Hound Under the Wagon:
Faulkner and the Southern Literati

FLOYD C. WATKINS

From the late 1920s through the early 1940s—the years of the composition and publication of William Faulkner's first great fiction—he remained isolated from organized groups of writers, schools of critics, and gatherings of high-toned practitioners of the literary arts. He talked often with the local pretender in Oxford, Phil Stone, and he knew Sherwood Anderson and the small coterie of writers who converged on New Orleans. Even with his friends there seems to have been more tale-telling than literary theorizing, and writing was seldom the major subject of conversation in the parties of those who sometimes wrote silently and alone. Faulkner in all the formative years was an observant and pondering loner.

In September, 1931, prominent Southern writers made their first significant gesture toward Faulkner. Professor James Southall Wilson invited him to attend a meeting at the University of Virginia of most of the well-known and accomplished Southern writers. Surprisingly, Faulkner was pleased to accept with a few reservations. The "loopholes" Professor Wilson mentioned for those with "peculiarities about social gambits" pleased him. He described his literary character among assembled literati: "You have seen a country wagon come into town [one wonders whether Mr. Wilson really had], with a hound dog under the wagon. It stops on the Square and the folks get out, but that hound never gets very far from that wagon. He might be cajoled or scared out for a short distance, but first thing you know he has scuttled back under the wagon; maybe he growls at you a little." So William Faulkner agreed to go to Charlottesville, to stay mostly under the wagon, and possibly to growl a little[1]— probably a very little. That was his manner, especially among those of literary pretensions and credentials.

The conference had no carefully prepared agenda; it was a time for authors to get acquainted. The aristocratic writers of the Atlantic seaboard had their difficulties understanding the new man from Mississippi. Ellen Glasgow was just beginning to learn of the Fugitives, Thomas Wolfe, and William Faulkner.[2] The other great aristocratic Virginia novelist of the time, James Branch Cabell, thought that Faulkner was "a young man who would develop,"[3] but the comment is as vague as a printed rejection of a manuscript submitted to a periodical. Forty-four years later Cabell admitted that he had never read any of Faulkner's books. First, he had had "to dispose of" *Gone with the Wind, Anthony Adverse,* and "some of Pearl Buck."[4] Josephine Pinckney (the South Carolina poet) could not lure him away from the wagon. She regarded him as "an important if elusive light on the Mississippi horizon," but she wrote with a sigh that he was only "spasmodically" present at the meetings.[5] For most of the assembled writers the Virginia conference was their first glance at the strange and reserved little man from Mississippi.

Faulkner and the other assembled writers were not at that

1. William Faulkner, *Selected Letters of William Faulkner,* ed. Joseph Blotner (New York: Random House, 1977), 51.

2. William W. Kelly, *Ellen Glasgow: A Bibliography* (Charlottesville: University Press of Virginia, 1964), xxvi.

3. Desmond Tarrant, *James Branch Cabell: The Dream and the Reality* (Norman: University of Oklahoma Press, 1967), 243.

4. *The Letters of James Branch Cabell,* ed. Edward Wagenknecht (Norman: University of Oklahoma Press, 1975), 108.

5. Josephine Pinckney, "Southern Writers Congress," *The Saturday Review of Literature,* 8 (November 7, 1931), 266.

time great literary personages. Faulkner told a young reporter that Southern writers of the time were "only pioneers" and that "nothing 'of any real value' was likely to come out of the South for at least twenty-five years."[6] His motive apparently was to taunt, to enjoy the consequences of his rudeness, and perhaps to salve his own ego for not having yet achieved literary recognition. The hound was not coming from under the wagon and growling; he was lying under its shade and sometimes barking.

Blatantly Faulkner stated his disapproval of the conference despite his agreement to attend. All the talk was too much for him. "The fellows who are going places," he once said, "are too busy working to sit around and talk about it."[7] The eccentricity, shyness, and rudeness revealed in Faulkner's public moments were unusually apparent at the conference. In the two days he was there his conduct and his drinking amazed the University of Virginia and his fellow Southern writers. Usually he spoke only three words at rare intervals: "I dare say," he would utter over and over with apparent acquiescence—a phrase which certainly does not dare to say very much. He drove through the Virginia hills with several writers, drank, sang "Carry Me Back to Ole Virginny," and avoided talking about novels.[8] On one occasion, the hound, drunk under the wagon, said he didn't "give a damn about Ellen Glasgow or any of them" and again during a talk by Miss Glasgow he frequently raised his head to repeat an uncharacteristic opinion, "I agree. I agree."[9]

The strange thing about Faulkner at the conference is that he attended it. Given his presence, the complexities of his personality have already been so well delineated by his enemies,

6. Joseph Blotner, *Faulkner: A Biography* (New York: Random House, 1974), 715–16.

7. *Lion in the Garden: Interviews with William Faulkner 1926–1962*, ed. James B. Meriwether and Michael Millgate (Lincoln: University of Nebraska Press, 1968), 36.

8. E. Stanly Godbold, Jr., *Ellen Glasgow and the Woman Within* (Baton Rouge: Louisiana State University Press, 1972), 186.

9. Blotner, 711.

friends, and biographers that one would expect to be both stunned and amused by his conduct. When all the Nobel Prize winners dined in state with President Kennedy at the White House, Faulkner said it was too far from nearby Charlottesville for him to go. Again when a literary festival was held in Faulkner's own Oxford, Mississippi, in the spring of 1949, Faulkner "stayed well clear of it" although he might have moved among such literary lights as Harry Harrison Kroll, Elizabeth Spencer, Stark Young, and John Crowe Ransom.[10] Such groups were not his cup of tea—or Jack Daniels. So he was speaking the truth when he told a group of Japanese, "I don't know any writing people and I am not really too interested in writing people"; and he meant especially those gathered in groups.[11] Occasionally Faulkner moved socially among writers, and he associated individually with other writers with some frequency, but I can find no indication of any literary conferences he attended in all his life except the one in Virginia.

Faulkner did have a fair number of literary friendships. Usually these were more friendly than literary. Phil Stone of Oxford and Faulkner exchanged books, stories, and opinions, but nothing in the long relationship except Stone's own opinions indicates that Stone was of substantial literary help. One prominent Southerner, the Fugitive and Agrarian John Crowe Ransom, was largely correct in 1951 when he said that Faulkner had "not had the advantage of the society of his literary peers discussing the realistic novel and performing it, not that of intellectuals with their formidable dialectic."[12] Of course if he had had such an advantage, it is quite possible that it would have changed or even ruined him. Ransom admitted that academics had not had

10. *Ibid.*, 1284.
11. *Faulkner at Nagano*, ed. by Robert A. Jelliffe (Tokyo: Kenkyusha Ltd., 1956), 194.
12. John Crowe Ransom, "William Faulkner: An Impression," *The Harvard Advocate*, 135 (November, 1951), 17.

the chance to "adulterate the natural directness of his style."[13] A possible result of the lack of formal literary associations was imperfections "large and small, to the extent almost of whole books sometimes," Ransom thought,[14] but "he recovers us from an immense torpor," perhaps because of his own solitary and lonely knowledge of reality.

If there were no dialectic literary friendships, there were friendships. One of the most significant was with Sherwood Anderson, who became the prototype for a character in Faulkner's second novel, *Mosquitoes*, and who did most of the talking. Those heated and face-to-face swift exchanges of the Fugitives were no precedent for the encounters with Anderson. When Faulkner finished his first novel, Anderson agreed to recommend it for publication provided that he did not have to read it first. Hardly a tutorial and advisory twosome, that.

In New Orleans, also, Faulkner knew Anita Loos, author of the best-selling *Gentlemen Prefer Blonds*. She was more his kind of literary friend than those who wished to discuss the niceties and technicalities of the arts.[15] Hamilton Basso and Faulkner were thrown together during Faulkner's New Orleans days, but not a great deal. "Faulkner and I," Basso said, "never spent much time together." When they were in the same group they did not talk about "art, or meaning, or the meaning of meaning."[16] Both were, Basso believed, "ill-educated," but Faulkner was much more a homebody, a Southern provincial: "I think it has been proven . . . that Faulkner was never really at home anywhere except in Oxford, Mississippi"; according to Basso, Faulkner was even "landlocked."[17] It was a great oppor-

13. *Ibid*.
14. *Ibid*.
15. Faulkner, *Selected Letters*, 32.
16. Hamilton Basso, "William Faulkner: Man and Writer," *Saturday Review*, 45 (July 28, 1962), 11.
17. *Ibid*., 12.

tunity for Basso to claim a formative influence on a much greater writer than he was himself, but he did not claim so much. When Basso wished to write an article on Faulkner in 1925, Faulkner objected.[18] Truly there were no formative influences in the early New Orleans days.

Faulkner's friendship with Stark Young was a rather long and sustained one, but it seems to have involved literature and discussions of Faulkner's writing little more than the one with Anderson. Later Young became an admirer if not an adviser. Bill, he said in 1936, "has more of the real thing in his little finger than all those New York writers put together."[19] But about twenty years later Young stated a still different view: "I am an old friend and appreciator of William Faulkner but not a raging admirer."[20]

So as a literary man Faulkner stayed by himself. Even in that closest of relationships in his older years with the novelist Joan Williams, writing was not the primary interest even when it was one of the subjects of letters and talked about in occasional encounters. His first intentions toward her do not seem to have been literary. If there were no long and sustained and influential discussions with anyone about writings, there were many brief visits with Southern writers, sometimes a few hours or even days spent together, and a good number of casual encounters. Paul Green and Faulkner seem to have traveled on short trips and to have drunk together.[21] Faulkner knew Roark Bradford especially during his days in New Orleans.[22]

When Faulkner saw or met a significant writer, Southern or not, there was almost no literary talk. Once he saw Pound, whom he admired, and he saw Joyce, but apparently they never spoke. As a young man when Faulkner went to Europe he made

18. Faulkner, *Selected Letters*, 276.
19. *Stark Young: A Life in the Arts: Letters 1900–1962*, ed. John Pilkington (Baton Rouge: Louisiana State University Press, 1975), 1156.
20. *Ibid.*, 1408.
21. Blotner, 722.
22. *Lion in the Garden*, 11.

"some effort to go to the café that . . . [Joyce] inhabited to look at him." He commented later that Joyce "was the only literary man that I remember seeing in Europe in those days."[23] Later Faulkner said that he had read *Ulysses* "in the middle 20's."[24] He also met Zelda and Scott Fitzgerald and Dos Passos, but little passed between them.

Except for Tennessee Williams (more cosmopolitan than Mississippian or Tennessean), Faulkner found his fellow Mississippi writers more likeable than those from other worlds. An evening with Williams was not conversational. Williams offended Faulkner by asking him about "Negroes in the South. He refused to answer and remained silent for what seemed two hours." No wonder that Williams thought that Faulkner's eyes seemed "terrible, distraught."[25] In contrast, in 1933 Faulkner, though not a man to go out of his way to see theatrical productions, drove to Memphis to see Marc Connelly's *The Green Pastures*.[26] Lillian Hellman, another Southern dramatist, thought that Faulkner seemed to talk "very well about books."[27]

Eudora Welty and Faulkner in their few encounters seemed to develop a silent rapport. The two great Mississippi novelists—perhaps the greatest American man and woman writers of fiction of their age—were congenial and much aware of the close presence of each other. They were friendly but remote. He said little about his writing neighbor. She remarked in an interview that "it was like living near a big mountain, something majestic—it made me happy to know it was there, all that work of his life. But it wasn't a helping or a hindering presence."[28]

When Miss Welty visited Oxford, Faulkner invited her to Rowan Oak and even took her sailing on Sardis Lake. Theirs was

---

23. Blotner, 452.
24. *Faulkner at Nagano*, 203.
25. Blotner, 1576–1577.
26. *Ibid.*, 821.
27. *Ibid.*, 741.
28. Eudora Welty, Interview, *The Paris Review*, No. 55 (1972), 82.

a sort of neighborly friendship, not a literary festival. "Out on the lake he seemed to her a comforting person, sensitive yet undemanding and restful to be with."[29] Later they stood at the piano at Rowan Oak and sang old favorites. Their personal harmony, no doubt, surpassed that of the music. Later she said that she "liked him ever so much."[30] When Faulkner was awarded the Gold Medal for fiction, Welty formally presented it to him. The occasion was different. As if Welty were a companion ship on dark and unknown seas, Faulkner kept turning to her and asking when the ceremony would be over.[31] Another Mississippian, Shelby Foote, and Faulkner enjoyed each other's company on more than one occasion. He too had dinner at Faulkner's home, and they went together to walk over the site of the Battle of Shiloh on the ninetieth anniversary commemoration of that bloody conflict. Their entire shop talk was as indirect as it was brief. Faulkner observed that you should "never work when you're tired."[32]

Written criticisms of other writers' works by Faulkner are rare, but on one occasion he took elaborate pains to write a Southern black writer, Richard Wright, about two of his works. Here for once the hound came from under the wagon wagging his tail. Faulkner had liked *Native Son* better than *Black Boy* because he preferred art to polemics, and *Native Son* says it, Faulkner thought, "as an artist." The implication is that art may work for a particular cause more successfully when it is written in the interest of all mankind: "I think you will agree that the good lasting stuff comes out of one individual's imagination and sensitivity to and comprehension of the suffering of Everyman, Anyman, not out of the memory of his own grief."[33] The princi-

29. Blotner, 1289.
30. Welty, Interview, 81.
31. Blotner, 1824.
32. *Ibid.*, 1414.
33. Faulkner, *Selected Letters*, 201.

ple in Faulkner's letter to Wright is the same as that in his attitude toward being a Southerner: a writer does not write of the Compson family as declining Southerners or Thomas Sutpen as a symbol of the South or even a large part of the South or Joe Christmas as a black man or a social figure. The writer faces a human question, and thus he supports any and all in adversity, especially those in most adversity.

One of the strangest of Faulkner's literary relationships was that with Thomas Wolfe. Perhaps they met each other at the Virginia Conference; Wolfe said in 1936 that he had met both Hemingway and Faulkner, but he said nothing beyond that, and Faulkner never mentions having met the North Carolina writer. The most noted encounter was not face to face. Again and again (more by repetition than by added information) Faulkner rated Wolfe first as a modern American writer, mainly, he usually said, because of the grandioseness of his attempt; that is, he tried "to put the whole history of the human heart on the head of the pin."[34] Since Wolfe did not succeed at this enormous task, Faulkner rated him first as a failure. He put Hemingway rather far down the list because he succeeded at everything he tried, but he did not try enough.[35] Those are the well-known statements, but in some ways they are puzzling. Faulkner does not say what he read by Wolfe and never discusses the content beyond the statement about the pinhead attempt.[36] More confusion arises about Faulkner's criticism of Wolfe in a statement he made in the 1950s: "I haven't read much of Wolfe. I've read one or two of his stories. I've opened his books and read pages or paragraphs."[37] Thus the issue is beclouded. Faulkner could have been almost unacquainted with Wolfe's writings, or he could

34. *Faulkner in the University: Class Conferences at the University of Virginia 1957–1958* (Charlottesville: The University of Virginia Press), 144.
35. *Faulkner at Nagano,* 61.
36. *Ibid.; Faulkner in the University,* 15.
37. *Faulkner in the University,* 206.

have read rather extensively in them. On one occasion, Faulkner said simply, "He bores me."[38]

Apparently Wolfe was not well acquainted with Faulkner's fiction either. In 1937–1938 he believed that Faulkner had written three or four novels, and thus there were at least five novels by Faulkner whose very existence was unknown to Wolfe. He had read three: *The Sound and the Fury, As I Lay Dying,* and, as he said, "of course," *Sanctuary*. He admired them greatly, but after all of Faulkner's novels through 1935, after his great period had slowly begun to come to an end, Wolfe still had a "deep feeling" that he had not "begun to reach full maturity."[39] About this time the only additional way for Faulkner to reach "full maturity" would have been for him to have discovered some new music of the spheres. Perhaps the only real explanations of these off-the-cuff opinions of these two writers about each other are the lack of thought given to responses to reporters writing for the moment.

Most of Faulkner's comments on Southern writers are as broad and general as those on Wolfe. Once he said that he "esteems" Ellen Glasgow, but he provided no evidence of having read in her work.[40] Erskine Caldwell began with a "plain, simple style" which was "first rate," but he "gradually grew towards trash."[41] When some dowager told him with assumed graciousness that she enjoyed his book *Tobacco Road*, Faulkner "froze, . . . pained at this confusion with the Southern writer he least liked to be confused with."[42] For once, at least, he made no pithy and memorable comment.

In 1952 Faulkner was one of a literary panel in Paris. After the event, Glenway Wescott and Katherine Anne Porter went to

38. *Lion in the Garden*, 268.
39. May Cameron, "An Interview with Thomas Wolfe," *Press Time* (New York: Books, Inc., 1936), 247–48.
40. *Faulkner in the University*, 202.
41. *Faulkner at Nagano*, 57–58.
42. Blotner, 1404.

meet him. Faulkner walked by their extended hands without heeding them, and "Miss Porter was furious."[43] It seems to have been simply another situation of Faulkner's not acknowledging a stranger. Later, in 1959, he was seen in "animated conversation" with Miss Porter at a party at the University of Virginia. By this time they must have been introduced.[44]

Faulkner read Styron's *Lie Down in Darkness* but made no revealing comment on a novel which was supposed to have been modeled in some ways on *The Sound and the Fury*.[45] He said that he had read two plays by Tennessee Williams.[46] He considered H. L. Mencken a "mad man."[47] Of Welty's works that he had read (there is no indication of how many there were), he preferred the remarkable blend of Old Southwest humor and American and European folk and fairy tales in the first novel, [48] *The Robber Bridegroom*. Once Faulkner wrote Welty "a two-line letter" from Hollywood. "This was long before we met," she said. "He liked a little book of mine called *The Robber Bridegroom*, and said would I let him know if he could ever do anything for me. It was on a little piece of notebook paper, written in that fine, neat, sort of readable hand, in pencil—and I've lost it."[49]

Faulkner liked much of the plain or bawdy older Southern literature: Mark Twain (if he was a Southerner), *The Arkansas Traveller*, *Sut Lovingood's Yarns*. Sut, Faulkner said, "did the best he could; at certain times he was a coward and knew it and wasn't ashamed; he never blamed his misfortunes on anyone and never cursed God for them."[50] Probably because of the extremely provincial character and the ridicule of the great bu-

---

43. *Ibid.*, 1422.
44. *Ibid.*, 1724.
45. *Faulkner in the University*, 13.
46. *Ibid.*
47. *Ibid.*, 55.
48. *Ibid.*, 24.
49. Welty, Interview, 81.
50. Blotner, 146; *Lion in the Garden*, 251.

reaucratic machines of government and modern warfare, he liked Mac Hyman's *No Time for Sergeants,* which he called "one of the funniest stories of war or peace either, of the functioning at its most efficient best, of man's invincible and immortal folly, that I ever read."[51] He liked Cabell's *The Rivet in Grandfather's Neck,* but he ignored or did not like or prejudged most recent Southern best-sellers. He did not read *Anthony Adverse* or even *Gone with the Wind.* Miss Mitchell treated him in kind. She asked a reviewer to send her a copy of his review of *Absalom, Absalom!* She would not be able to read the book because she was harassed in the library by talkers and autograph seekers. Apparently she never thought of buying a copy.[52] A curious footnote here is that little Miss Mitchell from Atlanta sent the gruff little man in Oxford a catalogue from the Italian publisher who published both their work. She wanted him to see "the reproduction of the 'Sanctuary' jacket."[53] The creators of Reba Rivers and Belle Watling were not wholly strangers.

Given the general principles agreed on by agrarians in the last few centuries, one would expect to find many close personal, intellectual, and political affinities among them. In truth, however, that has not been the case. The individualism inherent in agrarian thinking has led to differences that amount almost to intellectual altercation. Even in the small group in Nashville, one Agrarian often could not accept another's formulations. Further, an agrarian thinker often becomes intellectual and moves to the academies or to the cities and away from the farm. The Nashville Agrarians never viewed themselves as close disciples of the French Physiocrats or of their American predecessor, President Thomas Jefferson. Indeed, Robert Penn Warren's *Brother to Dragons* attributes many of the evils of American life

---

51. Faulkner, *Selected Letters,* 371.
52. *Margaret Mitchell's Gone with the Wind Letters 1936–1949,* ed. Richard Harwell (New York: Collier Macmillan Publishers, 1976), 88–89.
53. *Ibid.,* 421.

to thinking like Jefferson's idealism, which in turn is related to his agrarianism. In spite of the fact that there seem to have been almost no major ideological differences between Faulkner and his Nashville contemporaries, there were few interrelationships between them.

Personal encounters between the Nashvillians and Faulkner were few. Unless they talked at the Virginia conference, I do not know that Ransom or Davidson ever spoke with Faulkner in their lives. One book by Ransom was in Phil Stone's library, but there is no evidence about whether or not Faulkner ever read it. He did not mention Davidson in print, I believe. Between Robert Penn Warren and Faulkner I know of only one personal encounter, but it was very pleasant. Warren's editor and friend, Albert Erskine, brought the two writers together for dinner before Erskine became Faulkner's editor.[54] After a moment of Faulkner's customary reserve, he began to describe carefully the details of a story he had read, and Warren soon discovered that Faulkner was discussing Warren's story. Then he described a scene between a boy and his grandfather—this time from Warren's novel *At Heaven's Gate*. The evening progressed with such pleasure that the three went on a ferry ride together after dinner—at Faulkner's suggestion.

The man-to-man relationship between Faulkner and Allen Tate was much less cordial. Tate saw him "not more than five or six times,"[55] and on these occasions there was no real cordiality. In Rome once Tate thought that Faulkner was "arrogant and ill-mannered in a way that . . . [was] peculiarly 'Southern'; in company he usually failed to reply when spoken to, or when he spoke there was something grandiose in the profusion with which he sprinkled his remarks with 'Sirs' and 'Ma'ms.'" Further, Tate was annoyed at what he considered Faulkner's

54. Blotner, 1426.
55. Allen Tate, *Memoirs and Opinions 1926–1974* (Chicago: The Swallow Press, 1975), 82.

105

pretense of being a farmer.[56] Disregarding his critical opinion of Faulkner's writings, Tate said he was "a man I did not like."[57] Himself constantly in the company of Fugitives and Agrarians and then numerous writers of all sorts of international sets, Tate did not approve of the company Faulkner kept: "He was usually surrounded," Tate said, "by third-rate writers or just plain sycophants."[58] Except for Malcolm Cowley—I am sorry that I cannot regard Cowley as a notable exception—Faulkner was not, Tate believed, "a friend of anybody who could conceivably have been his peer." The remark is notable because Tate tended to preside autocratically over literary groups in the manner of Ezra Pound, Dr. Samuel Johnson, or Sherwood Anderson. Tate's social values and literary friendships were at odds with the usual solitude of Faulkner.

Faulkner did not subscribe at all to any belief in the values of communal criticism followed in those famous meetings of the Fugitives when they wrote their poems and published them in their magazine. Faulkner was "too busy writing" to "need to discuss" it. If it pleased him, he felt no need to talk about it. If it did not please him, talking about it did not help him to improve it.[59] One remembers the elaborate collaborations of several Fugitives on such poems as Tate's "Ode to the Confederate Dead" and Davidson's "Lee in the Mountains." Warren even wrote a line or so for Tate's poem. Faulkner, on the other hand, believed that "an artist shouldn't talk too much. If he talks then he works that much less. . . . I always knew whether what I'd done was right and good or not. There wasn't anyone who could tell me that."[60]

Faulkner resented criticism from some editors and occasion-

56. *Ibid.*, 82–83.
57. *Ibid.*, 83.
58. *Ibid.*
59. *Lion in the Garden*, 252.
60. *Ibid.*, 219–220.

106

ally tolerated brief views from others. Except for the late correspondence and talk with Cowley and perhaps some of the early talk in New Orleans, I know of no other relationship with any writer which was really formative in his career. Cowley's influence was perhaps harmful. The early exchanges with Phil Stone were, I suspect, no more helpful than the story-swapping between Faulkner and his local and hunting friends. All of his literary help and training came from his heritage, from his blood, and from the classics he read.

Judging by a few reviews and oral comments, Faulkner was a visceral critic, a responder, not an analyzer like the poets from Nashville. He said what he liked and what he disliked. He knew the Bible as intimately as a country preacher. Once on a trip he claimed that he did not know Joyce, but perhaps a little more in his cups he recited from Joyce extensively later on the same trip.[61] Usually he liked unsophisticated Southern writers, Mac Hyman and Sut Lovingood. He did not read many of the works of the Fugitives and Agrarians. He knew Eliot and followed the patterns and images and themes of his poems, but he did not, I believe, know the poetry of Ransom and Tate. Once Faulkner asked his publishers to send him the works of Donne,[62] but if he studied Donne, he never demonstrated his knowledge of the seventeenth-century poet. The only Fugitive-Agrarian whose works Faulkner ever commented on was Robert Penn Warren, and then he made only passing remarks after Lambert Davis had sent him a copy of *All the King's Men*. Himself an occasional modernistic author of an urbane and sophisticated story—as in *Pylon* and *The Wild Palms*—Faulkner was seldom drawn to peculiarly modern fiction; so it is not surprising that he did not like most of *All the King's Men*. He felt that he could "throw away" the story of Jack Burden and Willie Stark and not miss it.

61. Blotner, 716.
62. *Ibid.*, 1746.

Faulkner thought there was a deficiency in the character of Warren's fictional Southern governor. It is also predictable that the creator of Thomas Sutpen and the McCaslin family and the early Sartorises would like Warren's embedded story of Cass Mastern. This account of a guilty adulterer and slaveowner was the kind of yarn that settled in close to Faulkner's heart, and he believed that Warren "should have taken the Cass story and made a novel"—an entire novel—out of the part.[63]

If Faulkner said little about the Fugitive-Agrarians, they said a great deal about him. They were academicians, teachers, critics, reviewers, and students of literature and of Southern culture, bound to speak about this strange new writer William Faulkner. It is impossible to summarize briefly the almost un-equaled contributions to the study of Faulkner by the Fugitive-Agrarian Robert Penn Warren (who has been writing about the Mississippi novelist from the earliest days) and by his friend and collaborator Cleanth Brooks. But other members of the group also had much to say about Faulkner. It is somewhat surprising that the most conservative and perhaps the plainest of the Fugi-tive-Agrarians in intellectual terms, Donald Davidson, was the first to speak out loud and bold for the formally uneducated but complex Mississippi novelist. He was the first of the Fugitives and among the first of prominent Southern writers to praise Faulkner highly. Indeed, his reviews of Faulkner's early works make him almost a prophetic reviewer of future works rather than a commenter on what Faulkner had already done. He re-viewed favorably *Soldiers' Pay, Mosquitoes,* and *Sartoris*. After *Sartoris,* that first book of the Yoknapatawpha series, Davidson wrote that "Mr. Faulkner is the equal of any except three or four American novelists who stand at the very top."[64] Though an

63. Faulkner, *Selected Letters,* 239.
64. M. Thomas Inge, "Donald Davidson on Faulkner: An Early Recognition," *The Georgia Review,* 20 (Winter 1966), 460.

extreme conservative, Davidson was a literary and humane critic of Faulkner rather than a polemicist. He wrote in 1951 that for Faulkner as for the truly Southern writer "the people in the bend of the creek are not only sharecroppers representing a certain economic function. They are complete persons with significant personal histories."[65] Between those early favorable reviews and the late praise, Davidson did sometimes waver a little in his views of Faulkner. Perhaps W. T. Couch's emphasis on Southern culture in his volume of essays by many writers prodded Davidson to consider Faulkner's flaws. In 1935, not long after Faulkner's *Sanctuary*, Davidson commented that "horrors" in Faulkner's fiction had reduced "his own theme to something like absurdity."[66] He did not have a high regard for Faulkner as a Southern thinker outside the realm of fiction. Davidson found his comments on "public affairs . . . ignorant, gullible, and sophomoric."[67] Such an adverse view in this respect, however, would not negate Davidson's view that Faulkner was "our most notable single example" of a novelist of "sensibility" and "control."[68]

Ransom did not have such a sustained favorable view of Faulkner as Davidson had. Although in 1935 he regarded Faulkner as "the most exciting figure in our contemporary literature just now,"[69] in the 1930s he was also uneven.[70] Like Davidson, Ransom appreciated Faulkner's creation of Southern characters "low in their social and literary standing."[71] He was disappointed in

65. Donald Davidson, *Still Rebels, Still Yankees and Other Essays* (Baton Rouge: Louisiana State University Press, 1972), 177.

66. Donald Davidson, "The Trend in Literature: A Partisan View," in W. T. Couch, ed., *Culture in the South* (Chapel Hill: The University of North Carolina Press), 206.

67. Davidson, *Still Rebels*, 168, n.

68. O. B. Emerson, "Prophet Next Door," in *Reality and Myth: Essays in American Literature*, William E. Walker and Robert L. Welker, eds. (Nashville: Vanderbilt University Press, 1964), 258.

69. John Crowe Ransom, "Modern with a Southern Accent," *The Virginia Quarterly Review*, 11 (April 1935), 197.

70. Ransom, "William Faulkner: An Impression," 17.

71. Ransom, "Modern with a Southern Accent," 197.

Pylon, which he thought "might mark the end of William Faulkner."[72] Faulkner, he said, "is spent."[73] Though Ransom did not regard novels as "primarily moral or immoral," he believed that perhaps Faulkner had "worn out" his "artistic conscience."[74] The adverse views persisted into the 1950s. Ransom regarded *Sanctuary* as "aimless virtuosity" and *Requiem for a Nun* as a "poor theatrical" affair which all of "Faulkner's talents cannot change. . . ."[75] Ransom despaired of Faulkner's views of mankind. In 1936 he placed him in the company of such eminent renegades as Tolstoy, D. H. Lawrence, and Joyce as one of the "novelists of futility."[76]

Allen Tate did not let his dislike for Faulkner as a person control his critical views. In an obituary in 1962 he maintained the attitude that he had had all along: "a profound admiration of his works."[77] Since the 1930s he had believed that Faulkner was the "greatest American novelist after Henry James."[78] This view was, as Tate said, consistent with that in the middle forties, when Tate had called him "the most powerful and original novelist in the United States and one of the best in the modern world."[79] Indeed, Faulkner, isolato that he was, controlled and reflected the direction of the entire Southern Renaissance. The "historical moment for the climax" of that literary phenomenon came after "the middle nineteen-thirties," Tate said, "at the high point of William Faulkner's genius."[80] Thus some of the highest praise of Faulkner comes from a fellow Southerner whom he had met only a few times and who had a low personal opinion of him.

72. Emerson, 255.
73. Blotner, 889.
74. Emerson, 255.
75. Ransom, "William Faulkner: An Impression," 17.
76. Ransom, "The Content of the Novel: Notes Toward a Critique of Fiction," *The American Review,* 7 (Summer 1936), 318.
77. Tate, *Memoirs,* 82.
78. *Ibid.,* 83.
79. Tate, "The New Provincialism: With an Epilogue on the Southern Novel," *The Virginia Quarterly Review,* 21 (Spring 1945), 272.
80. Tate, "The Novel in the American South," *New Statesman: The Week-end Review,* 57 (June 13, 1959), 1931.

Tate's view is high credit to his own willing suspension of personal feelings and to Faulkner's accomplishment. Caroline Gordon (Mrs. Allen Tate) shared her husband's high view of Faulkner the writer, and no critic that I know has put more succinctly than she did Faulkner's love of the South and his people. "He writes like a man," she said, "who so loves his land that he is fearful for the well-being of every creature that springs from it."[81]

The Agrarian John Donald Wade (not a Fugitive) felt some admiration for Faulkner's art but could not agree with Davidson, Warren, Tate, and Gordon. Wade's comments resemble the opinions of some of the outspoken Mississippians who felt personally insulted by Faulkner's work: "It is difficult indeed," he wrote in 1931, "to find anywhere a more horrible pageant of degeneracy than Mr. Faulkner sets forth. His characters are all incompetents, morons, idiots, and he presents them with the relentless faithfulness of the great Russians who probe so carefully into all that normal people in America (perhaps ever so wickedly) have been so consistently bent to ignore."[82] Two anti-Agrarians, prominent journalists at least if they were not entirely given to belles lettres—W. J. Cash and H. L. Mencken—shared the views of Professor Wade. Cash called Faulkner and Erskine Caldwell "romantics of the appalling" and said that Faulkner created in his works "a kind of fury of portraiture, a concentration on decadence and social horrors."[83] First, Mencken ignored Faulkner. He reviewed eighteen books in the fall of 1929 but did not review either Wolfe's *Look Homeward, Angel* or Faulkner's *The Sound and the Fury*.[84] When he did

81. Caroline Gordon, "Mr. Faulkner's Southern Saga," *The New York Times Book Review*, May 5, 1946, 45.

82. John Donald Wade, "The South in Its Fiction," *The Virginia Quarterly Review*, 7 (January 1931), 125.

83. W. J. Cash, "Literature and the South," *The Saturday Review of Literature*, 23 (December 28, 1940), 4.

84. Fred C. Hobson, Jr., *Serpent in Eden: H. L. Mencken and the South* (Chapel Hill: The University of North Carolina Press, 1976), 186.

read Faulkner he said that he could not understand him.[85] In what may be one of the most appalling statements ever written by a man supposed to be a prominent literary figure himself, Mencken wrote that "there was no more sense" in Faulkner "than in the wop boob, Dante."[86]

The variety of Faulkner's relationships with other Southern writers during the time when he was writing his greatest books was extraordinary. There were a few warm friendships, as with Miss Welty, indifference and remoteness, as with most other writers when Faulkner was envisioning himself as the hound under the wagon, and rudeness, insults, and verbal dogfights. On the whole Faulkner was probably more abused than abusing, except in one respect. No one equaled him in his amazing lack of response. If silences truly could kill, there would often have been great quantities of gore in the paths Faulkner left behind him.

From the beginnings the South has been a traditional society and a richly cultured one, but it has not been significantly literary. If you eliminate the local colorists (who have been mostly forgotten by this time), the gentlemanly poets of more sound than sense (like Poe and Lanier), and a number of second-rate writers (at best), little is left before World War I. There were major political philosophers, but little belles lettres. The most successful writers in their own genre were the humorists of the Old Southwest, and there is good reason for that. The humor was related to oral literature, and the Southerner often felt that he did not need to write and to read. He talked. And told stories. Much of that kind of old Southern talk survived into modern times and became the bases of some of the best Southern and American writing since the early part of the century. Not all Southern writers used the old folk sources. Of the Fugi-

85. Charles A. Fecher, *Mencken: A Study of His Thought* (New York: Alfred A. Knopf, 1978), 251.
86. *Ibid.*

tives, Ransom was a wit. Of the group, only Warren significantly developed lowly and humorous country folk. Much of the work of Wolfe, Welty, Warren, and Faulkner probably would not have existed without long-standing oral tradition. The Snopes trilogy and parts of many novels, perhaps especially *Sanctuary* and *Light in August,* might never have been written. Rural backwoods humor in writing was surpassed in quantity by the strong sweet smell of magnolia romances, which resembled the people far less than the bawdy humor did.

If Faulkner was a hound under the wagon among literary groups, he was also aware of his literary isolation from the Southern people. He told a group of students that Southerners "don't read books. They write them."[87] But the writers had to send them to Northern publishers. In all history no major commercial press has ever existed in the South; so the writer, Faulkner says, "is never unaware" that he has a Northern publisher. Whether the Southerner read the books or not, if he knew they were printed he did not like them. As Faulkner said, the Southern writer knows "that his home folks ain't going to like what he writes anyway. . . . They are good people but they just do not read books."[88] A few Southern cities and many Southern towns had writers. There were few readers, few books in the homes, few bookstores. Even some counties, including Warren's home county in Kentucky, Todd, do not have to this day county libraries or even bookmobiles.

Faulkner had good reason for not being much of a reader of Southern fiction and poetry. He and some of his contemporaries had to write it before there was much good fiction or poetry from the South. He read a few books over and over rather than covering a large literary territory. He liked classical authors generally better than recent ones, European writers better than American writers, Northern writers better than Southern ones. Richard

---

87. *Faulkner in the University,* 136.
88. *Ibid.*

Adams has written an excellent discussion of his reading. With his non-reading Southern compatriots Faulkner knew the rolling rhythms of the images and the language of the King James version of the Bible better than the capable and famous Bache broker knows *The Wall Street Journal*. But no scholar has written a study of Faulkner's extensive use of the Bible in his fiction.

Not much has been said either about Faulkner's non-reading. A few of his favorite writers were Americans, but the closest he came to a long and sustained admiration of a Southern writer was Mark Twain. Here it is Mark Twain's Southernism which is the question. In Faulkner's library, as it was catalogued by Joseph Blotner, there were about thirty books of Southern fiction, and a good many of these looked like gifts or complimentary copies or hopes for an unlikely blurb. Except for a very few books on Faulkner himself, I find only three books of Southern nonfiction listed. His comments reveal that he has read more, but probably not a great many. The library contained Southern poetry only by Irwin Russell and William Alexander Percy. Faulkner was like the Southerners who did not read Southern books, and it is unlikely that books he borrowed, owned, and gave away or lent to other readers, or read in libraries would significantly change the character of his reading of Southern writers. The stories he heard were better than the Southern books he could find to read.

Richard Adams says it is "incredible nonsense" that Faulkner lived in intellectual isolation "without any teaching or learning."[89] But he was isolated from Southern literary groups. Adams lists ten writers that Faulkner did not like—every one of them an American, not one a Southerner. Perhaps he had not read enough Southerners not to like them. Six American writers made the list of those nineteen whom Adams says Faulkner

89. Richard P. Adams, "The Apprenticeship of William Faulkner," *Tulane Studies in English*, 12 (1962), 113.

liked. Of the six only three had any slight connection with the South—Mark Twain in childhood, Eliot for a brief time in the Border State Missouri, and Cather for a few years in early childhood.[90] Faulkner's lack of Southern reading may not be so much a description of his mind and education as it is a commentary on the state of Southern literature before 1920, a reflection of the richness of Southern oral culture, and a tribute to Faulkner's classical tastes in literature.

Literary groups and literary talk to Faulkner were simply deadly. He avoided careful discussions on the writings of others. In all the interviews later in his life he seldom talked analytically as long as a paragraph. The most a listener could expect was a witty, brief, off-the-cuff comment. Faulkner troubled no one with requests for advice about his writing. He felt that he did not need it, and apparently he did not. He might rewrite a novel as he did *Sanctuary;* or he might allow someone else to rewrite one, as he did *Flags in the Dust,* but he did not talk about any work in progress. He might let a novel set a couple of years, but he went to no one else for help. The only instance of any significant effect on Faulkner is that of Malcolm Cowley in the work on *The Portable Faulkner,* and I am inclined to think that that relationship was more of a liability than it was a benefit. With Faulkner, there was reading, but there were no academics, no discussions, no shop talk, no exchanges of opinions and analyses, little attention paid to criticism or critics.

The beginnings of the Southern Renaissance took place in a time of young writers or old writers; few middle-aged writers indeed were living to preside over the transition. Old publishing houses fell by the wayside and new ones came, published several books, and went out of existence. One constant remained in the South: there were no popular literary magazines and no established and successful publishing houses. Old line pub-

90. *Ibid.,* 116.

lishers tend to stick tritely with the tried and the true, and in that time many young writers yearned to create and to see their creations in print, even if everything but the paper and the type had to be home-made. It was the time of the little magazines. They were a good place to be tested, and even Faulkner placed his first publications in occasional journals and newspapers while he was hanging around, I suppose you might say, at the University of Mississippi and New Orleans. Today the pieces are more noted as collectors's items and for the prices they bring than they are for literary merit—as is nearly always to be expected with fledgling writers.

Faulkner, however, did not linger long with new and little publishers. As has been charged against him by all his enemies, he wrote for money. (Not able to understand his art, they need to find some reason for his writing and their confusion.) Of the eighty-seven short stories (some of which were excerpted from novels ready for print), almost none were published in little magazines or Southern outlets. That was not where the money was. Let it be said that there is no reason why—the public to the contrary—an author should not write for money. What is sometimes forgotten is that when Faulkner had to choose between the money and his craft, he chose the craft. He wrote *The Sound and the Fury* "for pleasure."[91] He rewrote the galleys of *Sanctuary* at his own expense. But he did not try to publish in a Southern academic journal when a slick Northern magazine would buy his wares. He allowed the Book Club of Texas in Dallas to publish "Miss Zilphia Gant" only after he had received several rejections.[92] One of his remarkable Indian stories, "A Courtship," almost equally noted for its heroism and its humor, was published in *The Sewanee Review*—after it had been submitted to six higher paying magazines. That is the only Southern

91. Faulkner, "Introduction," *Sanctuary* (New York: Random House, The Modern Library, 1931, 1932), vi.
92. Faulkner, *Selected Letters*, 42.

academic periodical in which Faulkner ever published a story—
none in the distinguished *Virginia Quarterly, The Georgia Review*, Brooks and Warren's *The Southern Review*, or some of the
late comers which tried to come out with a bang, like *The Texas
Quarterly*. It was the money that counted, not the academic
connection or the region. Faulkner published parts of one long
story in a nearby friendly press, "Notes on a Horsethief," but he
also published it in *Vogue* and then as part of *A Fable*. So far as I
have been able to determine, Faulkner never published a word
in a Northern academic journal.

One of the subjects in American literary annals about which
scholars seem to know very little is editorial rejections. The
strangest curiosities would be the great authors and works
turned down and the reasons given. *All the King's Men*, for
example, was refused by Warren's early publisher because his
first two novels had not sold well. Of all the prominent American
writers that I know about, Faulkner received more rejections
than any other. It may be, however, that the truth is that the
records about Faulkner are more complete. Ordinarily rejections are not framed and hung on the wall. But rejections are not
the things that are remembered. The places where Faulkner
published his stories sound like the names of the money-makers
and the money-payers of the American magazine industry, the
"slicks," as they were called, of the trade: Faulkner sold twenty-
one short stories to the *Saturday Evening Post*, but there is no
coincidence at all in the fact that over the years it was the
highest paying magazine in the country. Distinction and money
both were responsible for the eleven stories published in *Harper's* and the nine in *Scribner's*. After the eight sold to the
American Mercury there was a falling off of the number published in particular places.

Some of the places in which Faulkner's stories appeared seem
unlikely and unexpected: say, *Vogue, Mademoiselle,* and perhaps, for a different reason, *Collier's*. He submitted stories to

117

such seemingly unlikely places as *The Cosmopolitan, Liberty,* and even the *Woman's Home Companion,* but they did not accept his work. The level of society or the capability of the reader or some other factor makes one puzzle over how those readers could be attracted to Faulkner. Possibly the lucrative and supplementary magazine income helped to define Faulkner's writing, as is sometimes the case with writers whose books are much changed from what they were when parts of them first appeared as stories. For decades it has been a frequent occurrence for the fringe readers of Faulkner to remark that he was a better writer of short stories than of novels. It may be that he wrote them so that any literate person could comprehend the story line. But the main reason, I suggest, was money. It is a part of Southern literary history that Faulkner's stories and his books did not appear in the South. In a paradoxical sort of way, it was a mark of preciosity and of integrity in the Fugitives that they published their poems for a different sort of audience, readers with more learning and a more high-toned taste.

In the study of any group of writers—Southerners, Fugitives, Transcendentalists, or Elizabethan dramatists, the scholarly and critical difficulties lie in defining the identity of the individual and the diversity of the literary group. Frequently there are more dissimilarities than similarities, more disagreements than agreements, more quarrels than personal harmonies. Usually, however, there are enough likenesses so that the qualities which are shared by the group give the reader and student of literature at least a start in defining the uniqueness of the particular writer he is working with or reading at the moment. Writing is a lonely task, and every writer must be a loner no matter how integrated he is into a literary group. When the pen is put to paper, only one hand is holding it. With some falseness and a great degree of truth it is possible to speak of the Romantic poets or of Johnson and his circle, or the Georgian poets. Faulkner lived and wrote in a time and place that provided America with one of its most

sustained literary movements, the writers of the Southern Renaissance. In broad terms he was one of the group, almost without doubt the greatest one. But he also was a writer without a
circle. The least likely name for a literary course in any college, I
suggest, would be one entitled "Faulkner and His Circle." He
had a writing brother and he knew fellow writers. He was a
member of a writing family. But he had no circle. When the
wagon came to the literary marketplace and the horses were
hitched, Faulkner withdrew and shyly and fiercely glared from
the shade.

Emerging as a Writer
in Faulkner's Mississippi

ELIZABETH SPENCER

Coming back to Mississippi after not so long away in terms of visiting, but a long time away in terms of living—though in another sense a real Mississippian is never really away—means the arousing of many memories, some of the most pleasant, in my case, being associated with the years I taught here in the '40s and '50s. Even if I hadn't ever taught here, it would be impossible to think of Oxford without thinking of her most famous citizen, William Faulkner.

When I was growing up in Carrollton, sixty miles west of here, where I was born, Oxford was mainly associated with the University, "Ole Miss," its various well-known professors, its law school, its football team, and several families, like the Somervilles and the Hemingways, with whom we—the Spencers, the McCains, the Youngs—were somehow "connected." Two of my uncles went here—one was to become the Admiral, John Sidney McCain, for whom the building on campus here has been named; and my brother came here also, and every one of them was Phi Delta Theta.

It was a long, twisting drive over narrow, gravel roads to get over here in the old days, but once here one immediately felt something distinguished about both town and campus, as though the cultural roots were firm and strong and secure. On the campus, the lyceum, the observatory, and the grove seemed to have been created to impart a sense of the past, of classical studies, of tradition. Some campuses have this meditative quality and one need know no one ever connected with them to feel it. Others, I believe, never acquire it at all. Ole Miss had it, and Oxford itself had a serene, golden quality all its own. I would be many long years, however, in associating Oxford and Ole Miss with William Faulkner. There was, in fact, during the '30s when I was growing up, almost no importance attached to Faulkner at all. Why was this? Didn't we read books? Yes, we not only read, but some of us read extensively and intelligently. There were those, it is true, who did not read much of anything but the *Commercial Appeal* and the *Farmer's Almanac* and the *Christian Observer*, but many were very attached to books. My mother's family had a pretty large library—they would have just said that "we had a lot of books"—and most of them loved talking about their reading, comparing thoughts and impressions and judgments. The emergence of a writer of real potential in their area should have been of great interest to them, and his work should have sustained that interest. But the truth is I never remember people at home talking about Faulkner very much though it was known he was a writer who had begun to publish. One book was mentioned, *Sanctuary*. It was usually said that he had written it to make money, but the implication was that the writer and the book both were flashy, and without substance. If more was said, it was that this writer and others like him (Erskine Caldwell comes to mind) were trying to paint the South in false colors, to drag our culture through the dirt, to degrade and make fun of our ideals. To go a little further with remembering, I think I recall someone saying, "No book of his will ever be in my house." I also have a vague recollection of one of my aunts, glancing about to see that no children or men were present, whispering the name of Temple Drake, but I failed to get the rest of it, and of my mother saying, "Oh, awful, just awful. How could anybody write such a thing?"

But mainly nobody spoke of Faulkner at all. When I say we had a life which made ready reference to books and literature, I feel I must back this up, as too many have fallen into the way of praising the South for its "oral tradition," letting this so-called "oral tradition" account for all we have enjoyed in the way of a literary flourishing. To me this is to simplify what our culture was like. It was no interruption in small town social life, or family life or church-going or hunting or fishing, to have your mother read to you every night out of Greek and Roman myths, the story of the Bible, Robin Hood, Arthurian legend, Uncle Remus, Hawthorne, Aesop, Grimm, Robert Lewis Stevenson, George MacDonald, Louisa May Alcott, and all those others, who followed naturally after Mother Goose and Peter Rabbit. Later there were Dickens, Thackeray, Jane Austen, George Eliot, Victor Hugo, all of the fine Victorians. The characters in these books were often discussed as though they were live people we had all known. My uncle had a fondness for *Les Miserables* and pressed me to read it when I was about ten; too young, I got lost in all the history, French geography, manners, and characters with unpronounceable names. A cousin of mine from up the street who often used to play with the rest of us at my house in the summer, used to quote Swinburne by the yard, and even before that, my brother, whose bent was certainly not "literary," would recite long stanzas from Macaulay along with Robert W. Service. His favorite book was *Moby Dick;* he had several copies around the house. My aunt taught Latin and relished reading fiction. Long scraps of original poems were to be found in the notebooks of some of the family members. All this was to be considered, I think, as a kind of liveliness. It made life more enjoyable, expanded it, to have feelings for somebody in New England, or France or England, or for never-never characters out of myths.

I should like here to say a word about my home town of Carrollton. They have a pilgrimage there now, for people to visit its old homes and gardens. However, Carrollton never grew very much. I guess maybe it has shrunk. I recently saw it listed in a study published in one of the Mississippi quarterlies as a "dying town." My mother always said that while nobody much was left *in* Carrollton, half the Delta was *from* Carrollton. Carrollton is a hill town, older than both Oxford and Holly Springs. It was close enough to the Delta to be a refuge place during floods and yellow fever epidemics. There was once a "female academy" there; it was the birthplace of two U. S. Senators; it was considered the ideal setting for Faulkner's *The Reivers* when this book was photographed as a movie. (Oxford itself had got too modern and no longer looked like "Jefferson," or so it was judged.) Carroll County is adjacent to Leflore County, Leflore being named for Greenwood Leflore, the last of the Choctaw chiefs, part French-Canadian, whose plantation was largely in Carroll County, as was his splendid plantation home, Malmaison. My own family's plantation was neighbor to his, being called Teoc, after the Choctaw name, Teoc Tillila, meaning Tall Pines.

Carrollton was a sleepy town in the '20s and '30s, when I was growing up. It was really two towns, separated by Big Sand Creek. When this creek got up and roared after a big rain it was always threatening to wash the bridge out. The town on the other side of the creek was called North Carrollton. North Carrollton got mad at Carrollton once, back in the mists of time, or Carrollton got mad at North Carrollton, I forget which. At any rate, we had, between us, never more than 1,000 souls, but two separate 12-year high schools, two separate post offices, two mayors and boards of aldermen, and any number of separate reasons to feel different and superior, each to the other. I think, though, that since Carrollton had the courthouse and the county records, we quite possibly were more successful snobs, if this is any distinction. There were no paved roads in the state then, except maybe one or two down around Jackson, or up near

Greenville. There was one half-paved road, I remember, that is, paved on one side only. It was up near Greenville and was done so the milk wouldn't get churned on the way to town. It was difficult to go any distance by car without getting covered in dust. We usually counted on one or two flat tires on the way to Jackson, a hundred miles away. A teacher who came to our town school in the '30s from elsewhere was astonished that we had no school library. Since everybody I knew had books at home, I never thought a library was necessary in the schoolhouse, yet we were glad at the signs of progress when she raised some money to order books, stuck reference cards in a shoe box, and entered fines in a nickel notebook. Before that, a teacher I had in the fourth grade, whose home was there, had thought the textbook prescribed by the state was boring and had got us to buy copies of a book called *One Hundred and One Best Poems*. She loved reading aloud, and I can see her yet, completely wrapped up in the words and rhythm, chanting Poe's "The Bells" or "The Raven," or Bryant's "Thanatopsis," or something of Robert Browning's or Tennyson's, shaking her head until the hairpins fell out and peppered the floor. She was a grand reader named Miss Willie Kennan, really Mrs. Kennan (everybody was "Miss" something), and really a Money, one of the Senator's family. Before Miss Willie, though, there had been Miss Jennie Nelson McBride in grades one, two, and three, one of which I was let to skip, I forget which. But for two years, along with arithmetic, spelling, reading, and penmanship, I was taught the alphabet by Bible verses, committed to memory and recited daily. I remember to this day: A—A good name is rather to be chosen than riches and loving favor rather than silver and gold. B—Be ye kind one to another, tenderhearted, forgiving one another. C—Create in me a clean heart, O God, and renew a right spirit within me.

After Miss Jennie and Miss Willie, we had a teacher from Agnes Scott, who happened into our town by accident of marriage to one of the local boys and who wanted to work. She got us into Latin about grade seven, instead of waiting for grade nine; so beating ahead toward Virgil, we were reading Caesar's Gallic Wars in the eighth grade and Ovid (probably expurgated) in the ninth. A friend of hers came to Carrollton in need of work, this one being quite fond of Shakespeare. We read the plays aloud, sitting around an iron stove with our knees toasting and our backs cold and hunks of plaster threatening to fall down on our heads, taking parts in *Romeo and Juliet, The Merchant of Venice,* or *As You Like It,* building up to grade 12, when she moved full-scale into *Macbeth.* She had studied it in Nashville under Walter Clyde Curry, and it was her favorite play. "Life's but a walking shadow . . . a tale told by an idiot, Full of sound and fury, signifying nothing." All this was great in itself, but we studied a lot of other writers too, even though my summertime attentions had gone to pot as far as literature was concerned. The boys and the cousins who played tennis at our house were hooked on Edgar Rice Burroughs and other adventure stories, so I read those, and the girls I ran around with had discovered picture shows and *Photoplay* magazine.

A mixed education, but it was much richer than statistics would lead anybody to believe. Down here we were all supposed, in little societies like mine, to have no culture at all, except possibly this famous "oral tradition." It does seem to me that every place has, in one way or another, an oral tradition. Ours, it may be, was extraordinary—varied and expansive. Our talkers were great talkers; but people do talk most everywhere. And a Southerner can be as big a bore as anybody. Evenings of swapping local stories lead to wonderful laughter and a good night's sleep, but not necessarily to literature. It was the church-going crowd who got the most out of the sermons, and the politically-involved sat drinking in every word at the "speakings." So I do believe that making books springs from a love of books, and that many cultural forces, some of a literary nature, were at work around those small, dusty, obviously "backward," apparently asleep, possibly dead, little old Southern towns.

We had books by Southerners back then, too, though I have not yet mentioned any. Thomas Nelson Page was pointed out to me as a good writer; his *Red Rock* was on our shelves. There was also Stark Young, a distant cousin, whose *So Red the Rose* met with general approval as being true to the South, as so it was. It was true to what this society thought of itself. Mr. Stark had no reason even to change the names of some of his families in that novel, as he was painting them just in the way they believed themselves to be. I think quite possibly they really were this way. I see no reason to believe that Hugh McGehee and Sallie Bedford weren't as good as Stark Young makes them out to be. There were people that noble and that fine in the society then; they never hesitated one minute to be as good as humanly possible. I was fortunate enough to be born when some of that generation was still around, plus any number of people who had known them, and I don't think he exaggerated. And I think *So Red the Rose* is a fine book. *Gone with the Wind* appeared and was immediately read and widely discussed. I remember long arguments. Scarlett O'Hara was not "representative of Southern womanhood." Melanie Wilkes was "representative of Southern womanhood." But just about everybody who read at all, read it, and thought it was a great story and true to "what our people had endured." This was often said.

I began to get the reasoning little at a time. Southern writers were supposed to be "loyal to the South." It was as if we were still in a war and if you weren't loyal to the South you were a traitor, a turncoat, and should be scorned and regarded as a pariah, if not actually shot. This was a sensitive society. Proud, it had been humiliated by defeat and Reconstruction. This humiliation, it seemed to me, the more I heard people talk about it, had been the worst part of the Civil War experience. Now here was somebody, one of us, right over here at Oxford, shocking us and exposing us to people elsewhere with story after story, drawn from the South's own private skeleton closet . . . the hushed-up family secret, the nice girl who wound up in the Memphis whorehouse, the suicides, the idiot brother kept at home, the miserable poverty and ignorance of the poor whites— (Now, the truth is I never heard the term "poor white," just as I never heard the term "Deep South," until I got out of the South. But anyway, he wrote about whites who were poor)—the revenge shootings, the occasional lynchings, the real life of the blacks. What was this man trying to do? Humiliate us again? Tell on his own people in order to make money? Few people wanted to try to sort it out. Those few who did, agreed, I think, that here was great talent. Talent should be recognized and encouraged, but how were you to "encourage" William Faulkner? (He did, as we know, find encouragement with friends like Phil Stone, Ben Wasson, and perhaps others.)

I wish to say that I think the question of what Mississippi was to think about William Faulkner really was a difficult one. Now, many years later, we come to his books after a world of critical work at the very highest levels has been accomplished. We can look back on critics, not confined to the South, who misjudged, underrated, and misunderstood his amazing vision and the variety of his efforts in fiction to make it all plain. Even today if you come to Faulkner by way of only one fragment, say, one story or one novel (I have an opportunity to do this because I live in Montreal and I teach students who have not been as widely exposed to Faulkner as we here have)—if you come to Faulkner by way of only one work, you are apt to be confused, not as to the brilliance or even value of this particular piece, if you have chosen a good one, but as to the motive for it, the writer's focus. Faulkner, of course, we know now, had read widely in modern literature from the first; there was not much he didn't know about the French writers, and a study of modern literature makes us know that the modern writer's attempt is to hide within the work. Faulkner had as much right to this method as did Flaubert, whose precise focus is also not discoverable. Looking horizontally, regarding the literary scene of his moment, which is the only moment the artist ever knows, he had every aesthetic right to mask himself. The question that arose with many Southerners was not of aesthetic but of moral right. Did Faulkner have a right to make use of his own society (that is to say by extension, his own family, as the South or Mississippi was, in those days, something like a vast family connection), to create a shocking literature?

I was sent to a small Presbyterian school in Jackson, Mississippi, Belhaven by name. There was something that met each spring around among those colleges, I guess it still meets, at Millsaps, Ole Miss, Southwestern, Mississippi State, Blue Mountain, Mississippi Southern, MSCW. It was known as the Southern Literary Festival. If I'm not mistaken Robert Penn Warren founded this.* Warren taught for a time at Southwestern, and as happened everywhere he went, something positive and creative resulted. He thought that if the students in this area could get together once a year, students interested in writing, that is, and talk about what was going on in the world of writing, perhaps have writers or literary critics as speakers, then good things might happen. He was right. One thing that happened was that it came the turn of Belhaven College to have this festival and several literary people, writers and critics, were about to show up and students from the whole area were about to attend. It was then discovered that here in 1939 not a single book by the man who had become Mississippi's best-known writer was in the college library, any more than any book of his was in the Carrollton High School library, or in the Spencer residence. Yet an exhibit of Mississippi writing was being set up.

---

*Editors' note: Warren spoke at the first Southern Literary Festival. Its founder was Charles D. Johnson of Blue Mountain College.

A quandary. The college president, Dr. Guy Gillespie, was a very fine and learned and highly religious man. If people sometimes seem to act or think narrowly out of convictions, we have to recall the overwhelming numbers of people who have no convictions to act out of. Anyway, Dr. Gillespie had his troubles with literature. At times, he speculated that Shakespeare probably should not be taught to his girls in college, because he personally could not tell what Shakespeare's theology was. (As a matter of fact, I can't either.) Milton was all right, but he had more trouble yet with the romantic poets—Wordsworth was probably a pantheist, Coleridge undoubtedly took dope, Shelley was a declared atheist, Byron a libertine, and Keats was a pagan. Dr. Gillespie taught the required course in philosophy himself, lest something go wrong. Now here were the college librarian and the English department wishing to acquire one or two books by the notorious William Faulkner. Fortunately, Faulkner himself had innocently furnished Dr. Gillespie with a solution, as some up-to-date person on the committee realized. He had just published *The Unvanquished,* his most gentle and loving book about the trials of the Sartoris family in War and Reconstruction times. I remember seeing this book on the display table in the library at the time of the festival and thinking I would certainly check it out and read it when the meeting was over. I did so and encountered disappointment. I was looking for sex and violence, but found little of either. I put Faulkner aside indefinitely.

I confess with shame that it wasn't until I was in my early twenties and in graduate school at Vanderbilt that I realized I must find out more about Faulkner. I had still read very little of him, maybe an anthologized story or two. Nevertheless in the Modern British and American Novel course under Donald Davidson, I dauntlessly picked out a book by Faulkner on which to base one of my required papers. The book was *Sartoris*. I admitted in the paper to never having read widely in the writer's work. I took it, however, from this book that Faulkner was trying to present a decadent picture of the South, especially Mississippi—a deteriorated society. Mr. Davidson did not agree with the paper or its thesis, but was intrigued by it enough to read it aloud to the class and tear it to shreds. Faulkner was not pointing the finger at a terrible place called Mississippi. He was not out to reform anybody. The secrets of his writing lay deeper than that. Davidson did not try to give them all to us at once, but he pointed the way by indicating criticism that was already beginning to outline the Sartoris-Snopes poles of character, that was probing the mystery of Quentin Compson, and suggesting how Faulkner really regarded, and meant the reader to regard, the outrageous Bundrens. Much more serious after my scolding, I began a long commitment to try to understand slowly and as thoroughly as possible the literary genius of my own locale. I had hoped to find a quick way out of doing this, but finally I was so challenged I had to go on with it, and I then read a great deal of Faulkner, all the books up through *The Hamlet, Go Down, Moses*, some as they were appearing, and finally *The Collected Stories*. And then I thought I understood enough, as much as I ever would, and being not so interested in the later ones, I called it as much as I could do.

But by that time I was thoroughly converted and baptized. More than baptized, I was saturated. More than converted, I was almost fanatical. If anybody said anything about Faulkner that wasn't thoroughly positive and to my mind correct, I would undertake to lecture them. I thought everyone should be enlightened about his work, read it, see it as I had come to. To discover Faulkner was a great experience, of the sort which few writers can offer a reader. In our time, Proust can offer it, as can Joyce. Who else? Perhaps others. I can think of none. The work is there, complex and difficult, but finally understandable; we read it as though we visited a new country—I should say, being from Mississippi, another county. We can read its history, meet its people, see its sights, learn its language. The characters become like people personally known, part of our acquaintance who crop up from time to time.

I saw, of course, the perils all this was letting me in for, as a young woman who had wanted to write since childhood and who, worse luck, came from what was rapidly getting to be known as "Faulkner country." Once you were in it, especially as a writer, how in the world did you get out of it? (That was the 1940s.)

I think now that writers, would-be writers, beginning writers, writers already publishing, all over the South (for the South did, as we know, experience a real flowering of literature, call it what you will) were facing the same question as I. Faulkner was a lion in the path, menacing further advance—or a bear in everybody's private wilderness, if you prefer. Maybe some of us gave up. But a lot of us didn't. Few got by without a claw mark or two. I thought my work was original, all my own, but critics inevitably compared me to Faulkner. Some of them must have been simply aware of superficial resemblances in the landscape or the architecture or the characters or the speech. I knew little about any world other than the North Mississippi world where I had been born and my parents and their parents before them. But some of the critics must have been right; perhaps resemblances are really there between my work and Faulkner's and also the work of many other Southern writers and Faulkner's. For one thing, the Faulkner style, once it gets into your thinking, tends to want to get out on paper. Faulkner found a way of expanding the English sentence from within, elongating its rhythms so that line after line of subordinate matter could be introduced without losing or damaging the presiding thought it was intended to qualify. He knew how to lay clause after clause in long, richly worded sentences, not like equal stones along a flat path, but builder's units, raising some complex image before us, involving it along the way with his story's history, feeling and character all together. All this he managed to tune into the idiom that was native to him, in all its range. Should this great gain in stylistic method then be lost to other writers because none are strong enough to use it without becoming imitative? Many writers have learned from Joyce, even though few would even covet his enormous interest in linguistics, and perhaps none, even if they wished, would have the learning to bring it into full play. Many have found in Proust the courage to let memory create symphonic fiction out of past event. Well, a good many writers have found a way to borrow from this extraordinary style of Faulkner's without sounding too much like the one who invented it. We can, of course, immediately mention William Styron and Robert Penn Warren. But every so often, these rhythms crop up in some New Englander's novel, or in a Midwestern Jewish family saga, or are heard in Canada from some lonely dreamer on some the prairies of Saskatchewan. Any day now I expect to find the Aurora Borealis—the Northern Lights—described in rolling Faulknerian rhetoric. When we run across these things, we have to wonder if new writers are catching hold, putting the style to good use, or if it has come sneaking up out of the swamps and bayous and caught them. The first way would be the right one, the second is a kind of cop-out. The question, as it says in *Alice*, is who's to be master.

I can remark on all this now, but twenty or thirty years ago for me, it was a stiff problem. I personally managed to work out the threat of the Faulkner style, by reading certain other writers I lavishly admired, who served as counter-influences, neutralizers. (It's a bit like chemistry, where the solution turns from pink to blue.) One writer I read was the Russian, Turgenev. I read him, of course, in translation, yet his style got through to me as flexible, apparently simple, certainly lucid, and capable of both subtlety and feeling. There was the strong direct appeal of Chekhov, also his lyrical vein; for someone writing a bit this way in English you could read Katherine Mansfield. There was also, right in our own Southern literature, the crystalline style of

Katherine Anne Porter. While Willa Cather bore a creditable resemblance to Turgenev, and Hemingway's strict economies of language, though almost ballet-like in their stylization, were always a good antidote to Faulkner's baroque flamboyance. There were many ways, then, to hack your way out of the jungle, praying not to get snake bit. Another way I found to escape from the Faulkner overdose was to go back to what I knew before I .ever encountered his work. The discipline of Latin phrasing, the patient diagramming of English sentences, the rhythms of the King James Bible, the plain admonitions of country teachers, to say nothing of one's parents, aunts, uncles, and grandfathers: "Say what you mean! Mean what you say!" There is no better advice for anybody, and for a writer you can't beat it.

I hadn't, until this invitation reminded me of it, read much of Faulkner in recent years. Occasionally I go through one of his wonderful stories in *The Collected Stories* with my students, in the old "creative writing" way, pointing out richness of texture, levels of meaning, language, character, humor, etc. (Faulkner's humor, by the way, to people of cultures other than ours doesn't seem to travel very well. Either that or I don't know how to teach it. Sometimes they catch on to it, but often not. Seems a shame.) These stories, incidentally, seem to have been too much overlooked. They did not all fit in with the novels, and many are not even related to Jefferson and Yoknapatawpha. One is set in Hollywood, one in the Tennessee mountains, one in New York City, two in Virginia, two in the Caribbean, several marvelous ones deal with the First World War in France and postwar times in England and France. I have also reread recently several of the major Faulkner novels, only to be swept anew, like the Bundrens' mules in the flood; this old river can do it every time.

There are certain questions about Faulkner's work that to me have never been, for my personal satisfaction, adequately answered. Maybe some of the other critics here can enlighten me.

133

Maybe they don't bother anyone but me. Since I'm not a critic I should say they're not criticism but worries. I would like now to mention three areas.

One is Faulkner's nihilism. For there is nihilism at work here, and in some of the greatest books. Mainly in *Sanctuary*, also in *The Sound and the Fury, Absalom! Absalom!, Light in August*, to some extent, and in many of the stories. We not only approach the abyss in this writer's work, we go right on over the edge. I think personally that Faulkner may have been stimulated by a nihilistic approach, finding in it that source of a feeling of danger—threat, doom, the impossible event—which informs many of his strongest works. Violence is one thing—I don't mean only violence; but beyond violence, beyond tragedy even, lies the blank-out, the complete destruction, the totality of blackness, darkness, nothing, nothing. Toward this end, this writer often is prone to move. His powerful writing demands that the reader move with him, experience a nothing without measure.

A second worry: Faulkner's treatment of women characters often disturbs me. Many, *if* they are sexually involved, are hysterical, violent, raving, unable to cope with desire. In fact, sexual passion in Faulkner is generally treated as disastrous rather than life-giving. This is one area where one cannot say, it ought to be this way rather than that way, because the imagined experience here relates too deeply to the writer's psyche to be anything more than remarked on by the reader. I remark on it myself, now, because I have found it a problem with his fiction.

A third question in my mind concerns the Snopeses: worry three. A lot of double-dealing must go on in Mississippi; I say this because it goes on everywhere in the world—in Georgia, and Tennessee, and Alabama and Texas; in Italy, France, Canada, Australia, and Mexico; in Patagonia and Madagascar, in Tahiti and Denmark, in Iceland and Portugal. If more than five of six people ever get up there for more than a week, it will go on on the moon. Even Jesus Christ couldn't pick out more than eleven honest men. What I wonder is, why does everything like this have to be put off on the Snopeses? Well, of course, you are already telling me, Jason Compson is a lot worse than any Snopes. Okay, but Faulkner didn't write whole trilogies about Jason Compson. The Snopeses have been set up for us to despise. During the Civil War they were camp followers, trying to turn a quick profit out of horse-trading; they are poor whites, they work themselves up in the world, they stand for materialism, meanness of every sort; devoid of emotion, ignorant of aristocratic feeling, they are destroying Mississippi, by extension the South, by extension the world. If we were to observe a minute of silence and cut off the air conditioning and open the windows, we could probably hear them eating out there like army worms in a field of corn.

But this is myth, says the critic. If a myth does its work, which is to find a place for itself in the imagination, whole and alive, then to ask it to be anything else is useless. It is simply there, just as an event, or a person, is there. Does the Snopes myth, in a literary sense, succeed? It succeeds marvelously; *The Hamlet* is a great work. We cannot expect, the critic points out, that Proust's world will accurately depict Parisian society during La Belle Epoque. Perhaps it does, perhaps it doesn't. Perhaps only a Parisian associated with those times and places would even care. The thing I find troubling here is that with the Snopeses Faulkner catches up not only the literature of myth but also the literature of social observation, one of the great traditional provinces of the novel. One remembers, as one must, Flaubert, Zola and Stendhal, Dickens and George Eliot, Henry James and Theodore Dreiser. And when I know that I must think of these, I am worried a little—like the worry from a hangnail or a sty.

I cannot call myself a critic. I remember Faulkner said once, or was quoted as saying, and I read it, when asked about a comment or article on his work which praised him for his "linear discreteness," "Look, I'm just a writer, not a literary man." Lest someone think I am a literary woman, let me put the Snopes question in more practical terms. It would not be a good idea to conduct your love affairs by what you read in D. H. Lawrence. It would not be practical to try marrying your daughter off according to Jane Austen. It might be disastrous for a young man to enter the bull ring and encounter a live bull after reading Ernest Hemingway. If you are trying to deal with business matters in Mississippi, you should not confine your wariness to Snopeses. While you are busy watching out for spotted horses, somebody with the bluest blood between the Alabama state line and the Mississippi River will sneak up behind you and take everything you've got to call your own. Literature is one thing, but let's not ask too much.

After the publication of *The Hamlet* and *Go Down, Moses*, I feel that the Faulkner I had learned to prize so highly, turned into a different writer, one who is not so interesting to read. He felt he had to choose, I believe, and he chose goodness. He was sincere about it. It was a noble, admirable decision. He came out definitely on the side of endurance, courage, honor, pride, compassion, the human heart. He was writing of the heart, not of the gland. The long work of redemption had begun. So in the context of redemption we see book after book appear. The Snopeses need it, certainly, though it's up hill all the way. Temple Drake needs it, too. These books are obviously great efforts and some day, like my late discovery of Faulkner himself, I may make a discovery of books like *Requiem for a Nun, The Town*, and *The Mansion*. But, I must speak in the present, and my feeling is this: I hope now that we have set up, after his death, a wonderful artist, a folk hero named William Faulkner, who loved Mississippi (he said he also hated it—but we know he felt passionately about it) and tried with compassion to bring our society his understanding as well as his genius—I hope we are not going to forget the man who shocked us, horrified us, who scared the living daylights out of us, whose books were not to be allowed in anybody's mother's house. There are many gentle and civilizing qualities about Faulkner. His compassion goes so deep sometimes it will almost hurt. We can cherish that, but let's not forget the old dangerous, complex vision, with wild-eyed crazy Compsons waiting to do some desperate act; with women on quiet streets apt not only to murder their faithless lovers with rat poison, but keep the corpse around for a play-mate; with at least one Snopes or maybe two as unredeemable as the devil himself. In other words, let's not ever get folksy and cozy about our great writer. Let's not ever make it pure and simple. Let's keep it pure and difficult—complicated, wild, passionate, dark and dangerous—the real thing.

Memory
and Tradition

RICHARD H. KING

What does it mean to live in a world in which cultural tradition
lacks compelling power? Indeed what does it mean to call into
question the value of culture altogether, to suspect that the
claims of the past are deadening, life-threatening claims? In
such a situation what can possibly be the role of memory, our
way of appropriating and locating ourselves in a tradition? How
can we remember and represent what is dismembered and absent?

These questions comprise what I would call the "problematic"
of cultural modernism, which is a crisis sensibility above all else.
Modernism is no simple set of responses to a crisis in culture;
still, one of its most important concerns is the loss of tradition
and the attempt to work out a satisfactory response to that loss.[1]
According to Hayden White, the modernist impulse has shown a

---

1. Clearly the problem of the relationship between past and present is a perennial
one in Western culture, at least since the Renaissance when the debate between the
"ancients" and the "moderns" got underway. Modernism continues and accentuates this
debate, but is much more extreme in its questioning of the relationship. For the modernist sensibility, it is not so much a choice between the present and the past as it is the
awareness that neither is adequate.

A definition of modernism is beyond the scope of my paper. I would locate its beginnings between 1890 and 1914 and its full fruition in the inter-war years. In the literary
realm modernism can be understood in a substantive-thematic and a formal-technical
sense. A central theme is certainly the "loss of the past," while "experimentalism"
describes its dominant formal impulse. It has generally been anti-representational and
expresses, as well as reflects, the loss of the common nineteenth-century bourgeois
cultural assumptions.

deep-seated "hostility toward historical consciousness" and toward history itself.[2] I would suggest, however, that rather than unambiguous hostility, the modernist sensibility has displayed a profound ambivalence toward the past's claims on the present and had strong doubts as to the capacity of memory to understand that past. Faced with the perpetual "mixing of memory and desire," we can never quite decide which, if either, should receive pride of place. Surely that April-haunted novel, *The Sound and the Fury*, thematizes this confusion of memory and desire, tradition and creativity, as few other modern works do.

If, in what follows, my emphasis falls upon the anxiety-ridden nature of modernism, we should not forget that much of modernist culture has celebrated this liberation from the past. No one who has read in or looked at or listened to the works of the modernist period can ignore its playful, joyous, parodistic side. One thinks here of Joyce's play with language and myth in *Ulysses* and *Finnegans Wake*, the celebration of pagan sexuality in Picasso, the delicate and delightful canvases of Klee and Miro, Duchamp's pencilled-in mustache on the Mona Lisa, modern design's rejection of ponderous clutter for the clean, spare line or John Cage's compositions of silence. The list could obviously go on.[3]

And yet from these examples one senses a kind of whistling through the graveyard, an artistic bacchanal among the gravestones of Western culture. "Free play," the central idea of the contemporary French thinker, Jacques Derrida, sounds bracingly liberating. But one has only to remember the terrifying, vertiginous feeling of free play in the steering mechanism of

2. Hayden White, *Tropics of Discourse* (Baltimore: Johns Hopkins University Press, 1978), 31.

3. Albert J. Guerard's "Faulkner the Innovator," *The Maker and the Myth: Faulkner and Yoknapatawpha*, 1977, ed. Evans Harrington and Ann J. Abadie (Jackson: University Press of Mississippi, 1978) stresses the "aesthetic playfulness" of Faulkner's fictional style (72).

one's automobile to realize that freedom from binding values can be experienced as profoundly disorienting and dangerous, that freedom can often be "just another word for nothing left to lose." Against Derrida's notion of free play, we must set Yeats's oft-quoted but still powerful "the center cannot hold."

This all may seem far from the Southern Renaissance or Faulkner's Yoknapatawpha. It isn't. The Renaissance had its party of the past (the Fugitive-Agrarians, Will Percy) and its party of the future (the Regionalists, W. J. Cash, Lillian Smith), its literary traditionalists (Donald Davidson), and its experimentalists (Faulkner, Tate, Agee). Moreover, if one dominant impulse of the Renaissance can be isolated, it is the intense preoccupation, even obsession, with the viability of the regional tradition and with the problems of memory and historical consciousness. As many have observed, the Southern Renaissance stood at the center of American cultural and literary modernism.

Of all the Renaissance figures, Allen Tate was perhaps the most intellectually sensitive to the paradox of traditionalism. In his "Remarks on Southern Religion" in *I'll Take My Stand*, Tate recognized quite clearly that to raise the problem of tradition was already to escape its power and to be forced to defend rationally what was essentially irrational. Later in *The Fathers* Tate has Lacy Buchan, a less agonized but no less troubled "rememberer" than Quentin Compson, observe that "people living in a formal society, lacking historical imagination, can imagine for themselves only a timeless existence." To become aware that one has or lives in a tradition is itself a kind of alienation from that tradition. Thus is historical consciousness engendered.[4]

In what follows I would like to pursue this modernist theme of

4. Allen Tate, "Remarks on Southern Religion," *I'll Take My Stand* (New York: Harper Torchbooks, 1962), 155–72; *The Fathers* (New York: The Swallow Press, 1960), 183.

memory and its vicissitudes by playing two thinkers and one novelist off against one another. The thinkers are Friedrich Nietzsche and Sigmund Freud; the novelist is, as you might suspect, William Faulkner. One reason for approaching Faulkner through Nietzsche and Freud is that Faulkner and the Southern Renaissance should be taken out of a particularly regional or even American context and seen against the background of cultural modernism generally. I want to emphasize here that I am not concerned with whether Faulkner read or was directly influenced by either thinker. That would be intellectual and literary history of the most questionable and uninteresting sort.[5] Rather my claim is the looser, yet more important one that Nietzsche, Freud, and Faulkner all explored (and suffered from) the modernist obsession with memory and cultural tradition. Indeed, an understanding of the phenomenology of historical consciousness, of memory in search of the lost past in Faulkner, can deepen our understanding of these same themes in the thought of Nietzsche and Freud. Strict chronology is not at issue.

To do this I would like to focus on certain key texts by each man: Nietzsche's *The Use and Abuse of History*, several of Freud's shorter essays on therapy, and Faulkner's "The Bear," specifically the fourth section of that work. Yet another disclaimer: I am not trying to psychoanalyze Faulkner or to read his works in psychoanalytic terms. Whatever the importance of those kinds of efforts, they are not my concern here. To engage in them would give Freud a privileged position in my discussion. Rather I want to place Nietzsche, Freud, and Faulkner on equal footing and see the ways in which their notions of memory and historical consciousness can illuminate one another and enlighten us.

5. Quentin Skinner, "The Limits of Historical Explanation," *Philosophy*, 41, No. 157 (July 1966), 199–215.

"Learn to Forget"

Nietzsche stands in a tradition in modern thought, exemplified most clearly by existentialism, which considers appeals to the past to justify action (or inaction) as cowardly self-exculpation, as what Sartre called "bad faith." History, in this view, becomes the source of alibis, a lie not so much against reality as against vitality. Nietzsche was educated as a classical philologist and was the product of a German culture dominated by Hegelian and historicist tendencies. It was enamored with the "historical" as the central category of individual and collective existence. At the same time, and in reaction to this, Nietzsche insisted that Western culture had reached the end of its tether: Christianity, philosophy, and politics all stood in an essentially hostile relationship to the claims of the living present. Though Nietzsche's hostility to the inherited perspectives of the Western tradition may seem shrill and wrong-headed to us as Americans, a people allegedly heedless of the past, that same hostility should seem strangely familiar, even liberating, to Southerners who have labored in various ways under the "burden of Southern history."

Nietzsche's essay, *The Use and Abuse of History*, is highly readable and seductive in its powerful persuasiveness. Its central assumptions and imperatives can be limned out in the following way.[6] Nietzsche begins by assuming that what differentiates humans from animals is the human capacity for remembering. But just as strongly accented is his belief that memory finds it very easy to give us excuses for not doing what it is that our vital impulses and present situation demand of us. Life is set over against memory. Thus, he says, we hear the plaintive cry that we are "all epigones," all latecomers on the historical stage. If we depend on our knowledge of history to tell

6. All quotations come from Friedrich Nietzsche, *The Use and Abuse of History* (Indianapolis: Bobbs-Merrill, 1957). Hereafter this work will be cited in the text as *UA*.

us when the time is ripe for action, we will never take action. One thinks here, of course, of Quentin Compson and his effort to escape time, to throw off its stifling effect and somehow to free himself from his own and the region's past. Quentin and Gail Hightower are latecomers to the core, the figures for whom Harold Bloom's "anxiety of influence" might have been coined.

More generally it follows that memory is always memory *of* something *for* a certain purpose: it is intentional and functional. The notion that history can be objective, that there can be a disinterested comprehension of the past is, for Nietzsche, a pernicious illusion. The question is not *whether* we use the past to justify this or that but *how* we use it.

With this established, Nietzsche then sets forth a three-fold typology of historical consciousness, what he calls the monumental, the antiquarian, and the critical. Monumental historical awareness is that mode of apprehending the past which searches for examples of heroic action to enliven the present and to teach the present how once more to be heroic. The historical consciousness of Southern culture is most essentially monumental; it looked traditionally to the glories of the antebellum days or the more tragic heroism of the War and Reconstruction for figures to be imitated. The dominant sensibility of the Agrarians and of a figure such as Will Percy was clearly monumental. In Faulkner's work, Miss Jenny in *Flags in the Dust,* Gail Hightower in *Light in August,* and Quentin Compson's father in *Absalom, Absalom!* all express a kind of monumental view of the past. Yet Nietzsche also warned of monumentalism's dangers— its tendency to mythologize, its refusal to acknowledge the difference between the present and the past, and hence its concealed hostility to the present altogether. Of these tendencies there have been more than enough in the Southern experience.

Nietzsche's second type—antiquarianism—is less interesting and less relevant for our purposes. The antiquarian view glories in the details of the past and dwells on them with loving rever-

143

ence. Though it satisfies our need for rootedness, it also threatens to become an indiscriminate preference for the past, regardless of the worth of that past. It fails to make the distinction made by monumentalism between the essential and the non-essential in the past. At its worst antiquarianism is the monumentalist view gone timid. The South has also had more than its share of the antiquarian.

In contrast, critical historical consciousness seeks to criticize the entire past in the name of the present and future, to be entirely free of the claims of the past. Those claims are a burden and must be totally rejected. The essential charge against Southern liberals from the pens of the Agrarians was that the liberals wanted to jettison the regional tradition and to change the South beyond all recognition. W. J. Cash and Lillian Smith represent this critical attitude toward the past at its best. In Faulkner's fiction the most extreme example of critical historical awareness can be seen in Thomas Sutpen, a figure whose entire life is devoted to a systematic effacement of who he was and what he had done. Sutpen possesses a willed rootlessness, and this makes his energy, even heroism, all the more frightening to Quentin and to us. Of Faulkner's other figure of critical consciousness, Ike McCaslin, I will have more to say shortly.

Finally, Nietzsche set forth one crucial injunction in *The Use and Abuse of History*—"learn to forget." If we pay close attention to this phrase, it can assume two slightly different meanings. Nietzsche is not saying that we can or should become as animals, even were it possible. We must first learn and then forget. The relationship is a sequential and even a vaguely causal one. We should only forget the past and throw off its claims once we have taken its measure. But if we take the phrase to mean "learn forgetting," something a bit different is implied—that the ability to forget is something we must practice and is a distinct capacity all its own. One can only escape what Nietzsche calls

144

the "historical malady" by understanding the historical historically and realizing that we think history is so important only
because we live in a time that considers it important. If we can
manage this, then we can be original and act in the present.
Thus in Nietzsche we see one of the earliest and clearest examples of the modernist ambivalence toward tradition and the past.
To live in the present, to be "modern," we must first learn the
past and then forget it.

REPETITIONS INTO RECOLLECTIONS: SCREEN MEMORIES AND CONSTRUCTIONS

Though both Nietzsche and Freud saw the past as a burden on
the present, Freud was less sanguine about the possibility of
fighting free of that past. Indeed Freud's life and work were
marked by conflicting moods and impulses; his personal normal-
ity and theoretical achievement hard-won. He was a scientist
whose case histories read like fiction, a thinker who wanted to
be a conquistador, and a man very much of his time and place
whose thought ranged far into the past and future. Few thinkers
have had such great influence on art and literature, yet Freud
has been dismissed as a terrible simplifier of artistic intention
and expression. As a non-religious Jew, Freud was a cultural
outsider, but he addressed, if not the only important question
about human existence, certainly one of them—why are we so
unhappy?

Conventional wisdom has it that Freud's thought is dominated (and thus distorted) by a heavy-handed emphasis upon
sexuality. Yet one might equally claim that memory is the central category in his theory. He grounded his therapeutic hope in
the belief that repetitions could be replaced by recollections,
that neurosis could be cured by remembering and re-
experiencing the past. But Freud worked against the grain of his

145

own therapeutic project by suggesting that all memory is founded on a wish, even those of the normal as opposed to the neurotic. Thus Freud vacillated between the hope that the past can be known and then transcended and the suspicion that we are hopelessly stuck with and in our pasts and can never entirely be free of them.[7]

Though the problem of memory in Freud's thought demands more space than is available here, one can point to some of the ways which Freud's analysis of memory and Faulkner's depiction of memory enrich one another.[8] To do this we must return to the relationship between repetition and recollection. There are several ways of defining neurosis in Freud's thought, but the most general way is to see it as "repetition," the drive to repeat in action and thought certain actual or phantasized experiences from the past. The neurotic seeks to deny time by acting in the present in ways which were once perhaps appropriate, but no longer are.

Now, as numerous Faulkner critics have pointed out, Faulkner's protagonists are often caught in patterns of repetition that they rarely succeed in escaping. And Faulkner himself claimed that the fundamental temptation of human existence is the attempt to stop time. This temptation—one wants to say with Freud this "compulsion"—to repeat is often connected with the theme of the power of the father and the tradition of the fathers.

7. See Sigmund Freud, "Screen Memories," *Early Psychoanalytic Writings*, introduction by Philip Rieff (New York: Collier, 1963) and "Recollection, Repetition and Working Through," "Analysis: Terminable and Interminable," and "Constructions in Analysis," in *Therapy and Technique*, introduction by Philip Rieff (New York: Collier, 1963).

8. David Minter's *William Faulkner: His Life and Work* (Baltimore: Johns Hopkins University Press, 1980) suggests that the three central themes of Faulkner's work are: (1) the relationship of inadequate parents and wounded children; (2) the power of the past over the present; and (3) romantic passion. The first two, and arguably the third, coincide clearly with Freud's main concerns. See also John Irwin's *Doubling and Incest/Repetition and Revenge* (Baltimore: Johns Hopkins University Press, 1976), David Wyatt's *Prodigal Sons: A Study in Authorship and Authority* (Baltimore: Johns Hopkins University Press, 1980), 72–101; and my *A Southern Renaissance* (New York: Oxford University Press, 1980), for various kinds of Freudian readings of Faulkner.

146

What is the personal Oedipal struggle in Freud's thought becomes in Faulkner's work an historical and cultural struggle as well.

How then can the power of repetition, i.e., fate and destiny, be broken, how can the past be prevented from becoming our future? For Freud the answer lay in a telling of one's story and thereby defusing or draining off its power. To tell one's story was to turn repetitious actions and feelings into recollections, articulated as part of the "talking cure." Cure, or something approaching it, involves the possibility of distinguishing phastasy and reality and thus constructing a coherent narrative discourse about one's life. One's story is one's identity. What else is the central action between Quentin and his father in *The Sound and the Fury* and *Absalom, Absalom!*, between Quentin and Rosa Coldfield and between Quentin and Shreve in *Absalom, Absalom!*, but the attempt to recapture the past and be free of it through the narrative act. Moreover, as any reader of Faulkner knows, this is not merely an intellectual, but also a highly emotional process of re-experiencing the past. It bears close resemblance to what Freud called "transference" of the past onto the present.

And yet, for Freud—and Faulkner—an objective narrative representation of the past was terribly problematic. The mirror of remembrance distorts as much as it mirrors. What one is sure was the case, the way things "really were," is for Freud a wishful remembering, what he called a "screen memory." He wondered in fact "whether we have any memories at all *from* our childhood; memories *relating to* our childhood may be all that we possess."[9] Memory seems always to be in the service of unconscious wishes and desires. Similarly, much in Faulkner tells us that memory is not to be trusted. It has alchemical powers that create tales of heroic action out of base materials. Of Miss Jen-

9. Freud, "Screen Memories," 243.

147

ny's version of the story of John and Bayard Sartoris, Faulkner's narrator in *Flags in the Dust* says: "As she grew older the tale itself grew richer and richer . . . until what had been a hair-brained prank of two heedless and reckless boys wild with their own youth, was become a gallant and finely tragical focal-point to which the history of the race had been raised from out of the old miasmic swamps."[10] What else is this but a kind of cultural screen memory and what else is Faulkner doing but trying to show the way what we take to be fact is really wish?

Nor was Freud or Faulkner sanguine about the possibility of fighting free of the past. If there is one thing Quentin Compson can not do, it is "learn to forget." Late in life Freud came to suspect that there is some basic human resistance to cure itself, a will to misremember or not to remember at all. We are the animals who not only remember, but also lie to ourselves and others about what we remember. We forget and forget that we forget. In Faulkner's words we "make trashy myth of reality's escape" and take that for reality.[11] Further Freud admitted that the "true" account of the past which the analyst suggests to the patient may be only a theoretically informed supposition, what he called a "construction." These constructions fill the gaps in the patient's narrative and allow closure on past experience; still they are at best very plausible guesses. One thinks here most immediately of Quentin and Shreve as they try to repair the break in the Sutpen-Bon-Henry story. They reason, they specu-late, they suppose: but we are never sure if their story matches reality.

Thus nothing escapes the inevitable circularity of memory and desire. We can never quite escape either or both. There are only relative victories, only precarious transcendences of the

10. William Faulkner, *Flags in the Dust* (New York: Vintage, 1974), 14.
11. William Faulkner, *Absalom, Absalom!* (New York: Modern Library, 1951), 143.

past. Next to Freud and Faulkner, Nietzsche only hints at the difficulty, bordering on impossibility, of learning to forget or to remember.

CHRONICLE INTO STORY

I have tried thus far to suggest affinities between the concept of memory in Nietzsche and Freud and Faulkner's presentation of the workings of memory in his fiction. Now I would like to turn to a specific text where we see Faulkner depicting the work of memory most clearly. In the early pages of Section IV of "The Bear," we find Ike McCaslin trying to make sense of, trying to work through, the ledgers that record the history of the McCaslin family. Unlike Quentin, Ike can engage his memory with a text and thus anchor himself in a written discourse.[12] The ostensible purpose of the ledgers is commercial; yet their implications bear on every important aspect of the family's history. If we did not sense it on our own, Faulkner makes it clear that more is at stake than just the story of the McCaslin family. For, as he writes, the ledgers are a "chronicle which was a whole land in miniature, which multiplied and compounded was the entire South."[13] They are meant to stand as a text, obscure and cryptic though it is, of "that whole edifice intricate and complex and founded upon injustice and erected by ruthless rapacity and carried on even yet with at times downright savagery not only to human beings but the valuable animals too" (*GDM*, 298). In short, the ledgers stand for the history of the South.

12. In his stimulating *Friday's Footsteps* (Columbus, Ohio: Ohio State University Press, 1979) Wesley Morris claims that "the romantic association of oral language with presence will serve as a refuge from the 'written' world that threatens to dismantle Ike's dream wish" (17). Yet the articulation/mediation of the story by a text, i.e., the ledgers, also prevents Ike's engulfment in and by the past.

13. William Faulkner, *Go Down, Moses* (New York: Modern Library, 1942), 293. Hereafter this work will be cited in the text as *GDM*.

149

To grasp the complexity of this text, we must remember that four levels of interpretation are involved: (1) the ledgers as the effort of Buck and Buddy McCaslin to make sense of events; (2) the written text as Ike's attempt to understand what the ledgers mean; (3) the text also as Faulkner's efforts to recreate and represent this situation; and (4) our interpretive efforts as readers. We are not presented with the finished story of Ike's interpretive quest in straightforward form, but, as all readers of modernist texts, we must participate in the process of construction and comprehension of narrative coherence. Working backwards: we read and interpret Faulkner's attempt to read and interpret Ike's reading and interpretation of his ancestor's chronicle. At issue is something akin to what Freud aimed for in the therapeutic process—the production of a "full" story, a coherent narrative, to replace the fragmentary, cryptic account initially presented by the patient.

In analyzing this section of "The Bear," I will assume a rough distinction between a chronicle and a historical narrative. A chronicle is a record of historical facts and events of the form: "This happened and then this and then this." An historical narrative integrates these facts and events into a coherent story which has a beginning, middle, and ending and is informed by causal connections. A narrative's prototypical form is: "This happened because of that and as a result. . . ." What we have in Section IV of "The Bear" is initially a proto-chronicle which Ike (and the reader) must turn into a coherent chronicle and then further transform into a narrative.

With this in mind we can try to reconstruct in our own minds what Ike makes of what he reads. (Even here we are offering a plausible narrative account of Ike's reconstruction of the ledgers rather than anything absolutely certain.) "The Bear" tells of Ike's reading the ledgers on several occasions, but most importantly when he is sixteen years old. The first ledger entries we are given are set in the 1850s. We are then taken back to 1837 and then 1832–33. Thus the ledgers are presented to us out of chronological order and are written in the nearly illegible script of Ike's barely literate uncle and father.

A redaction of the ledgers reveals the following fragments taken in order of presentation: 1856—the Percival Brownlee entries, which record his incompetence, the desire of Buck and Buddy to be rid of him, but Brownlee's refusal to leave the land; 1836—the death of Carothers McCaslin, followed by brief entries concerning several of his slaves, the last, Thucydus, refusing ten acres of land and $200 left him by Carothers; 1832–33— Eunice's suicide on Christmas day, which is the subject of puzzlement between the brothers and which elicits "But why?" from Ike; and finally that which "he knew . . . he was going to find before he found it" (*GDM*, 270), the record of Tomy's death in childbirth in June of 1833, the birth of her son, Turl, and the cryptic phrase "Fathers will." Through these pages we move from the comic to the tragic, from Ike's bemusement to a dreaded confirmation of what he sensed he would find.

Following these entries we have Ike's attempt to make sense of the entries, a process which forces us to order them chronologically and then transform them into a narrative. Our ordered chronicle goes something like this: Eunice and Thucydus have a child, Thomasina (Tomy) in 1810; on Christmas 1832 Eunice drowns herself; and six months later Tomy dies while giving birth to Turl. But then comes the crucial interpretive "action" which is occasioned by Ike's effort to understand why Eunice commits suicide. The result is a meaningful narrative; the narrative, not the chronicle, delivers the meaning and indeed is the meaning. The narrative runs as follows: Carothers fathers a daughter, Tomy, by Eunice, but Tomy is recorded as Thucydus's child; at the age of twenty-two Tomy becomes pregnant by Carothers, her own father; when Eunice discovers this horror, she commits suicide, and finally the "Fathers will" entry refers to what Carothers wills to Turl as material compensation.

151

This is the story which Ike reconstructs from the cryptic and confusing ledger entries and which we must reconstruct with him.

Even now, we need to be clear about what meaning Ike carries away from the story he has constructed and the one he will try to bring to a close once and for all. For just as the facts fail to tell us anything significant, just as they never simply speak for themselves but have to be arranged by narrative action, we must try to distill from Ike's reactions the essence of the horror which leads him to relinquish his patrimony and to reject the tradition of the fathers.

Here it is crucial that we distinguish Ike from Quentin. Unlike Quentin, who is not a Sutpen and can thus view Sutpen as an interloper and despoiler, Ike is a McCaslin and must judge the order founded by his grandfather from within. He cannot place blame on others for having disrupted the community order. His South—and by implication Faulkner's—is not riven by conflict between the values of the Sartorises and those of the Snopeses; rather the very values upon which the dominant order is based are flawed. Thus Ike's problem with the tradition is not that it is beset by outside forces, but that it is fundamentally flawed, less that it has grown too weak than that it is still too strong.

The key to Ike's horror lies in the phrase "Fathers will," one which carries obvious religious resonance. It refers to at least three different things: to the actual legal document; to Carothers McCaslin's specific instructions as to the disposal of his property; and, most crucially, to Carothers's wish that his will be done, whatever that will might be or entail. Taken generally, then, "will" implies violation and imposition. It overrides the order of nature, while property in persons violates the human order. Within the Southern context, miscegenation represents a kind of violation of (pseudo-) biological boundaries, while incest is, of course, the primal transgression of cultural life. Finally Old

Carothers's refusal to say "My son to a nigger" violates the patriarchal order of inheritance which lies at the foundation of the tradition. This refusal points to the way in which the master-slave relationship takes precedence over the father-son relationship. As with Sutpen and Charles Bon, the refusal to recognize the product of one's desire defeats the desire for recognition. History is the history of the will to power, and this lies at the core of what Ike wishes to reject.

The vexing question remains, however, as to whether the action of memory, informed by the moral insight gained in the woods from Sam Fathers, leads Ike to a new capacity for living in the present. Has Ike escaped the order of will and domination which memory uncovers at the center of the Southern tradition? And what does it mean, as I began this paper, to live outside one's tradition? By transforming repetitions into recollections, by breaking the repetitive pattern of the tradition through remembering it, has Ike somehow attained what Nietzsche called the "superhistorical"? Or has he seceded from his family experience, only to live off the proceeds of his patrimony without fully facing the consequences of his actions?

I confess I can't answer these questions with any certainty. They are ones which still dog us and nag at our own self-understanding. Numerous critics, most immediately Louis Rubin in his eloquent, "The Dixie Special,"[14] have been extremely critical of Ike's decision; indeed even Faulkner was later to confess to being unimpressed by Ike's moral heroism. There seem to be three distinct, though clearly related, reasons for criticizing Ike. First, his relinquishment is a kind of withdrawal from history. This seems to be Rubin's position. Second, after making his grand moral gesture, Ike lives off proceeds from the land which he had given up. Third, in "Delta Autumn" he is guilty of

14. Louis Rubin, "The Dixie Special," *Faulkner and the Southern Renaissance*, ed. Ann J. Abadie and Doreen Fowler (Jackson: University Press of Mississippi, 1982).

a failure of imagination and of love, for he wants Roth's mistress to disappear rather than to challenge the existing attitudes and arrangements in the South concerning miscegenation.

But I want to enter a measured defense of Ike here. The form of historical consciousness he displays is an example of Nietzsche's critical form of memory which has it that "every past is worth condemning." Nietzsche goes on, however, to say that this is dangerous, since "we are also the resultant of their [*our predecessors*] errors, passions and crimes; it is impossible to shake off this chain . . . we cannot escape the fact that we spring from them" (*UA*, 21). This is always the dilemma of those who criticize the past; it must be rejected, yet it can't be.

What we have in "The Bear" is an authentically tragic dilemma. If we remember Hegel's notion of the tragic as involving the conflict between two "goods" and not the melodramatic defeat of the "good" by the "bad," then Ike McCaslin and McCaslin Edmonds, who speaks as a representative of the tradition, both express plausible, even compelling views. I must confess that I don't quite follow Rubin's reading of the story which allows him to claim that because Old Ben is finally killed, Ike tries to halt any further change and to secede from his historical responsibility. Rather, the moral values learned from Sam, as well as the end of Old Ben, compel Ike precisely to confront the past and to take action in history. This action is an intervention in a repetitious family and regional pattern and seeks, however ineffectively, to break that pattern. Nor can I see how Ike's act of relinquishment keeps him from rectifying injustice in "Delta Autumn." In that story Ike repeats his much earlier protest to Fonsiba in the form of a panicky "not yet." But in neither case does Ike's failure of nerve follow causally from his decision to give up his land. Finally, Ike is at least aware of these various dilemmas and conflicts. It is against him, not his kinsman Roth, that Roth's mistress directs her withering charge of being incapable of love.

154

The other important issue in connection with Ike's action concerns its political implications and the political role of fiction generally. As I have written elsewhere, what renders Ike's act of relinquishment abstract and without significant effect is the lack of a political context for his action. Unlike John Brown, who surprisingly is one of Ike's models, Ike acts in a political vacuum. He acts as an isolated individual; and his decision neither touches off nor occurs in a political movement aimed at challenging the tradition of the fathers. In "The Bear" the mythical world of the hunt stands beyond history, while the historical weight of the family tradition smothers any but a negative sort of freedom. Thus Ike's tragedy is political as much as it is personal. Indeed, it has been little noted that, for all the richness of Faulkner's world, it is one which presents no political "space" within which collective, public action can be taken seriously.[15]

Here in response to Rubin, I want to emphasize that not all fiction should be written with political or moral effect in mind. (I would argue that such intent does not automatically lessen the quality of the work where it is expressed.) Nor, more importantly, should all fictional depictions of political action suggest that the reader go and do likewise. It is extremely difficult, for instance, to figure out the political "message" of *All the King's Men*. But much of the richness of Warren's novel derives from the way Warren creates politically serious actors and actions within the world of the novel. *Within* "The Bear," however, Ike has available no political space for action. This is not to demand that Faulkner should have made him a radical or Populist or whatever. Nor is to say that "The Bear" is fatally flawed as fiction. But since Ike does make a moral gesture, having potential political implications, it is not far-fetched to note the lack of a political realm to "register" that gesture.

15. The notion of politics in its most general sense is drawn from the work of Hannah Arendt.

This whole issue of politics in Faulkner demands a brief discussion of *A Fable*, his only novel in which a group of men engage in collective action with a broadly political purpose, but not connected with making war. It would seem to be Faulkner's political novel. And yet, *A Fable* mystifies rather than clarifies the issues of war and peace, authority and the resistance to authority. Unlike Ike, the Corporal and some of his men are outsiders with only the haziest of pasts. There is some suggestion that a "class" issue is involved, i.e., the "men" versus the "generals," but Faulkner never sharpens this point to any significant degree. Most crucially, we never observe the Corporal and his men actually talking to and trying to convince the soldiers on both sides of the trenches to put down their weapons, to say "enough." All we really learn is that they would materialize quite mysteriously on both sides of the lines; indeed the Corporal is himself so elusive as to be identified as several different people. Finally, in the crucial dialogue (really more of a monologue) between the Corporal and the General, it is not history but metahistory, not politics but cosmic principles which are debated. And they are fuzzed over as much as they are clarified. Thus I don't think *A Fable* counters my contention that Faulkner fails to create convincing images of political consideration or action in his fiction.

Finally, then, Ike's choice to relinquish his inheritance is an individual solution to a political and, more generally, a cultural problem. What does it mean to liberate oneself from outworn social, racial, and cultural imperatives when nothing lies at hand to provide an alternative order within which the self can find meaning? It means, provisionally, to live "between" times, at the closing time of one culture and prior to the time when a new order of binding authority has emerged. Nietzsche was one of the first to be fully aware of the necessity of living in a time of transition. But after his desperately "joyful" dithyrambs to the superman, he succumbed to insanity. Ike clearly lacks the spiritual attractiveness of a Quentin Compson, whose descent into derangement and then suicide and his failure to make his way back from where memory and desire led him are more appealing to us modern readers. There is something compelling about the *frisson* of psychosis, our contemporary form of higher spirituality. And thus we are tempted to prefer Quentin for it. Fortunately or not, Ike lives on; there is no second act to his life. For all his faults, however, he did survive, even endured. It isn't enough. But, then, what in the modern world—or in Faulkner's—ever is?

Faulkner
and Continuance of the
Southern Renaissance

ALEXANDER BLACKBURN

Generally, I believe, it is agreed that the memorable Southern literature of the twentieth century appears at a time when the older South's moral order, the old notions of certainty and belief, has ceased to suffice as an explanation and an adequate basis for daily experience. Although the term "Southern Renaissance" seems a bit highfalutin and vague as a description of this literary activity, we would agree that a peculiarly Southern consciousness is revealed in it. C. Vann Woodward, following Allen Tate, defines the Southern Renaissance as "literature conscious of the past in the present"; this consciousness disdains nostalgic myths and romantic dreams of the South's past and turns instead to the South's real experience with history, with defeat and failure, with long periods of frustration and poverty, as well as with human slavery and its long aftermath of racial injustice.[1] Similar conclusions are pressed by Cleanth Brooks in *William Faulkner: The Yoknapatawpha Country* and by Louis D. Rubin, Jr., in *The Faraway Country: Writers of the Modern South*, two books published the year after Faulkner's death and still, eighteen years later, invaluable studies of the relationship of modern Southern letters to a view of man as an inextricable part of a living history and community. Brooks emphasizes the pastoral

1. C. Vann Woodward, *The Burden of Southern History*, rev. ed. (Baton Rouge: Louisiana State University Press, 1970), 24.

mode in Faulkner's fiction, what man has done to his fellow man and to nature, a kind of Wordsworthian lament for an Edenic world lost as irrevocably as Benjy Compson's pasture and Ike McCaslin's wilderness. Rubin discerns in such various writers as Faulkner, Thomas Wolfe, Robert Penn Warren, and Eudora Welty a spiritual detachment from values of community, history, and society and an emotional emigration from the geographical South into a country of the mind—not Asheville but Altamont, not Northern Mississippi but Yoknapatawpha—and emphasizes a tragic sense of the literature, one born out of the feeling that an old order is passing away. At all events, the pastoral and the tragic combined give Southern writing much of its gravity of tone.[2] As a literary phenomenon, the Southern Renaissance does indeed bear credible resemblance to that period of Europe's dark radiance when the medieval synthesis was breaking up and men no longer believed with a living faith. Here, very loosely, we are comparing a fifty-year period of Southern writing with an almost two-hundred-year period of European, from Fernando de Rojas and Cervantes to Marlowe, Shakespeare, Donne, and Milton, so, to make the comparison just, not merely a product of provincial enthusiasm, we would have to consider the novels of Faulkner, at least, as representing an achievement more or less equivalent to the plays of Shakespeare. That case, I believe, can be made and later I shall return to it. For the moment let's accept the Southern Renaissance as a fact beyond dispute. What I want to do here is raise some questions as to its boundaries. In what ways, if at all, has a Southern tradition in literature been continued since, say, 1950?

First, who qualifies as a Southern writer? John M. Bradbury's *Renaissance in the South: A Critical History of Literature, 1920–1960* deals with 700 writers, thus bringing us perilously close to admitting what we've long suspected, that every hamlet

2. See Cleanth Brooks, *William Faulkner: The Yoknapatawapha Country* (New Haven: Yale University Press, 1963), and Louis D. Rubin, Jr., *The Faraway Country: Writers of the Modern South* (Seattle: University of Washington Press, 1963).

in Dixieland shelters more inglorious rustic bards than Gray's *Elegy* ever contemplated. Clearly, this kind of approach won't do, this *renaissancing* of every Southerner not demonstrably illiterate. Do we swap non-Southerners for those who decamped, recalling that it was recently fashionable to give T. S. Eliot for W. H. Auden at an arbitrary rate of international poetic exchange? We are of course traditionally hospitable. Take, for instance, Hervey Allen of Pennsylvania: one of the few distinguished American writers who actually served in the gas-green trenches of France and survived, he recuperated in Charleston, helped DuBose Heyward found there the Poetry Society of South Carolina in 1921 (thus pipping the Agrarians at the post), and wrote of Southern mood and history in his poetry, his biography of Poe, and in two of his historical novels, *Anthony Adverse* and *Action at Aquila*. Or take Sherwood Anderson of Ohio whose sojourn in New Orleans provided young Faulkner with some encouragement. But neither Allen nor Anderson, welcome as their presence may have been, qualifies as a Southern writer. Southernness has to be bred in the bone, has to do with roots. (And it excludes no one on the basis of race: Richard Wright and Ralph Ellison belong to Southern tradition.) As long as we are talking about a general cultural manifestation of the literary imagination, we are probably safe in assuming that a writer need have spent only his or her formative years in the region—until the age of twelve at most—to become forever a Southerner, which is to say, with Wolfe, forever lost. For instance, in William Styron's *Set This House on Fire* (1960) the Virginia-educated Peter Leverett declares he is "estranged from myself and from my time, dwelling neither in the destroyed past nor in the fantastic and incomprehensible present" (18–19).[3] Such estrangement is peculiarly rooted in Southern experience.

3. All quotations from William Styron's novels are from the first editions as published by Random House, New York.

But roots also have to do with a whole complex of values bodied forth in language. The Southern man-of-letters (or woman-of-letters, if you will) need not have written poetry or fiction in order to establish credentials in a poetics of Southern discourse. Permit a pious example here: my father, William Blackburn, was born to a South Carolinian mother but not in the South, was born in fact in an antediluvian village in Persia where he was held for several years hostage to the twin terrors of his missionary parents' poverty and Presbyterianism; terror which I wouldn't say he escaped when the family moved to Seneca, S. C., but he grew up sufficiently at home in and disenchanted with Southern historical consciousness and language to inspire, as a teacher at Duke, their grieving in the poetry and fiction of a new generation of writers. To write as a Southerner, seriously that is, one learns early on the emptiness of the old rhetoric of Cloud-Cuckoo-Land (as W. J. Cash called it), of innocence and success and invincibility, and one also learns early on to contract out of our All-American, urban, anti-pastoral values of imperial politics and flash merchandise. On your own and not because of a literary influence, you come upon the richness and variety of Southern speech. For instance, long years before I read *As I Lay Dying*, I knew that countryfolk in Moore County, North Carolina, 800 miles from Lafayette County, Mississippi, say "right well" and "right smart" and "studying up them Ten Commandments what taken the Lord forty days when he done done the world in seven." The point of course is a truism: Southern writing is the outgrowth of an early collective experience of a certain kind of people spread over a land bigger than France, a marrow-deep experience of land and blood. From childhood, Wordsworths all, we inherit the real myth of our dispossessed and dispossessing land, with both wonder and irony, coming the hard way up to our common heritage and our common toil.

There is, I surmise, no intrinsic reason to believe that a vigorous Southern tradition in literature should cease with the passing of its first geniuses. True, the so-called extended family may be breaking up in the South, as elsewhere, and small towns get larger. True, television wreaks philological havoc. I don't suppose you could go now to the Outer Banks of North Carolina and hear one of Blackbeard's descendants say, "When's hoigh toide on th'oiland, goin oot in me bo-at." True, the assumptions of permanence, out of which Faulkner's great art arises, no longer come with the territory; that is, with the memory of the territory. On the other hand, we can readily recognize the durable strength of our emotional pieties when these are tested by the flip conceptions of non-Southerners. To hear them tell it, you would think Southern literature is a sort of parody Annunciation: thus once, amidst magnolias and wild grits, the deity disguised as Poe's raven ravished still unravished Dixie, and in that lethargic rush engendered there the burning shacks of Atlanta and Elvis Presley dead. Whatever else they know, Southerners know what it's like to feel insulted and injured. A literature of outrage and defiance is certainly a continuing possibility.

If there is no intrinsic reason to doubt the continuance of Southern literary tradition, there is nonetheless evidence that it continues in a mode differing from that of the elder generation of writers. This, I take it, is why Rubin describes a boundary between the Faulknerian mode of novel and the kind of novel William Styron began writing in *Lie Down in Darkness* (1951). As we all know, Styron's extraordinary first novel, written in New York in his early twenties, owes more than echoes to *The Sound and the Fury* and *As I Lay Dying*. I have no desire to rehash the matter here; Rubin, among others, has performed that function admirably and demonstrated beyond any lingering

4. Malcolm Cowley's review of *Lie Down in Darkness*—"The Faulkner Pattern," *New Republic*, 125 (Oct. 8, 1951), 19–20—concentrated attention upon that book's apparent similarities to *The Sound and the Fury*. Such a comparison thereafter became a sort of mandatory critical exercise, to the point of irrelevance in John W. Aldridge's chapter called "William Styron and the Derivative Imagination" in *Time to Murder and*

doubt that Styron did not exhibit the "derivative imagination" once so absurdly attributed to him.[4] Loveless families are *not* all alike, nor are funeral processions, nor are Southern girls lost for the same reasons; and the uses of interior monologue did not grow stale after Faulkner's. Styron *couldn't* have written as Faulkner did. Absent from *Lie Down in Darkness* are the historical dimension and community perspective of Faulknerian tragedy: "Where Faulkner created a Greek-like tragedy reminiscent of the fall of the House of Atreus," writes Rubin, "Styron produced a domestic tragedy that had no element of fated dynastic downfall about it."[5] Quentin Compson's alienation from Yoknapatawpha County is *em*blematic of his failure to cope with the modern world; Peyton Loftis's alienation from Port Warwick is *symp*tomatic of her parent's selfishness and weakness. Moreover, where *The Sound and the Fury*'s juxtaposition of Compson decadence and Dilsey's theologically validated compassion gives a powerful sense of living myth, in *Lie Down in Darkness* only the semblance of such juxtaposition exists, there being no authenticity either to Carey Carr's or to Daddy Faith's versions of Christian ethics. Styron's positives lie elsewhere, implicitly in *Lie Down in Darkness*, explicitly in his second novel, *Set This House on Fire:* the way to human survival lies through personal choice and maturation. Cass Kinsolving, hero of the later novel, creates his own salvation and brings to the community his own stability. Southern attitudes toward history and society have been tested and finally made to depend for

Create: The Contemporary Novel in Crisis (New York: David McKay, 1966), 30–51. A sensible approach becomes evident in Louis D. Rubin, *The Faraway Country*, 185–230, and in Jonathan Baumbach, *The Landscape of Nightmare: Studies in the Contemporary American Novel* (New York: New York University Press, 1965), 123–37, and thereafter in Marc L. Ratner, *William Styron* (New York: Twayne, 1972), who emphasizes Styron's talents as satirist. Styron's indebtedness to Faulkner is of little moment in the essays printed in *The Achievement of William Styron*, edited by Robert K. Morris and Irving Malin (Athens: University of Georgia Press, 1975).

5. Rubin, *Faraway Country*, 201.

their reality on Cass's own inward acceptance of them. This proceeding would certainly seem to evince a new mode in Southern writing.

Somewhat parenthetically I might say at this point that the most "Faulknerian" moment in Styron's writing occupies four pages of *Set This House on Fire* (88–92). The rich, sleazily corrupt boy, Mason Flagg, has been sent home from school for seducing (in the school's chapel!) the witless thirteen-year-old daughter of a Chesapeake oyster fisherman, who, outraged and hellbent on retribution, suddenly appears outside the Flagg family's Virginia mansion. Then, just as suddenly, Mason's father commands the oysterman to put down his murderous lead pipe. He does so. End of scene. Styron of course is merely foreshadowing how Mason's later life leads to the rape of an Italian peasant and to Cass Kinsolving's more or less remorseless murder of him. But just think what Faulkner might have done with these materials! Our oysterman might have founded a dynasty in order to avenge himself upon the Flaggs; and we can see the poor ravished but unwoebegone daughter riding in the last mule-drawn wagon toward Jefferson through the quiet dust of the world's last worthless, umbrageous twilight, she thinking, *My mother is an oyster.*

Although Styron himself evidently rejects the idea of a new mode, his novels dispose one to think otherwise.[6] A rejection of "Southernness" is just a protest, quite wholesome, against being tagged as a regional writer. But a modal proposition, one that involves differing affirmation of possibility, impossibility, necessity, or contingency, is not a limiting tag. Thus a new mode of Southern writing may easily accommodate an extension of the South's experience with history stretching beyond geographical frontiers. The South, more than any other American region, has

6. Styron's statement in a *Paris Review* interview ("I don't consider myself in the Southern school") is cited as evidence that he doesn't belong to a "new mode" by Willard Thorp, "The Southern Mode," *South Atlantic Quarterly*, 63 (1964), 576–82.

a common bond "with the ironic and tragic experience of other nations and the general run of mankind."[7] This, Woodward's fine observation of universality in Southern thought and feeling, may help to explain why Styron, among other writers of the post-1950 era, has refused to limit his "faraway country" to Virginia. Of course, he makes in *Set This House on Fire* some memorable imaginative excursions to "Port Warwick" and to the Carolinas, but New York is in there, too, (as it had been in *Lie Down in Darkness*) and above all Paris and parts of Italy. *The Confessions of Nat Turner* (1967) takes place in the Tidewater, to be sure, and what Styron calls a "meditation on history" could have meant, but doesn't mean, a renewal of Faulknerian meditations on race in *Absalom, Absaslom!* and in *Go Down, Moses*. The publication of *Sophie's Choice* (1979) clarifies what Styron has been doing: it is a Southerner, and no surrogate Albert Camus either, who confronts the hardest existential choices wherever his imagination may lead him, to the despair of a Black revolutionist in nineteenth-century Virginia or to the despair of a Holocaust survivor in New York. Styron remains a representative Southern writer when he views the hell of dehumanization anywhere and everywhere, the special vantage point being the tragic-pastoral poet's. Like Virgil in the *First Eclogue*— sometimes called "The Dispossessed"—a Southern writer (more so than other American writers, I would judge) sees an alien world of dehumanizing power encroaching on the ideal landscape, and he or she faces, behind the masks of contemporary Arcadians, the prospect of unending deprivation and despair.[8]

Although Styron does not create a Yoknapatawpha on native soil, he extends his vision of the South to a country quite literally faraway—Poland—as in this passage from *Sophie's Choice:*

7. C. Vann Woodward, *The Burden of Southern History*, 230.
8. American pastoralism in general has been brilliantly studied by Leo Marx, *The Machine in the Garden: Technology and the Pastoral Ideal in America* (New York: Oxford University Press, 1964). I find his argument peculiarly applicable to discussion of Southern writers.

Poland is a beautiful, heart-wrenching, soul-split country which in many ways . . . resembles or conjures up images of the American South—or at least the South of other not-so-distant times. It is not alone that forlornly lovely, nostalgic landscape which creates the frequent likeness—the quagmiry but haunting monochrome of the Narew River swampland, for example, with its look and feel of a murky savanna on the Carolina coast, or the Sunday hush on a muddy back street in a village of Galicia, where by the smallest eyewink of the imagination one might see whisked to a lonesome crossroads hamlet in Arkansas these ramshackle, weather-bleached little houses, crookedly carpentered, set upon shrubless plots of clay where scrawny chickens fuss and peck—but in the spirit of the nation, her indwellingly ravaged and melancholy heart, tormented into its shape like that of the Old South out of adversity, penury and defeat. (*SC*, 246–47)

In both Poland and the American South, Styron continues,

the abiding presence of race has created at the same instant cruelty and compassion, bigotry and understanding, enmity and fellowship, exploitation and sacrifice, searing hatred and hopeless love. While it may be said that the darker and uglier of these opposing conditions has usually carried the day, there must also be recorded in the name of truth a long chronicle in which decency and honor were at moments able to controvert the absolute dominion of the reigning evil, more often than not against rather large odds, whether in Poznan or Yazoo City. (*SC*, 247–48)

In speaking, then, of the possibility of the continuance of Southern tradition, I would lay stress upon universality. Writers like Styron continue to affiliate with the victims and dispossessed of this world, to withdraw with them from the world's mad society, and to shape their quest for renewed life by first, Prospero-like, mastering nature through mind, through the kind of civilized control that makes possible the growth of love. Literature, as Solzhenitsyn said in his Nobel Lecture, is a nation's soul. The long sad memories of the Southern writer compel a change of wording: literature is the world's soul.

166

Faulkner and Continuance of the Renaissance

Every artist revolts against a previous form of possession. Axiomatic as this saying is, a good deal of criticism over the past thirty years has seemed impervious to the fact of revolt where Southern writers are concerned. We are supposed to be mesmerized by Faulkner's style, cowed by his stature. It is curious but one doesn't receive the impression that Styron, Flannery O'Connor, Reynolds Price, Walker Percy, Fred Chappell, Elizabeth Spencer, and a host of other new writers have been writing in a daze or lying down on the tracks waiting for the Dixie Special to come helling along. We—they—must usually answer to two charges of "influence": Faulkner's language and techniques did a trick on us, and we all came trailing clouds of Gothicism.

Reynolds Price issues a correct defiance: "Serious writers of fiction born in the American South, setting their work in the region which they possess and must comprehend, do not imitate the obsessive themes of the private language of a single distinguished elder, William Faulkner; they imitate the South, their South, as Faulkner imitated his South, his private relation to a public thing, a place . . . inhabited by millions of people united by an elaborate dialect formed in syntax and rhythm (like the people themselves) by the weight of land, climate, race, religion, history."[9] It is a case, in other words, "of Southern writers, almost to a man, *not* being involved in an imitation or mimicry of Faulkner but of Mr. Faulkner and other Southern writers being involved in an imitation of a given original, of a common original—which is the way men and women have talked in the South in the last fifty or sixty years."[10] Having read the work of Eudora

9. Reynolds Price, "Speaking of Books: A Question of Influence," *New York Times Book Review* (May 29, 1966), 2.

10. Reynolds Price in *Conversations: Reynolds Price and William Ray* (Memphis: Memphis State University Press, 1976), 24. Although Price has successfully fended off the claim that his own fiction, especially *A Long and Happy Life* (1962), was heavily shaped by Faulkner's, he writes generously of Faulkner's art in an introduction to the Signet edition of *Pylon* and has reprinted this essay in *Things Themselves: Essays & Scenes* (New York: Atheneum, 1972), 91–108.

167

Welty when he was in high school, Price feels that she, not Faulkner, is the one who revealed to him possibilities for fictionalizing landmarks of his own world. This is self-discovery through a writer, not imitation of one.

As for the charge of Gothicism, Flannery O'Connor refuted it wonderfully: "I have found," she wrote, "that any fiction that comes out of the South is going to be considered grotesque by the Northern critics, unless it is grotesque, in which case it is going to be considered realistic."[11] And it is not to Faulkner but to Mark Twain and Nathanael West that one must turn to find her literary precursors.[12]

The impact of Faulkner on other writers cannot be simply assumed. His first encounter with Faulkner's works left Reynolds Price cold, and many new writers nowadays have probably not read them at all. Although Faulkner's reputation is in a solid state, the fact of the matter may be that his impact on other writers may have just begun. Few of us born in the twenties and thirties ever heard of Faulkner until Malcolm Cowley brought out the Portable Edition in 1946, and even then, I strongly suspect, most of us strung out our reading of the novels—not all of them either—over the next thirty years, a period almost as long as that which elapsed between the publication of Shakespeare's First Folio and the appearance of Dryden's criticism. Perhaps Faulkner's star is just now looming in our previously unfocused lens.

The post-World-War-II generation of writers felt distanced from Faulkner. Wright Morris, commenting on the Nobel Prize

11. Flannery O'Connor, from an unpublished lecture cited in Stanley Edgar Hyman, *Flannery O'Connor* (Minneapolis: University of Minnesota Press, 1966), 44. Similar remarks about misunderstanding of "gothicism" and "grotesque" may be found in Flannery O'Connor, "The Fiction Writer and His Country," in *The Living Novel: A :Symposium,* edited by Granville Hicks (New York: Macmillan, 1957), 157–64.

12. Hyman, *Flannery O'Connor,* 43.

speech about the ding-dong of doom, observes, "It is the *nature* of the future, not its extinction, that produces in the artist such foreboding, the prescient chill of heart of a world without consciousness."[13] William Styron's *Esquire* article on "My Generation" has something similar to say: "We were traumatized not only by what we had been through and by the almost unimaginable presence of the bomb, but by the realization that the entire mess was not finished at all. . . . When at last the Korean War arrived, . . . the cosmos seemed so unhinged as to be nearly insupportable."[14] So the new generation's doubt over humanity, over the survival of the humane within humanity, became an intense preoccupation; Faulkner's strategies for human recovery seemed to unfold from a desperation not somehow quiet enough to confront the new facts.

This sense of distance from Faulkner has led and might still lead to serious parody, a literary stance definable as both a compliment and a deliverance, a testament of real and, yes, loving devotion to *il miglior fabbro* but also a ceremony of disaffiliation. It is as if the imaginative power, far from being derived from the artist parodied, derives him from itself—reproduces him through a process of refictionalization. Thus Faulkner's techniques, themes, settings, and presumed style can be approached and imitated as if they symbolize a whole culture, the Old South, old, that is, to a writer from the urbanized New South. Styron's *Lie Down in Darkness*, for example, exploits the Faulknerian mode in the fashion of parody: Styron obtains his visa from the Old South, so to speak, in order to travel to the new Southern presence, now an urbanized landscape that brings Virginian shipyards, country clubs, and frater-

13. Wright Morris, "The Territory Ahead," in *The Living Novel*, ed. Granville Hicks, 145.
14. William Styron, "My Generation," *Esquire*, 70 (October 1968), 123.

nity houses into easy conjunction with New York subways and flats.[15]

To explain how a parody-intention comes into play, I will have to risk solipsism and a kind of presumptuousness by disclosing what I myself did in a novel called *The Cold War of Kitty Pentecost* (1979). It was a composition that took many years and various drafts to complete, but in the final draft I was more or less fully conscious of a partial Faulknerian parody, because I wanted to juxtapose New South and Old, contriving to exhibit the latter as pseudo-Faulknerian, a world of strong-willed and violent people accursed by racial fears. At several points I even put Faulkner himself on the scene. I had seen him in Virginia, nattily attired, head held dreamily high, walking along the highway between Charlottesville and Farmington, so when I first introduce the reader to Mrs. Pentecost, representative of the Old South, I fused that image of Faulkner into the portrait, pictured her walking along a highway, and let the description echo "A Rose for Emily":

> Transcontinental eighteen wheelers were expresstraining past this figure in black mourning clothes of a bygone era, this figure with head and shoulders almost as stiff as a waxwork at Madame Tussaud's, sounding horns at her, raking her with cyclones of diesel exhaust, yet there she was walking, a scarecrow in black whose flesh, he remembered, sagged off high gaunt cheekbones like drippings of candlewax and was of that pallid hue—a figure fragile, indomitable, ludicrous, haughty, and mad. (*KP*, 32)

Faulkner is not Mrs. Pentecost—good grief! But I confess to a ghostly presence. At a later point in the novel I wanted a character who would sum up its theme; I needed a sort of disembodied

15. One critic suggests that Styron's whole procedure in *Lie Down in Darkness* is "elaborate literary pastiche," a kind of sympathetic mockery of Faulkner's techniques. See Melvin J. Friedman, *William Styron* (Bowling Green, Ohio: Bowling Green Popular Press, 1974), 29–30.

voice with sepulchral tones and Mt. Rushmore monumentality, a Melvillean Dansker, the *Agamemnon* man, and so I gave the speech to a lawyer from Charleston named Buck McKay. That passage, rather godawful to me now, reads:

> The voice of Buck McKay was communicative in a reserved way. "Extending sympathy with the mind is easy, and it's not enough. Besides, it can be dangerous to liberty. But, as for the other, extending sympathy with the heart, the glacier-show movement of man towards some frail kinship with his kind—kinship of his own desiring and making from love and hope and sacrifice—it also may well not be enough. Nevertheless it is now the only movement in which his liberty has meaning. What is needed is a change in the human weather, atonement, compassion. But what we are likely to have instead is a kind of spiritual Stone Age in which whatever fire first stirred in whatever brutish and fetid cave our nearer ancestors to cherish and to fear the new god of themselves will be gradually extinguished and finally forgotten, and then our cold, lonely, unsupported souls shall be set adrift, like the planet itself, among myriads of unknown stars." (*KP*, 107–08)

In this scene Buck McKay is addressing and consoling a highly sensitive, potentially revolutionary black student from the modern industrial city of Poe's Hill, North Carolina; the distant shade of Faulkner is his Virgilian guide to an old Inferno but capable of hinting at the New South's hope for redemption from ways of the past. There are deliberate echoes from *Go Down, Moses*—the love-hope-sacrifice incantation, the brutish cave, the ancestral self-worship—but the full weight of the passage falls upon the rather unFaulknerian conceptual word, "unsupported." The image of our drifting planet owes much, in fact, to that photograph, taken from the Apollo spacecraft, of Earth shimmering and green in a black void of space. As for the two kinds of possible human community, that of the intellect and that of the heart—their conflict forming the "cold war" of the narrative and title—such a theme runs so deeply in American

171

literature, as well as in an English writer like D. H. Lawrence, that I can feel comfortable in presenting a personal variation.

Odd as it may seem, few of the methods and materials of *The Cold War of Kitty Pentecost* have a parody-intention. There are multiple restricted points of view, interior monologues, collo- quies of conjecture about the past, running rhythms, strings of viscid epithets, a domineering mother, a fated girl, a chain of crimes leading into an Old South darkened by incest and mis- cegenation and perjury and religious fanaticism, and even, in- evitably, a statue of the Confederate Soldier. Admittedly, Faulkner's technical innovations form a precedent, but in point of fact my adoption of multiple viewpoints was the result of a vision which I can date quite precisely. In November, 1951, as a R.A.-all-the-way buck-private in the Army Signal Corps, I had the dubious privilege of participating in an atom bomb "experi- ment" in Nevada. Our dutifully radiated contingent from Geor- gia afterwards took a slow train east, and as it coughed and throbbed into the thin blue air of the Grand Canyon country, I was visited by a sudden realization of life as fragmentation and motion, of solitudes within the symmetries of sublimely beauti- ful nature. Recording the vision at once, I determined to find use for it at a future time and hence it became the structural metaphor of that novel. Out of a world fragmented by loneliness and fear and mendacity there would emerge a new society based upon personal choice and mutual acceptance.

The architectonics of *The Cold War of Kitty Pentecost* came originally out of a meditation over *The Tempest*, my working title, *Reason Against My Fury*, being lifted from that soliloquy when Prospero, enemies in his grasp, relinquishes vengeance and elects civilization. My Prospero, Max Stebbins, focus of consciousness and conscience, has, I fear, dwindled from a princely magician into an English professor at a riotous univer- sity in a Carolina tobacco-manufacturing city. Guilt-ridden by war and by thwarted love for Kitty Pentecost, Max is perplexed by his apparent loss of humanity; what he does not know, but through reason and self-realization is able to discover, is that Kitty had sacrificed happiness in order to spare Max the Pentecost's ancestral violence; and his discoveries arm him against Kitty's husband, an Oxford-educated, Marxist millionaire Yankee psychiatrist, who arrives at Bermuda Farm in hopes of dishonoring Max and of having him executed by government agents. The novel is a parable of violence, a search for its sources in history, society, and self. Although the literature of the Southern Renaissance also offers parables and versions of pastoral (*Light in August* comes to mind), the dramatic focus in *Kitty Pentecost* is upon spiritual salvation *from*, not in, the past. The mood, moreover, is romantic: Eros, that is, is not for me the Dark God of American puritanism but the creative source of well-being and of freedom from heartless authoritarianism.

I recognize in my first novel "Southernness" and continuance of tradition, and I confess that such limited knowledge of Faulkner as I possess played a part in the writing. But I feel no need to apologize for the connections, for they are fewer than appearances might suggest.

I have argued that the Southern tradition in literature continues in a new mode emphasizing individual salvation and accommodating the tragic experience of outsiders everywhere. Further, I have observed how a reductionist criticism, with stress upon "influences," produces misunderstanding of the South and of the nature of narrative art. Now, I wish to present the view that Faulkner the *artist* belongs to a literary tradition that reaches back to antiquity—the tradition of verse drama. Faulkner's poetics aligns his greatest novels more closely to the plays of Aeschylus, Sophocles, and Shakespeare than to the novels of Dostoevsky, Conrad, or Joyce, anti-realistic as these sometimes are.

Needed here is Denis Donoghue's definition of verse drama: "A play is 'poetic' when its concrete elements (plot, agency, scene, speech, gesture) continuously exhibit in their internal relationships those qualities of mutual coherence and illumination required of the words of a poem."[16] By these terms even a silent film may achieve a high style in both tragedy and comedy: the poetry inheres in the structure of a drama as a whole and in the manner in which, and the degree to which, all the elements act in cooperation. And, as Donoghue noted as early as 1959, a novelist like Faulkner succeeds as verse-dramatist where so many poets, confined to theatrical conventions, have failed. Those conventions prove recalcitrant to the poet's efforts to discover a form commensurate to the depths of individual modern experience. On the other hand, the novelist, released from theatrical conventions, may present large dramatic actions that focus a civilization in all its complexity.

T. S. Eliot believed verse has advantages over prose; there were possibilities of reinforcing and deepening the dramatic effect by the musical effect of a varied pattern of style. Tension would be slackened when, for example, a character has to come off the high style and order a cup of coffee, so Eliot tried in his plays to give characters credible speech that would also, almost surreptitiously, remain heightened. But the trouble with "high" speeches is like that with the police: once you invite them into your home, they refuse to go away. Moreover, because actors look like real people, radical departures from credible speech are difficult to sustain. Finally, Eliot and other modern dramatists struggled to construct, however artificially, a code that could be broken and affirmed, that would set limits to a hero's conduct. That is to say, to achieve an authoritative style, one must establish without showing one's hand a decorum of ceremony, to

16. Denis Donoghue, *The Third Voice: Modern British and American Verse Drama* (Princeton: Princeton University Press, 1959), 10.

dissolve realistic terms into a self-subsistent universe wherein the values of human choice and action can be asserted. One would have to affect the sublime, the elegiac, or the apocalyptic—and "get away with it," as Donoghue remarks. And to get away with it is to seize the opportunity of "framing one's own rules." Yet modern verse drama has discovered no truly satisfactory convention "by which the dramatist may indicate more of the truth about an agent than that agent may be expected to know."[17] The omniscient dramatist cannot step forward to comment and expect to get away with it.

Faulkner's verse dramas, secured from theatrical conventions by the novelistic convention of authorial omniscience, get away with it. The Sole Proprietor of Yoknapatawpha County enjoyed the privilege of making an internally consistent world; of defining human action against a convincing background of communal code and ceremony; of creating characters with a force of will behind their words and acts; and above all of devising strategies to establish and maintain a high style of epic, tragic, and comic decorum. He doesn't need to lug in the machinery of rusty Classical or Christian mythology, for he consistently *sees* his material as mythical. His poetics carries and lends necessary distance to events of tragic, mythical grandeur. His characters wear masks larger than life, and for them he contrives, as Albert Guerard observes, a "notlanguage" that tells you what is in a character's soul: "what the whole personality (conscious, preconscious, unconscious) would say if it could speak."[18] Indeed, Guerard surmises that Faulkner's view of his characters may well have been Mr. Compson's in *Absalom, Absalom!*: "people too as we see, and victims too as we are, but victims of a different circumstance, simpler and therefore, integer for integer,

17. *Ibid.*, 260.
18. Albert J. Guerard, *The Triumph of the Novel: Dickens, Dostoevsky, Faulkner* (New York: Oxford University Press, 1976), 323.

larger, more heroic and the figures therefore more heroic too, not dwarfed and involved but distinct, uncomplex who had the gift of loving once or dying once instead of being diffused and scattered creatures drawn blindly limb from limb from a grab bag and assembled."[19]

Realistic novels are usually submerged in the stream of time, the aesthetic equivalent of formlessness, but anti-realistic dramatic art demands that time be made important through ideas of order. Some sense of the timeless, of the sacred, is called for. Belief in (or merely the adoption of) the eschatological, that is, the doctrine of judgment and historical consummation, gives daily happenings an unrusting patina, and this, however, mysterious, does fulfill a profound human need for family and corporate continuity. In the eschatological view, the past flows into the present, the timeless is co-existent in time, so that a person may incorporate into himself what is scattered and passing and give it a meaning and an identity. What we love, we become— other persons, the land—renewing without change what is free and growing as well as what is old and past. Here, where it is not necessarily a question of Faulkner's belief in Christianity, we discern that his greatest works, taken singly or as a whole, dramatize the act of the mind in *defining* the relations of man to himself, to society, to history, and to the cosmos. His typical strategy is a *juxtaposition* of negative and positive polarities; he suspends dramatic illumination and choice until what is *not* (not-love, not-life) has exhausted its power in outrage and despair and then what *is* (love, life, no-time) returns us to wonder.[20] The defining mind produces dramatic structures so remarkably

19. William Faulkner, *Absalom, Absalom!* (New York: Vintage Books Edition, 1972), 89.

20. I have adopted and enlarged the approach to structure taken by the late Lawrance Thompson, "A Defense of Difficulties in William Faulkner's Art," *The Carrell* (University of Miami, Florida), 4 (December 1963), 7–19. Thompson's essay is devoted to discussion of dramatic structure in *Absalom, Absalom!* and *Go Down, Moses*.

unified as to seem Aristotelian. In *The Sound and the Fury*, Dilsey's numinous reality defines the mad loveless world of the Compsons: her positives are fourth after three prior negative sequences of narrative, so we have a Classical reversal except that it is *our* peripeteia, the audience's. In *As I Lay Dying*, the positives of family and of community are defined by the negative of Addie Bundren's strategically located soliloquy from death-in-life and life-in-death. Addie's revealed wilful vindictiveness looks ahead to the "not-love" of characters in later books. In *Light in August*, the stories of Lena and Joe Christmas are juxtaposed throughout: timeless and time, life and death, community triumphing over alienation, comedy over tragedy. But these juxtapositions precipitate the climactic dramatic action whereby Gail Hightower defines and comes to knowledge of his own selfishness and is prepared to believe in the good of himself, the good which is close to God. The whole structure of *Absalom, Absalom!* is poised as powerfully and as delicately as the cornerstone of a Gothic arch on the moment of Quentin's surprised definition: "But that's not love. That's still not love." Self-love had established the matrix for Sutpen's tragedy and for the tragedy which eventually lost him both sons, in that moment when one son lay dead and the other became a fugitive from justice. And in *Go Down, Moses,* in Part IV of "The Bear," Ike McCaslin discovers why his family and the wilderness are accursed and consequently chooses to relinquish all forms of possession. Ike is "juxtaposed . . . not against the wilderness but against the tamed land which was to have been his heritage," and he is "juxtaposed" against his kinsman and heritage; like the bear, who is "widowered childless and absolved of mortality," Ike paradoxically recovers the "nothing" of sacred earth and the "anonymity" of human brotherhood. Nevertheless, the truly profound peripeteia of *Go Down, Moses* is reserved for "Delta Autumn" when old Isaac realizes one cannot repudiate the inheritance of guilt: he is astonished and diminished by the fact that the old ritual of incestuous miscegenation has repeated itself in the white great-grandson and the part-black great-granddaughter of Carothers McCaslin. Such summaries as these leave much untold, but it should be clear that Faulkner's structures of definition are a component of his poetics and provoke insights into moral values in human relationships.

Faulkner's rhetoric, it should be self-evident, reinforces the structures of definition. Reality is constantly being forced into corners in order to reveal its "uncomplex" and irreducible terms, usually by means of absolutes such as timeless, motionless, soundless, immemorial, eternal, indivisible, infallible, indestructible, and so on. This rhetoric, righly available to him as novelist, has eluded the verse-dramatists *per se*.

We arrive, then, at a conclusion more surprising than we might have anticipated from our initial discussion of the historical consciousness in the literature of the Southern Renaissance. Faulkner's elevation of that consciousness into the poetics of verse drama means that his art, as all great art, transcends its time. It is creative mythology which performs myth's ageless function of arousing and reconciling waking consciousness to the mystery and terror and beauty of the universe as it is. We might expect the continuance of the Southern tradition not only in the South but also in parts of the world where artists feel the need of "faraway country" to focus civilization. And, indeed, Faulkner's influence has helped a Colombian to write a masterpiece of "magic realism": I refer to *Cien Añōs de Soledad* or *One Hundred Years of Solitude* (1967) by Gabriel García Márquez.[21] The

---

21. Faulkner's inspiration of García Márquez has been explored (on intuitive rather than historical grounds) in Mario Vargas Llosa, *Gabriel García Márquez: Historia de un deicidio*, Barcelona: Barral Editores, 1971, 140–50. Vargas Llosa stresses Faulkner's creation of Yoknapatawpha, a unified world, as a model for Macondo and Aracataca in the fiction of García Márquez.

next Faulkner will appear, like as not, in China, Nigeria, or Peru.

Yet to speak of a "next Faulkner" is misleading. That is why, I believe, the concept of a Southern Renaissance is validated as an ongoing expression of literary vitality. If we may allow comparison of Faulkner with Shakespeare, let us welcome a William Styron as, say, an American and Southern John Donne. Just as Shakespeare and the younger Donne represent different aspects of their times, so do Faulkner and the younger Styron. Faulkner creates the world of Yoknapatawpha and rules it omnisciently; Styron's voice is more intimate than Faulkner's and calls to mind the John Donne of playful and passionate lyrics, disconsolate elegies, urbane satires on human corruption, and above all of vehement, compassionate, and doom-haunted sonnets and sermons. Donne's world is no longer the fixed, timeless, sacramentalized one of the Middle Ages and Renaissance but a world that has lost the old coherence and, under pressure of that loss, has twisted itself into all kinds of restless and elaborate shapes connoting the fellowship of terror. Surfacing from the heart of self-doubt, Donne's writing, typically Baroque, is cathartic—in a new sense of a purging away of passions and a stimulus to virtue—and usually meditative. Donne's writing is still in anguished contact with the problem of organic community, of what it means to be fully human, but the world-view is out of joint. His thought no longer feels itself a part of things; it disengages itself from them in order to reflect upon them. One exists in one moment, and life is a continued creation of such moments unless or until God withdraws creative power from the next moment. The gift of existence is still regarded as divine, but anguish is born from two related senses, first the sense of man's sin, second the sense of separation between the timeless and the temporal. Thus every moment of consciousness is actually a sense of the instant of slipping away—a mad, headlong course which is, declares Georges Poulet, "less like the flight of a projectile than the ceaseless beating of wings by which a bird manages to support itself from moment to moment."[22] Now, William Styron's sensibility seems remarkably similar to Donne's. Ostensibly Styron's novels address the tragic-existential condition of victimization— by Freudian complexes, by systems of enslavement—and invite our feelings of pity and terror by making the central action (save in *The Long March*) one involving the persecution and death of a beautiful young woman. Yet the poetic urgency of these novels derives, Donne-like, from the refusal of God to reveal Himself, from, in other words, a metaphysical dilemma. How, Styron repeatedly inquires, can there be personal redemption in a world without God? *"Then what I done was wrong, Lord? I said. And if what I done was wrong, is there no redemption?"* Nat Turner's cry at the end of Part I of his *Confessions* (115) and toward the end of the novel (423) evokes a final Donne-like response as Nat experiences remorse at having killed the gentle, potentially loving Margaret Whitehead. To be purged of moral blindness, of self-absorption, and of the self-destructive element is, in Styron's world, to achieve a measure of salvation. Cass Kinsolving's retribution, Nat Turner's revolt, and Sophie Zawistowska's sexual rejuvenation together represent not only existentialist life-values but also, out of a victim's long subjugation by others and self-conviction of guilt, a form of spiritual reconstitution. Styron's affirmations of unity, though, are as precariously poised as Donne's—which is to say, more precariously than Faulkner's.

A Southern writer is compelled to confront his inheritance of guilt and the historical loss of parental and social authority. Faulkner in one generation and Styron in another have made of their confrontations quite different fictions, but they share with one another and with other Southern writers—and, curiously,

22. Georges Poulet, *Studies in Human Time* (New York, 1956), 16.

180

with writers of sixteenth and seventeenth-century Europe—a refusal to abandon the notion of guilt or the quest for atonement. For them, the human drama still unfolds from a necessary correlation of the individual with society and of both with God. For them, mankind still desperately needs to be battered back into human wholeness.

181

Family, Region, and Myth
in Faulkner's Fiction

DAVID MINTER

Family, region, and *myth* are terms that have been prominent in
the evaluation and interpretation of Faulkner's fiction for several
decades, almost in fact from the beginning. Of all major American writers, Faulkner is the one most clearly associated in our
minds with large, extended, elaborately entangled families and
with a region, both as actual Mississippi and as imaginary or
mythical Yoknapatawpha. Mindful that Faulkner began his life
with a strong, even inescapable, sense of family, region, and
history; mindful too that he began early to hear and remember
stories about his own and other prominent, extended families, as
well as stories about his region—about its history and traditions,
its victories and defeats, its customs, folkways, mores, and
myths; mindful too, that he began early to locate in the stories
he was hearing two complementary impulses, one a loyalty to
nuance and specificity that rooted stories in local habitations and
endowed them with authenticity, the other a revisionary impulse that made room for elaboration and condensation, for displacement and rearrangement; mindful, finally, that Faulkner's
own decisive move toward the writing of great fiction coincided
and interacted with his imaginative return to family and region
as resource and subject—mindful of all these things, many
critics have viewed discussion of family, region, and myth in

182

Faulkner's fiction as appropriate, salutary, even inevitable. From this perspective, Faulkner comes to us as our great provincial, not only because he came from our nation's most distinctive province, but also because, in creating his own elaborate corollary to his inherited province, he raised so many of its particulars to distinctness.[1]

Cleanth Brooks begins *William Faulkner: The Yoknapatawpha Country* with a chapter called "Faulkner the Provincial," and throughout his work he stresses the importance of the sense of community to the fabric of Faulkner's fiction.[2] In an article published in 1974, Joseph Blotner states that "William Faulkner used and transformed more of his own family for his fictional purposes in more books than any other major author."[3]

Other critics, however, have viewed critical emphasis on Faulkner as a provincial artist with jaundiced eyes, seeing in it yet another instance of the South's vain effort to thumb its nose at the North or, more significantly, as an unfortunate distraction. Near the beginning of a recent review, Sean O'Faolain reiterates the first of these objections, interpreting the statement Faulkner "is our great provincial" as a Southern challenge to the Northern assumption that "great writing can only thrive on big cities."[4] Near the end of *Faulkner's Narrative Poetics*, Arthur Kinney states succinctly the second of these points: "European critics and writers have best discerned Faulkner's European roots for a narrative poetics [in Symbolist and Impres-

---

1. Wesley Morris, *Friday's Footprint: Structuralism and the Articulated Text* (Columbus: Ohio State University Press, 1979), 47–48. Here and elsewhere in this paper, I am indebted to Morris's discussion of Faulkner, which centers on *Go Down, Moses* but has implications that extend well beyond it.

2. Cleanth Brooks, *William Faulkner: The Yoknapatawpha Country* (New Haven: Yale University Press, 1963).

3. Joseph Blotner, "The Falkners and the Fictional Families," *The Georgia Review*, 30 (Fall, 1976), 592.

4. Sean O'Faolain, "Hate, Greed, Lust and Doom," *The London Review of Books* (April 16, 1981), 16.

sionist literature and art] while we in America have been distracted by Southern regionalism, folktale, and myth."[5]

In raising again the question of Faulkner's relation to his region (this paper might well be entitled "Faulkner as Provincial: Yet Again"), and all that relation implied, I intend to assume several things—first, the legitimacy of the issue as estabished by several decades of critical discourse; second, the advantage of exploring it, as demonstrated by the advances Cleanth Brooks and Joseph Blotner, whom I have quoted, as well as several other critics have made; and third, the partial validity of Kinney's stricture. For Kinney should serve to remind us at least of this: that stress on Faulkner's regionalism need not and should not result in separating his stories from his fictional techniques, a danger Kinney himself seems to me not to have avoided, though his erring in this regard is as it were from the other side. As stories, many of Faulkner's stories strike Kinney as ranging from the "simply unappealing" to the "unattractive and absurd"; for him they are redeemed only by style and form as determined by Faulkner's angle of vision, or as Kinney also puts it, by Faulkner's "narrative poetics."[6] The issues I want to address in this paper are, then, three: whether it is possible at this late date to say anything new about Faulkner's tie to his region; whether, if it is possible to do this, it is possible to do it in a way that helps to explain Faulkner's (and for that matter other Southern writers') continuing preoccupation with family and region, history and myth; and third, whether it is possible to do it in a way that helps to clarify the relation between Faulkner's stories as stories, however unappealing, unattractive, and absurd, however pathetic, comic, or heroic they may seem to us, on one

5. Arthur F. Kinney, *Faulkner's Narrative Poetics: Style As Vision* (Amherst: University of Massachusetts Press, 1978), 246.
6. *Ibid.*, 243–49.

side, and his fictional procedures and techniques, however experimental, innovative, and sophisticated they may seem to us, on the other.

In examining these issues, I want, first, to draw on the work of two writers who share several concerns, the most obvious being their concern with America's political history and traditions. In two recent essays Michael Rogin, who teaches political science at the University of California, Berkeley, argues, convincingly I think, that proper understanding of the fiction of Herman Melville depends, among other things, of course, first, on our gauging the importance of Melville's sense of his own family's history as a history of decline; and second, on our discerning in Melville's work a sense, less conscious and therefore less directly articulated, but no less deeply felt, that the history of his own family mirrored the history of the family as an institution, the latter as well as the former being a story of decentering and decline.[7]

Although it is impossible for me to do justice to the range and subtlety of Rogin's argument as it pertains to Melville, I do want to suggest some of its pertinence to our understanding of Faulkner. Melville, Rogin's argument runs, felt his family threatened; its status, its power, its very existence seemed to him imperiled. Yet, though he felt this threat with singular force, he did not think of it as singular. Like his cousin Henry Gansevoort, Melvin saw his own family fading during an era in which the "family as the unit of government" was also fading: "Today a man is better off without a family at his back. Our Presidents and legislators are selected . . . because they hardly know who were their fathers, our Railroad Kings are foundlings," his cousin wrote.[8] In

7. Michael Rogin, "Herman Melville: State, Civil Society, and the American 1848," *Yale Review*, 69 (Autumn, 1979), 72–88; and especially, "The Somers Mutiny and *Billy Budd:* Melville in the Penal Colony," forthcoming.

8. Quoted in Rogin, "The Somers Mutiny and *Billy Budd*," 4–5.

an effort to describe the historical context that gave rise to Melville's sense of this fundamental shift, Rogin writes as follows: "By the Gilded Age many [aristocratic] families had disappeared, and with them the family-based order they epitomized. Family was 'the unit of government' and the economy at the [time of the] Revolution; corporation, entrepreneur, politician and party had replaced it a century later." This lost world, Rogin goes on to point out, Melville sought to elegize in varied ways, most transparently in a series of portraits of Major Jack Gentian, the eldest son of two aristocratic descendants of the Revolution and the wearer, by right of "primogeniture," of the "inherited badge of Cincinnati."[9]

In the language of modern social theory, the shift Rogin describes as marking the mind and art of Melville is a shift from a "class society," with its premium on loyalty to family, to a "mass society," with its premium on loyalty to state. Now, as we all have reason to know, Faulkner was not on easy terms with big ideas, social, political, or otherwise.

> Q. "Sir, to what extent were you trying to picture the South and Southern civilization as a whole, rather than just Mississippi—or were you?"
> A. "Not at all. I was trying to talk about people, using the only tool I knew, which was the country that I knew. . . . I don't know anything about ideas, don't have much confidence in them."[10]

Certainly it is not my intention to make Faulkner sound as though he wrote his fiction mindful of large-scale interpretations of Southern history and Southern society, let alone the institution of the family. He did not.[11] But he came from a prominent,

9. *Ibid.*, 5.
10. Frederick L. Gwynn and Joseph L. Blotner, eds., *Faulkner in the University* (Charlottesville: University Press of Virginia, 1959), 9–10.
11. David Minter, *William Faulkner: His Life and Work* (Baltimore: Johns Hopkins University Press, 1980), 85–86.

extended family which retained a sense both of its privileged position and of its glamorous history and which saw its own story (or stories) as inseparable from the story (or stories) of its region. In the context from which Faulkner inherited both familial and regional stories, moreover, we can locate a strong political theme as well as a strong aristocratic theme. Writing in 1853, William Gilmore Simms noted that "no periodical can well succeed in the South, which does not include the *political* constituent. The mind of the South is active chiefly in the direction of politics."[12] Looking back a century later, Allen Tate described Southern society as "hag-ridden with politics," adding that since "all aristocracies are obsessed politically" their "best intellectual energy goes into politics and goes of necessity."[13]

Interpreted broadly, as Simms probably intended and as Tate almost certainly did, *politics* describes as well as any single term can the concerns that dominated the lives of William Faulkner's ancestors, particularly his great-grandfather, the figure who had raised the family to prosperity and prominence. Mississippi, after all, is several hundred miles west of Tidewater Virginia, and is a considerably younger society. Its mansions, gardens, and plantations were still new when the Civil War came, and so was its aristocracy. At the time of Faulkner's birth, his family had been prominent for almost as long as North Mississippi had had prominent families, but it had not been prominent very long. As it turned out, moreover, it had become prominent just in time to witness and participate in the disappearance of the Old South as a class- and family-based society and the decline of the family as an institution. Although it is not clear that Faulkner's family as a whole was troubled by a sense of its own and its region's decline, it is certain that his family was aware of the

---

12. Quoted in Jay B. Hubbell, *The South in American Literature, 1607–1900* (Durham: Duke University Press, 1954), 367.

13. Allen Tate, "The Profession of Letters in the South," *Essays of Four Decades* (Chicago: The Swallow Press, 1968), 523.

displacement that accompanied what we now know as the rise of
the New South, and certain, too, that William Faulkner was
troubled both by what was fading and by what was rising. Each
of the old aristocratic families that he created—from the Sartorises to the Compsons to the McCaslins—assumes that it is
prominent, feels that it is entangled, and senses that it is en-
dangered, and so regards the world around it with alarm.

Faulkner's art was clearly grounded in his knowledge of family
and region, or as he put it, in "the country that [he] knew"; and
much of what he knew came from stories he had heard—stories
his family and region had lived, continued to recount, and by
recounting, bequeathed to him. One part of what he gathered
from the live traditions around him, beyond, as it were, the
stories themselves, was the sensed significances of those stories
and the motives imbedded in their telling. With Rogin's work in
mind, we can place Faulkner's familial and regional heritage in a
context that ties Faulkner's art not only to the work of older
writers, such as Melville, or for that matter to Henry Adams,
whose three great works elegize the fading of the Middle Ages,
the fading of the early Republic, and the fading of the Adams
family, but also, as we shall see, to other more recent writers,
some Southern and some not.

Before expanding this last point, however, I want to turn to
another political thinker, one who speaks briefly about Faulkner
and his art, and in doing so helps us to understand not so much
why Faulkner became absorbed in the history of his family and
his region but why he remained absorbed in them and why his
absorption took the fictional forms it took. In a footnote to a
section of *On Revolution* called "The Revolutionary Tradition
and Its Lost Treasure," Hannah Arendt writes as follows: "How
such guideposts for future reference and remembrance arise out
of this incessant talk, not, to be sure, in the form of concepts but
as single brief sentences and condensed aphorisms, may best be
seen in the novels of William Faulkner. Faulkner's literary pro-

cedure, rather than the content of his work, is highly 'political,' and in spite of many imitations, he has remained, as far as I can see, the only author to use it."[14] I want to come back toward the end of this paper to the issue of whether other writers have used "incessant talk" as Arendt suggests Faulkner used it, but before doing that several things need sorting out, the first being the context in which Arendt links "Faulkner's literary procedure" to "incessant talk."

Arendt's subject, and her regret—that America has lost touch with its revolutionary tradition—need not concern us here. But her sense of how and why that loss occurred should. Her argument runs like this: it is because America has failed "to remember" its revolutionary tradition, and failing "to remember" it has failed to talk of it, or rather to talk of it incessantly, and failing to talk of it incessantly has failed to understand and appropriate it, that it now fears and resists the revolutions of others. For Arendt there is a clear connection between the failure of a people to remember, the failure of a people to talk, and the failure of a people to understand. The gist of her argument together with several of its implications and pertinences emerged clearly in the passage to which her statement about Faulkner is a note. If it is true, she writes, "that all thought begins with remembrance, it is also true that no remembrance remains secure unless it is condensed and distilled" in language. "Experiences and even the stories which grow out of what men do and endure, of happenings and events, sink back into the futility inherent in the living word and the living deed unless they are talked about over and over again. What saves the affairs of mortal men from their inherent futility is nothing but this incessant talk about them, which in its turn remains futile unless . . . certain guideposts for future remembrance, and even for sheer reference, arise out of it."[15] Arendt's position in a passage such as this is obviously tied

14. Hannah Arendt, *On Revolution* (New York: Viking Press, 1963), 318, n.4.
15. *Ibid.*, 222.

to a familiar theme in recent intellectual history: to Ernst Cassirer's sense of man as a creature possessing a distinctive symbolic faculty; to Noam Chomsky's sense of man as a creature possessing a distinctive linguistic faculty; and to Roland Barthes's sense of man as a creature possessing a distinctive literary faculty. For Arendt both memory and talking are of critical importance. On our willlingness to remember and recount, not knowledge but civilization itself depends, the alternative being not only the loss of living words and living deeds but also a gradual sinking into "ignorance, oblivion."[16] In Arendt's context, no people is without a history but no people possesses its history unless its memory is raised to an active pitch and so becomes articulate, becomes, if we take the word *incessant* seriously, almost compulsively articulate.

Faulkner's fiction, as we all know, is filled with remembering that becomes incessant talking, and I want to turn now to what this implies regarding the nature and motive of Faulkner's imagination, what we might term its "conserving" or "preserving" bent. For Faulkner himself, one factor in the equation was personal: "All that I really desired was a touchstone simply: a simple word or gesture . . . nothing served but that I try by main strength to recreate between the covers of a book the world as I was already preparing to lose and regret." A part of what Faulkner wanted, we may conclude, was to convey his own sense of his world: to "capture" and "preserve" the "feeling of it."[17] This personal motive is one he shared with many of his characters, including Rosa Coldfield. Among the several things that shock and offend Miss Rosa, one is her awareness that her story, like her life, will soon be lost, that it will most likely never be told in any other way than that in which she is telling it, and that when

16. *Ibid.*, 221.

17. Untitled manuscript in Beinecke Rare Book and Manuscript Library, Yale University. For a published version, see Joseph Blotner, "William Faulkner's Essay on the Composition of *Sartoris*," *Yale University Library Gazette*, 47 (January 1973), 121–24.

she is dead, her story as told will be the only story she ever had: "It's because she wants it told," Quentin thinks, early in *Absalom, Absalom!;* "It's because she wants it told."[18]

Finally, however, Miss Rosa's motives are more than personal. In her incessant voice ("Her voice would not cease, it would just vanish."), we sense loyalty that overcomes deep ambivalence. Sitting in an over-tall chair in which she resembles "a crucified child," her "wan haggard face" becomes almost a mask. But as her voice comes and goes, "not ceasing, but vanishing into and then out of the long intervals like a stream," we locate loyalties that, however painfully divided, run deep and touch everything, including family and not-family, region and not-region (8–9; see 11–18). All of Miss Rosa's relations—mother, father, sister, niece, nephew, not-husband—are failed relations. In the only town and country she has ever known, she remains curiously at home yet not at home, a native who is also an alien. Finally, however, despite everything, her voice speaks of and for her family, of and for her region: "It's because she wants it told," Quentin says, "so that people whom she will never see" will know at last the story of "the blood of *our* men and the tears of *our* women" (11; emphasis added).

In *Absalom, Absalom!*, as in the statements of Arendt quoted earlier, remembering and talking have a powerful, even an indispensable social function. On one side, they provide the only adequate means we have of taking possession of the culture we inherit. "How may the Southerner take hold of his Tradition?," Allen Tate once asked. Mindful that the world around him was hostile to the tradition-, family-, class-, and agrarian-based society of the Old South, Tate answers, "by violence"—meaning, as Louis Rubin has noted, a deliberate, aggressive act of will.[19]

18. *Absalom. Absalom!* [1936]. (New York: Random House, 1972), 10, 11. References to this novel hereafter appear parenthetically in the text.

19. See Louis Rubin, *The Writer in the South* (Athens: University of Georgia Press, 1972), 90, where he quotes and comments on Tate's remark.

In order to be absorbed by individuals, tradition must first be created and possessed by a society; when a society functions properly, moreover, tradition is among the gifts it bequeaths. Violence of the kind that Tate refers to becomes necessary only when a society begins to lose its coherence and force. The world in which Take found himself—I am referring specifically to his essay called "Remarks on Southern Religion" in *I'll Take My Stand*—was after all the world in which Faulkner also lived. It was not only a world undergoing rapid change (most worlds seem so to people living through them); nor was it merely a world deeply antagonistic toward the fading culture—the land-, family-, and class-based order—of the Old South; it was also a world almost wholly committed to not remembering. What Arendt implies, Faulkner's fictional strategies establish: that the primary sign of the violence to which Take refers, its almost inevitable form, is a human voice become more insistent and more incessant.

Although *Absalom, Absalom!* is many things, it is among others a drama of incessant voices in which remembering becomes talking, talking in turn becomes remembering, and remembering, talking. In it we move back from Quentin's beleaguered and divided voice through his father's and Miss Rosa's to Thomas Sutpen's "patient amazed recapitulation" (263). Or, seen another way, we move forward from Miss Rosa's haggard, haunted voice in the first scene to Quentin's still-divided voice in the last. Even the calmest, least insistent of the voices we encounter, Mr. Compson's and Shreve's, speak from and of bafflement, about things that aren't known, that don't add up, that can't finally be taken hold of. Yet, time and again, despite repeated consternation and failure, we see Faulkner's characters moved to remembering and then to talking. Or perhaps it is because of the consternation and failure that they are so moved: "The very disintegration and inadequacy of the world," Lukacs once noted, "is the precondition for the existence of art and its becoming conscious."[20] The scene with which we begin *Absalom, Absalom!*, an insistent Miss Rosa talking to a reluctant Quentin Compson, is repeated later with Quentin become insistent and Shreve now reluctant. Similarly, the process by which Quentin abandons his reluctance and becomes insistent, is later repeated as Shreve moves gradually from a manner and tone that are flippant, even faintly condescending, toward full participation in remembering and recounting. Like Quentin, Shreve moves through a kind of apprenticeship in which listening is the central human act toward moments in which listening gives way to talking. Following an extended collaborative dialogue with Quentin, in chapters six and seven, Shreve begins, first, to recall and repeat, and then, slowly to rearrange and elaborate all he has heard and absorbed.[21] As he assimilates and appropriates, he also begins to talk and talk and talk. "No," he says in chapter seven, "you wait. Let me play a while now" (280). In the next chapter, he stands beside a table, wearing an "overcoat buttoned awry . . . look[ing] huge and shapeless like a disheveled bear," and insists on talking until he has gone over everything (293; see 329). Later still he sits with Quentin, as they stare and glare at one another, to go over it again, so that, finally, together, they may move beyond it (see 299, 303), at which point listening and talking become so closely allied as to be virtually indistinguishable. "They stared—glared—at one another. It was Shreve speaking, though save for the slight difference . . . inculcated in them (differences not in tone or pitch but of turns of phrase and usage of words), it might have been either of them and was in a sense both: both thinking as one, the voice which happened to be speaking the thought only the thinking become audible, vocal; the two of them creating between them, out of the rag-tag and bob-ends of old tales and talking, people who perhaps had never existed at all anywhere" (303). In the eyes that stare and glare as well as in the voice that insists on doing as it will with what it has been given, the voice that Faulkner first describes and then renders (see 303–304), we observe several things, including a kind of violence that manifests itself less obviously in the eyes that glare than in the voice that insists on remembering and talking and playing, on constructing, deconstructing, and reconstructing a long, complex, convoluted story, itself made out of recounting and elaborating on "the rag-tag and bob-ends of old tales and talking." Still, it is not the violence of what Quentin and Shreve do that impresses us so much as the union of mind with mind and of mind with tradition. What Quentin and Shreve come to is not only a kind of creative collaboration; it is also a sense, however fleeting, of atonement, a sense of community.

> "And now," Shreve said, "we're going to talk about love." But he didn't need to say that . . . since neither of them had been thinking about anything else; all that had gone before just so much that had to be overpassed and none else present to overpass it but them . . . That was why it did not matter to either of them which one did the talking, since it was not the talking alone which did it, performed and accomplished the overpassing, but some happy marriage of speaking and hearing wherein each before the demand, the requirement, forgave condoned and forgot the faulting of the other— faultings both in the creating of this shade whom they discussed (rather, existed in) and in the hearing and sifting and discarding the false and conserving what seemed true, or fit the preconceived—in order to overpass to love, where there might be paradox and inconsistency but nothing fault nor false. (316)

The unions on which this passage turns include a union between Quentin and Shreve; a union between each of them and the story they tell, as well as the sources and the protagonists of that story; and a union between each of them and not only their story, its protagonists, and its sources, but also the history, the

20. Georg Lukacs, *The Theory of the Novel; A Historico-Philosophical Essay on the Forms of Great Epic Literature,* trans. Anna Bostock (Cambridge: M.I.T. Press, 1971), 38.
21. Terrence Doody, *Confession and Community in the Novel* (Baton Rouge: Louisiana State University Press, 1980), 163–83.

culture, and the traditions that both gave birth to and are captured by that story, its protagonists, and its sources. In addition to being several, these unions are complex, intricate, shifting, and partial. What they share is Faulkner's insistence, first, that each is made possible by a prior union, "some happy marriage between speaking and hearing"; second, that each involves a kind of transcendence, an "overpassing"; and third, that each involves a kind of love—since it is not only love that Quentin and Shreve begin to discuss; it is love they begin to experience.

The sense of community thus created is remarkable on several counts, particularly its inclusivity. For it embraces Quentin and Shreve and the shade and story which they both discuss and exist in; it embraces the other characters who hear and recount and participate in Sutpen's story; and it embraces author and reader alike. Those activities that bring Quentin and Shreve to the happy marriage between speaking and hearing, then to overpassing, and then to love have after all much in common with the habits and activities of mind and spirit that lie behind the making of *Absalom, Absalom!,* just as they have much in common with the habits and activities that any reading of *Absalom, Absalom!* requires. Faulkner is widely thought of as a difficult, uncompromising writer; several readers have felt that he treated most of his characters and all of his readers as Vince Lombardi was said to treat all of his football players, like dogs. There is, of course, some truth in these sentiments. But the other side of Faulkner's demands, the varied difficulties that he strews in our paths, is a remarkable generosity. No writer has shared more fully the tasks and even the prerogatives of the writer with his characters, and none has shared them more fully with his readers. In the listening and talking in which Quentin and Shreve engage—their remembering and sorting and recounting, even more their creative extensions of the rag-tag and bob-ends given them—we locate primitive versions of Faulkner's larger labor; in their willingness to listen and listen and

195

listen, to try, as it were, for total recall, in their willingness to arrange and rearrange, to remember and surmise and speculate, to work and play endlessly, we locate models of many things required of us as readers.

Like them, furthermore, we come curiously to view all knowing as re-knowing, all cognition as re-cognition, even as we come to view all knowledge and cognition as tentative, provisional, imperfect. "Really, universally," Henry James once remarked, "relations stop nowhere, and the exquisite problem of the artist is eternally but to draw, by a geometry of his own, the circle within which they shall happily *appear* to do so."[22] No such geometry exists for Faulkner's characters, nor even in James's triumphant terms, for Faulkner himself. His novels—at least his Yoknapatawpha stories, clearly the heart of his achievement— reach beyond themselves to one another. They give us the sense of beginnings, the sense of endings. We know without being told that Miss Rosa's talking and Quentin's listening have been going on a long time before we too begin to listen and talk. On the last page of the novel, Quentin's voice, with its curious blend of affirmation and denial, vanishes without ceasing. In between we come repeatedly to moments of illumination in which we at least feel ourselves on the verge of seeing everything clearly, only to discover again our bafflement.

> "You cant understand it," [Quentin says to Shreve]. "You would have to be born there."
> "Would I then?" Quentin did not answer. "Do you understand it?"
> "I don't know," Quentin said. "Yes, of course I understand it." They breathed in the darkness. After a moment Quentin said: "I dont know." (361–62)

Of Quentin's and Shreve's inventions, on which so much of the novel depends, we know that they are "probably true enough"

22. Henry James, Preface to *Roderick Hudson*, in R. P. Blackmur, ed., *The Art of the Novel* (New York: Scribner, 1934), 5.

(335), but we also know that they involve people and events that "perhaps had never existed at all anywhere" (303). From beginning to end, the mood of the novel is interrogative and tentative.

> Maybe we are both Father. Maybe nothing ever happens once and is finished. Maybe happen is never once but like ripples maybe on water after the pebble sinks . . . Yes, we are both Father. Or maybe Father and I are both Shreve, maybe it took Father and me both to make Shreve or Shreve and me both to make Father or maybe Thomas Sutpen to make all of us. (261–62; italics omitted)

A few years earlier, around 1931, Faulkner had played with related contingencies wondering whether he had created the world of his fiction with its "shady but ingenious shapes" or "it had invented me."[23] Given such fundamental contingencies, tentativenesses that touch everything, Faulkner's characters are doomed to circle almost endlessly. "Wait, I tell you!" Quentin says to Shreve; and then to himself: "Am I going to have to have to hear it all again . . . I am going to have to hear it all over again I am already hearing it all over again I am listening to it all over again I shall have to never listen to anything else but this again forever . . ." (277). Yet, even as everything Quentin and Shreve learn remains tentative, hedged here with statements that seem to balance and cancel one another, or there with a long string of maybes, it also comes to us as something already known. For Quentin in particular everything heard or seen, including those things we have heard him hear or say or seen him see, come to him always as both strange and familiar, new and old.

> But you were not listening, because you knew it all already, had learned, absorbed it already without the medium of speech somehow from having been born and living beside it, with it, as children will and do: so that what your father was saying did not tell you anything so much as it struck, word by word, the resonant strings of

23. See work cited in n. 17 above.

remembering. You had been here before, seen those graves more than once . . . just as you had seen the old house too, been familiar with how it would look before you even saw it . . . No, you were not listening; you didn't have to. . . . (212–13; cf. 229–30)

Quentin listens, of course, listens even when he does not appear to be listening, even when weariness and reluctance well up in him. He has grown up with more stories than we will ever know, with names "interchangeable and almost myriad." His "very body," we read early, "was an empty hall echoing with sonorous defeated names; he was not a being, an entity, he was a commonwealth" (12). For him all knowing begins with remembering and depends upon talking. The stories that come to him, word by word, to strike "the resonant strings of remembering," provide the only access he has to his cultural heritage; the stories he hears, tells, and seeks to finish are the only means he has of absorbing, appropriating, assimilating his culture. In addition, they are the only means he has of moving beyond both the dangerous desires and the harsh judgments that memory and knowledge arouse within him. Although the stories he hears complicate everything for him, provoking contradictory desires and judgments, they provide his only hope of mastery and his only hope of peace. What this suggests proves in fact to be of crucial importance, for the stories that come to Quentin word by word to strike "the resonant strings of remembering," also create the only avenue he has for exploring the depths of his own consciousness. In Faulkner's fiction remembering serves a personal function in addition to the socially indispensable function Arendt helps us to locate. What is curious, if not striking, about this, however, is the loose analogy Faulkner seems to establish between the social and the personal, between our explorations of culture and our explorations of consciousness. Like our access to culture, our access to consciousness, at least so far as Quentin is concerned, turns on our willingness to remember, our willingness to talk incessantly, even our willingness to listen interminably. In *Absalom, Absalom!*, the shadowy past toward which remembering, listening, and talking take us is always double; although it forever remains just beyond our reach, it holds the secrets of our people and the secrets of our selves. Such glimpses as we gain, within and beyond us, are always of things remembered and discovered, familiar and strange, old and new, and they always come as sights desired and pursued, dreaded and shunned, and therefore as things held, if at all, tenuously. On both the cultural and personal levels, moreover, such seeing, if it is to become knowing, must be in part a matter of absorbing and in part a matter of constructing. *Knowing* may begin with copying, but as Piaget has suggested, it always involves acting: "It means constructing systems of transformations. . . . Knowing reality means constructing systems of transformations that correspond, more or less adequately, to reality. Knowledge, then, is a system of transformations that become progressively adequate."[24]

Viewed from such a perspective, *Absalom, Absalom!* remains, whatever else it is, a drama of incessant voices: a drama in which the human acts of remembering, talking, and listening become "interchangeable and almost myriad" (see 12); a drama in which these acts provide man's only means of taking hold of the experiences and traditions that have shaped his family and his region, as well as his only means of exploring his own consciousness; and a drama in which these acts, given the stakes they entail, must under proper force prove as dangerous as they are necessary. In addition, however, *Absalom, Absalom!* becomes a model, a trying out, of what *knowing* in its fullest sense actually means. Knowing in *Absalom, Absalom!* begins with remembering, talking, and listening; and it involves considerable *copying* in the form of repetition, not only of countless details and events but

24. Jean Piaget, *Genetic Epistemology*, trans. Eleanor Duckworth (New York: Columbia University Press, 1970), 15.

even of voices: to Quentin, Shreve "sounds just like father" (181), and for the reader the several voices of the novel seem to merge into a resonant medley charged with echoes.[25] But *knowing* moves in the novel toward transformations—toward arrangements and re-arrangements, toward inventions and creations. What Quentin and Shreve do overtly, even boldly—which is to transform the givens they receive—other characters in the novel do covertly or timidly. *Absalom, Absalom!* traces, then, a series "of transformations that correspond, more or less adequately," to its givens, its reality; and though knowing, for its characters and readers alike, remains tentative and imperfect, unfolding and unfinished, the series "of transformations" it traces do "become progressively adequate."

My long look at *Absalom, Absalom!* notwithstanding, it is my intention in this paper to make suggestions pertinent both to the larger reaches of Faulkner's Yoknapatawpha fiction and to the writings of other Southern writers. As a move in that direction, I want to invoke a term from my title that I have thus far almost wholly ignored. In his "Foreword" to *Brother to Dragons*, Robert Penn Warren remarks that "historical sense and poetic sense should not, in the end, be contradictory, for if poetry is the little myth we make, history is the big myth we live, and in our living, constantly remake."[26] History or the past is, as we know, never dead in Faulkner's fiction, and sometimes it is not even past; his characters are often preoccupied or obsessed with the past, and even when they are not, they and their worlds are shaped by it. Still, Faulkner is not in the usual sense of the term an historical novelist. His sense of the past is neither nostalgic nor sentimental, which means that his art is dedicated neither to recapturing the past as it was nor to investing or charging it with the emotions of the present. In the remembering and talking

25. Doody, 173.
26. Robert Penn Warren, Foreword, *Brother to Dragons* (New York: Random House, 1979).

and listening, in the assimilations and the transformations that take place in *Absalom, Absalom!*, the explorations of history and the creation of myth occur simultaneously. Although one part of the process is "the hearing and sifting and discarding" of what seems false, and another part the hearing "and conserving" of what seems true, neither the one nor the other separates history from myth. For another part of the process, somehow beyond yet continuous with the discarding of what seems false and the conserving of what seems true, but no less important and no less legitimate, is the game of transformation: the game of inventing and creating people and events that seem right, people and events that are "probably true enough" even though they perhaps never "existed at all anywhere," or more radically, even if they never existed. In this context, man makes myth as he explores history.

Another part of the figure I am trying to describe here can, I think, be got at by recalling an observation of W. B. Yeats, that it is of our quarrel with society that we make rhetoric and of our quarrel with ourselves that we make poetry. If for Faulkner we may say that it is of our quarrel and struggle with our traditions, our culture, that we make myth, and of our quarrel with ourselves that we make poetry, we no doubt simplify too much, leave too much out. But we gain this at least: a clear sense of how inseparable the two parts of this process were for him, and a clear sense of why he made every instance of one at some level a version of the other. Remembering, talking, listening, as activities and as terms, get mixed up in Faulkner's fiction in a thousand ways. Finally, however, there is a seamlessness to them, just as there is a seamlessness to the stories they yield, to the form those stories take, and to the hedged and tentative knowledge they bequeath. Every exploration of family becomes an exploration of region, and every exploration of either becomes an exploration of self. If we distinguish myth from poetry, allying "myth" with culture and history, and allying "poetry"

201

with consciousness and self, we do so in the name of convenience, knowing that in *Absalom, Absalom!* myth and poetry alike, the hold we have on culture and the hold we have on self come from stories that in turn come from remembering and talking and listening incessantly.

"What shall we say who have knowledge carried to the heart?" asks the protagonist of Allen Tate's "Ode to the Confederate Dead," in a line that puts as succinctly as any I know the question Faulkner's characters and readers alike face repeatedly. Some such question also lies behind books as different as *All the King's Men* and *North Toward Home*, as well as Tate's "Ode" and much of Warren's recent fine poetry. In *I'll Take My Stand*, to take a very different case, a book of essays whose reputation continues to rise and fall, remembering, talking, and knowing, if not seamless activities, are at least closely allied, as are history, myth, and poetry. The form of *I'll Take My Stand*, its motives and procedures, may well be of more historical, or in Arendt's terms of more "political," significance than its explicit themes, as they are certainly of more aesthetic significance. Arendt suggests that Faulkner alone, despite "many imitations," has succeeded in turning "incessant talking" into art. But Faulkner's career coincided, from the mid to late twenties into the thirties and beyond, with the remarkable flowering of Southern writing that we now call the Southern Renaissance, and like the years of his life, the concerns that manifest themselves in his art were shared. Those concerns touched family, region, and the past as they impinge upon consciousness, but they also touched his sense that knowing begins with remembering, follows talking and listening, and ends in transformations. Tradition, to borrow Tate's inclusive term, is important, then, not because it is fixed and finished but rather because it is not; nor, to paraphrase Marianne Moore's description of poetry, "because a/highsounding interpretation can be put upon" it, but rather because, given its fluidity and incompleteness, it invites play as well as loyalty and so enables poets to present "for inspection, imaginary gardens with real toads in them," which may be as close as poets come to offering us "guideposts for future remembrance, and even for sheer reference."[27]

27. Marianne Moore, "Poetry." Different versions of this poem have been published. For the one quoted, see Richard Ellmann and Robert O'Clair, eds., *The Norton Anthology of Modern Poetry* (New York: Norton, 1973), 421–22.

Faulkner's
Poetic Vision

PATRICK SAMWAY, S.J.

In the March 24, 1920, issue of *The Mississippian*, an Ole Miss student who referred to himself as "J" chided a fellow student—William Faulkner:

> Mr. Editor . . . wouldn't this be a fine University if all of us were to wear sailor collars, monkey hats, and brilliant pantaloons; if we would 'mose' along the street by the aid of a walking prop; and ye gods forbid, if we should while away our time singing of lascivious knees, smiling lute strings, and voluptuous toes? Wouldn't that be just too grand?

Such jabbing from a campus rival indicates, to some degree, how Faulkner's peers regarded his poetic posture. Our own appreciation and critical judgment of Faulkner's poetry, however, unlike "J's" apodictic views, must remain more tentative since one major booklet of poetry, *Vision in Spring*,* which Faulkner gave to Estelle Franklin in the summer of 1921 has not been commercially printed. On the other hand, Faulkner's *The Marble Faun* (1924), *A Green Bough* (1933), both reprinted in a single volume in 1965, and the recently published *Mississippi Poems* (1979) and *Helen: A Courtship* (1981) do provide a sufficient amount of poetry so that a general and tentative assessment of Faulkner's poetry can be made. In addition, there is a strong likelihood that previously unaccounted-for poetry in private hands will become available in the next few years; these

*See footnote 3.

204

poems will undoubtedly alter our appreciation of Faulkner as poet.

To an audience at the University of Virginia on June 5, 1957, Faulkner defined poetry as "some moving, passionate moment of the human condition distilled to its absolute essence."[1] Likewise in an interview in 1955, Faulkner distinguished between the poet and the novelist: "the poet deals with something which is so pure and so esoteric that you cannot say he is English or Japanese—he deals in something that is universal. That's the distinction I make between the prose writer and the poet, the novelist and the poet—that the poet deals in something universal, while the novelist deals in his own traditions."[2] Although Faulkner did not explicitly paraphrase or refer to Pater's intention to "burn always with this hard, gemlike flame," he had something analogous in mind insofar as he wanted to refine human experience in his poetry so that life's universal and quintessential nature could be captured in the final process, one which involves a contraction or reduction of experience rather than an expansion of it. Faulkner's emphasis on the passionate moment also suggests, as the Latin *patior/passus* indicates, that his poetry emerges from a fusion of intense love and intense suffering, a late Romantic view which seems at odds with his Nobel Prize address where he puts greater value on the moral dimension, the edifying, uplifting aspect of literature.

Although Faulkner actively wrote, revised, and published poetry over approximately a fifteen-year period from 1918–1933, he concentrated on writing poetry in a formal sense between 1918 and 1926.[3] In retrospect, Faulkner never considered him-

1. *Faulkner in the University: Class Conferences at the University of Virginia*, ed. Frederick L. Gwynn and Joseph L. Blotner (Charlottesville: University Press of Virginia, 1955), 202.
2. *Lion in the Garden: Interviews with William Faulkner 1926–62*, ed. James B. Meriwether and Michael Millgate (New York: Random House, 1968), 96.
3. For a census of Faulkner's poetry, see Keen Butterworth's helpful "A Census of Manuscripts and Typescripts of William Faulkner's Poetry," *A Faulkner Miscellaney*, ed. James B. Meriwether (Jackson: University Press of Mississippi, 1974), 70–97; see also

self a successful poet, partly I believe because his own incre-
mental, widening, repetitious imagination never coalesced with
his own conception and definition of poetry: "I've often thought
that I wrote the novels because I found I couldn't write the
poetry, that maybe I wanted to be a poet, maybe I think of
myself as a poet, and I failed at that, I couldn't write poetry, so I
did the next best thing."[4] But this was not the way he felt at first.
Under Phil Stone's tutelage, Faulkner developed an interest in
poetry that dates back probably to the summer of 1914 when
Phil encouraged the young Bill to browse through the extremely
large library in the Stone house. As Faulkner relates in his
highly informative "Verse Old and Nascent: A Pilgrimage," he
discovered Swinburne when he was approximately sixteen years
old. Or rather it was the other way around:

> Swinburne discovered me, springing from some tortured under-
> growth of my adolescence, like a highwayman, making me his
> slave. . . . It seems to me now that I found him nothing but a flexible
> vessel into which I might put my own vague emotional shapes with-
> out breaking them. It was years later that I found in him much more
> than bright and bitter sound, more than a satisfying tinsel of blood
> and death and gold and the inevitable sea.[5]

Curiously, Faulkner found nothing terribly sexual in the poetry
of Swinburne whom he considered at one point more of a poetic

Cleanth Brooks's "Faulkner's Poetry," *William Faulkner: Toward Yoknapatawpha and
Beyond* (New Haven: Yale University Press, 1978), 345–54. All references to *The Marble
Faun* and *A Green Bough (AGB)* will be to the combined edition published by Random
House in 1965. I am grateful to Dr. Lola Szladits of the New York Public Library and to
the staff of the Alderman Library at the University of Virginia for their assistance.
William Faulkner's manuscripts and typescripts are under copyright. I am thus grateful
to Mrs. Jill Faulkner Summers for allowing me to quote from this copyrighted material,
"and to Judith Sensibar, the exclusive copyright licensee of Faulkner's unpublished,
eighty-eight page typescript, *Vision in Spring* (1921). Sensibar's Ph.D. dissertation,
William Faulkner, Poet: The Origins of His Art (the University of Chicago (1982),
discusses the relation of Faulkner's apprenticeship poetry, particularly *Vision in Spring*,
to the emergence of his fictional voice." The asterisks after each reference to this booklet
are to remind the reader about the nature of this copyright.

    4. *Faulkner in the University*, 4.
    5. William Faulkner, "Verse Old and Nascent: A Pilgrimage," *William Faulkner:
Early Prose and Poetry*, ed. Carvel Collins (Boston: Little, Brown and Company, 1962),
114. Hereafter cited as *EPP*.

mathematician than anything else; he did acknowledge, however, that there was eroticism here, but not to a significant degree since eroticism can be present whenever form, color, and movement are evoked or presented. Whatever, Swinburne's poetry satisfied him: "Perhaps it is that Swinburne, having taken his heritage and elaborated it at the despair of any would-be poet, has coarsened it to tickle the dullest of palates as well as the most discriminating, as used water can be drunk by both hogs and gods" (*EPP,* 115–16). While Faulkner explicitly pays tribute to Swinburne, Keats, Shelley, Shakespeare, Spenser, and the Elizabethans as being influential in helping him formulate his poetry, it was Housman above all who gave Faulkner a deep sense of how the living, as Faulkner's own epitaph in its several versions reveals, should project themselves into the beyond and deal with the relationship of the quick to the dead. One has only to take the poem entitled "The Gallows" in *Mississippi Poems* to see echoes of Housman's poems IX, XXXII, and XLVII of *A Shropshire Lad,* a book which I believe Faulkner praised more than any other book he commented on: "Here was reason for being born into a fantastic world: discovering the splendor of fortitude, the beauty of being of the soil like a tree about which fools might howl and which winds of disillusion and death and despair might strip, leaving it bleak, without bitterness; beautiful in sadness" (*EPP,* 117). This note of sadness, again a hallmark of the late Romantics and Victorians, was a characteristic of poetry which Faulkner saw as an ideal coming from his reading of poetry rather than rising naturally from his own imagination.

Metaphorically, Faulkner's entrance into the world of literature, including poetry, can be seen in his 1919 story "Landing in Luck," a heuristic title to say the least in which he shows graphically how difficult it is for Cadet Thompson to approach this earth when one is inexperienced in the art of flying—and landing:

For Thompson's nerve was going as he neared the earth. The temptation was strong to kick his rudder over and close his eyes. The machine descended, barely making headway. He watched the approaching ground utterly unable to make any pretence at levelling off, paralyzed; his brain had ceased to function, he was all staring eyes watching the remorseless earth. He did not know his height, the ground rushed past too swiftly to judge, but he expected to crash any second. Thompson's fate was on the laps of the Gods. (*EPP*, 48)

The plane did land solidly, with only one embarrassing consequence: it finally halted with its nose down and its tail-piece up in the air, which for Faulkner must have been how he felt after returning to Oxford in early December 1918 after spending 179 days as a member of the R.A.F. A poem fragment from his Canadian days, entitled "The Ace," presents a picture of a pilot in the early morning hours searching for some unspecified quarry:

> The sun light
> Paints him as he stalks, huge through the morning
> In his fleece and leather, gilds his bright
> Hair and his cigarette.
> Makes góld his fléece and leáther, aňd his bright
> Hair.[6]

This portrait of a rugged, cigarette-smoking, twentieth-century airborn Jason resembles the picture Faulkner tried to create of himself after the war.

The image of the returning soldier gave Faulkner sufficient thematic material both for much of his poetry and for his first novel.[7] In "A Dead Pilot," also called "Boy and Eagle," Faulkner builds on this theme of the returning soldier by depicting a young man on what he calls an "adolescent hill" who watches the "aircarved cummulae" and a lone eagle in the sky. This youth,

6. See Joseph L. Blotner's *Faulkner: A Biography* (New York: Random House, 1974), I, 220.
7. For a further analysis of the wounded pilot, see Margaret Yonce's "'Shot Down Last Spring': The Wounded Aviators of Faulkner's Wasteland," *Mississippi Quarterly*, 31 (Summer 1978), 359–68.

apparently both dead and alive, expresses the ambiguous feelings a soldier experiences after imaginatively meeting death; we
as the reader thus reflect on what the dead feel as they contemplate the earth they have left and the enveloping world:

> Here still the blue, the headlands; here still he
> Who did not waken and was not awaked.
> The eagle sped its lonely course and tall;
> Was gone. Yet still upon this lonely hill the lad
> Winged on past changing headlands where was laked
> The constant blue
>
> And saw the fleeing canyons of the sky
> Tilt to banshee wire and slanted aileron,
> And his own lonely shape on scudding walls
> Where harp the ceaseless thunders of the sun.
>
> (*AGB*, XVIII)

The earth will always retain the impact of war, and any memory
of it will be difficult to stamp out:

> He winnowed it with bayonets
> And planted it with guns,
> And now the final cannonade
> Is healed with rains and suns
>
> He looks about—and leaps to stamp
> The stubborn grinning seeds
> Of olden plantings back beneath
> His field of colored weeds.
>
> (*AGB*, XXXI)

In his imagination, Faulkner's quest, both as pilot and poet, is to
accept the inevitability of war and destruction, then search after
an unnamed young woman, and when a lasting union with her
seems impossible, he continues this quest, this time seeking
death and a final resting place in the earth.

The first poem in *A Green Bough*, "The Lilacs," showing the
influence of Eliot's "Portrait of a Lady" insofar as both these
poems contain three people discussing the inability of youth to
adapt to their current situations in an atmosphere permeated by

the abundance of lilacs, focuses on the plight of the returned pilot and his quest for an illusive, ideal woman who represents not so much the source of poetic inspiration, but of death, the same juxtaposition of the eternal moment of bliss and man's finitude and mortality that Keats achieved in his "Ode on a Grecian Urn." In "The Lilacs," three individuals, who might also be considered manifestations of a fragmented psyche, discuss a young man shot down over Mannheim. As in "The Ace," the pilot seeks a young woman:

> A white woman, a white wanton near a brake,
> A rising whiteness mirrored in a lake.

Just as the pilot is about to embrace the phantom woman, he is shot. And the poem's refrain, "One should not die like this," has the explicit approval of all present. In 1925, the same year in which "The Lilacs" was published, Faulkner probably wrote a sketch entitled "Nympholepsy," an expansion of "The Hill." This sketch can be considered a land-based prose version of "The Lilacs" arising as does "Carcassonne," "Black Music," and "The Leg" from the recesses of Faulkner's poetic imagination. In "Nympholepsy," a young man chases after a woman but never captures her, nor even touches her though he thinks he does:

> He plunged after her. His furrow broke silver in the wheat beneath the impervious moon, rippling away from him, dying again into the dull and unravished gold of standing grain. She was far ahead, the disturbance of her passage through the wheat had died away ere he reached it. He saw, beyond the spreading ripple of her passage arching away at either side, her body break briefly against a belt of wood, like a match flame; then he saw her no more.[8]

In "The Lilacs," the pilot is reproached for stalking the skies, seeking the feminine "mouth of death" when he himself has not known the bliss of home and children. As the air becomes cool

8. William Faulkner, *Uncollected Stories of William Faulkner* (New York: Random House, 1979), 335.

and the pale lilacs vanish from the pale lilac sky, the wounded veteran hesitatingly affirms, "I—I am not dead."

The poet, though barely alive, reiterates his preoccupation for *la belle dame sans merci* in "Une Ballade des Femmes Perdues," published in January 1920, and inspired directly perhaps by François Villon's *"Ballade des dames du temps jadis"* since he uses as his epigraph Villon's *"Mais òu sont les neiges d'antan"* or indirectly through the translations of Swinburne and Dante Gabriel Rossetti. Though only in his early 20s when the poem was published, Faulkner in the concluding stanza projects himself into later life:

> I am old, and alone
> And the star dust from their wings
> Has dimmed my eyes
> I sing in the green dusk
> Of lost ladies—Si vraiment charmant, charmant.
>
> (*EPP*, 54)

Faulkner's poems, indeed, are songs written for lost ladies: *Vision in Spring** was written for Estelle Franklin; *The Marble Faun* was dedicated to his mother; *Mississippi Poems* were written for Myrtle Ramey; and *Helen: A Courtship* for Helen Baird.[9] After 1918, Faulkner had left home often enough so that the influence his mother had on him had begun to diminish; he had lost Estelle Oldham to Cornell Franklin; neither Myrtle Ramey nor Helen Baird considered Faulkner a serious suitor, let alone a prospective husband. Faulkner's poetry did not arise from a vacuum, but emerged from deep-seated social and psychological contexts which certainly involved his relationship with women; this is not to say that Faulkner's poetry is autobiographical or provides a clinical chart to his love life. This could hardly be the

*See footnote 3.

9. I am grateful to Mrs. Summers for allowing me to examine a Xerox copy of this 88-page booklet. Recently two of Faulkner's booklets of poetry have been published: *Mississippi Poems* (Oxford: Yoknapatawpha Press, 1979) and *Helen: A Courtship* (Oxford; Yoknapatawpha Press, 1981).

case if we take seriously his belief that poetry removes the impurities from life's experiences so that only the universally significant remains.

Of the books and booklets of poetry that Faulkner wrote and either had published commercially or hand-bound himself, *Vision in Spring** is, in my opinion, the most significant. Not only was it written for a young woman Faulkner had wanted to marry in 1918 and who subsequently spurned him to marry someone else, but it was written while Estelle was still married, thus showing the depth of his affection for his future wife at that period in time. In addition, it does not have the artificial immaturity of *The Marble Faun* nor the fragmented, anthological quality of *A Green Bough*. Finally, because it is consciously varied in context and style, unlike *Mississippi Poems* or *Helen: A Courtship*, it reveals more characteristically the modalities of Faulkner's imagination and shows in an inchoate way something that Faulkner developed in such works as *The Wild Palms* and *Go Down, Moses*, that is, global unity is achieved by structuring and interlocking smaller independent segments. In passing, I should note that three poems in *Vision in Spring** were reprinted in *A Green Bough*, one in the 1920–21 Ole Miss yearbook, one in the *Double Dealer*, and two in *Contempo*, while eight poems in *Mississippi Poems* appear in *A Green Bough*, one of which was also printed in the *New Republic*. As William Boozer notes, ten of the sixteen poems in *Helen: A Courtship* were never published elsewhere. Five were published in *A Green Bough*, and the sixth, "The Faun," dedicated to "H.L." (Harold Levy), was printed in the April 1925 issue of the *Double Dealer*. The last stanza of poem XIV appeared as poem XXIII of *A Green Bough*, and part of one line of poem X in *Helen: A Courtship* was included in poem XL of *A Green Bough*.[10] While Estelle Franklin

*See footnote 3.

10. William Boozer, "'Helen: A Courtship' Joins *Mayday* in Facsimile and Trade Edition," *The Faulkner Newsletter and Yoknapatawpha Review* (July-September 1981), 4.

and Myrtle Ramey might have thought they had ultra-secret poetic nosegays locked up in their vanities, Faulkner took care to see that a good many of these private poems would also be available to a wider public.

The first two poems in *Vision in Spring** do not present us with explicit statements about the nature of the poetry in this booklet; rather, they give us a congeries of images which sets an overall tone. The title poem, "Vision in Spring," portrays a man who has followed a voice that trembles within him and about him until finally his heart breaks with the striking of a bell. When the dancers he dreams about float before him in the evening air, he is revived and touched by their beauty. Elderly and alone, he realizes that he has been seeking something that has been shattered and thus feels quite impotent in rectifying the situation. When the atmosphere becomes calm, he rises from his stiffened knees and the quest begins:

> Spring, blown white along the faint-starred darkness,
> Arose again about him, like a wall
> Beneath which he stood and watched, growing colder and colder,
> A star immaculately fall.
>
> (5)

Intensely involved in a private vision, which could be both exterior and interior, he summons up thoughts about music and nature. This first poem, a prelude, without specifically referring to a woman, hints that the falling star is an omen, a sign of luck just when he needs it. Almost imperceptibly in "Interlude," the second poem in this sequence, the protagonist feels the need to explore around him and become aware of his own finitude in contemplating the vast ocean of stars, and as he does so, he senses the presence of a young woman:

> Slowly, solemnly, and turn
> With lifted throats, and hair that floats
> With scarce moved knees, and soft-breast bare.
> Slow gigantic waters slowly burn
> The unstirred air.
>
> (7)

*See footnote 3.

213

However, in spite of the protagonist's desire to "bless in quiet pain, and kiss," he finds no consolation in trying to summon up and palpably speak what appears to be ineffable, and thus, a hollow man, he walks down a deserted street ringing the pavement with his feet. This exit is highly enigmatic since we have never really entered into the protagonist's true predicament. And while music and dance are elements which suggest sexuality and excitement, they also seem to have a calming effect.

With the third poem, "The World and Pierrot: A Nocturne," we return to a more familiar Faulknerian world, as the poet re-enters the dramatic landscape of "Nocturne" in the 1920–21 Ole Miss yearbook and that of his one-act play, *The Marionettes*, written probably in the fall of 1920. In this poem, Pierrot, the clown, spins and whirls about as he is caged in the moonlight while the moon, a spider, weaves "icy silver across his heart." Columbine, a female figure, flings a rose, a "severed hand," at Pierrot's feet in a sort of decadent *danse macabre,* and though the two remain silhouetted against the sky, they merely pose in each other's presence and do not communicate at all. Pierrot realizes, as the returning pilot and the solitary figure in the first two poems of *Vision in Spring** know, "He, alone, must die by growing old." In *The Marionettes*, with important drawings by Faulkner in the style of Aubrey Beardsley and John Held, Jr., Faulkner created a drama influenced by the *symbolistes*, Verlaine and Mallarmé, though as Noel Polk mentions in his admirable introduction to this play, one should not overlook the possible influence of Laforgue, Baudelaire, Valéry, and Gautier.[11] In fact, Verlaine's "Clair de Lune," which Faulkner translated, outlines *The Marionettes* in that we have a garden described where masked singers and dancers perform while all the time concealing their inner feelings, a variant of the picture in "Inter-

---

*See footnote 3.

11. William Faulkner, *The Marionettes*, introduction by Noel Polk (Charlottesville: University Press of Virginia, 1977), xi. All future references will be to this edition.

lude." A comparison of the two versions of "Clair de Lune" shows that Faulkner had a good knowledge of the French text, but remained a bit too faithful to the French with the result that he transliterates it in spots:

Clair de Lune

Votre âme est un paysage choisi
Que vont charmant masques et bergamasques,
Jouant du luth, et dansant, et quasi
Tristes sous leur déguisements fantasques.

Tout en chantant sur le mode mineur
L'amour vainqueur et la vie opportune,
Ils n'ont pas l'air de croire à leur bonheur
Et leur chanson se mêle au clair de lune,

Au calme clair de lune triste et beau,
Qui fait rêver les oiseaux dans les arbres
Et sangloter d'extase les jets d'eau,
Les grands jets d'eau sveltes parmi les marbres.

PAUL VERLAINE

****

CLAIR DE LUNE
(From Paul Verlaine.)

Your soul is a lovely garden, and go
There masque and bergamasque charmingly,
Playing the lute and dancing and also
Sad beneath their disguising fantasy.*

All are singing in a minor key
Of conqueror love and life opportune,
Yet seem to doubt their joyous revelry
As their song melts in the light of the moon.

In the calm moonlight, so lovely fair
That makes the birds dream in the slender trees,
While fountains dream among the statues there;
Slim fountains sob in silver ecstacies.[12]

—W. FALKNER

12. See *EPP*, 58. Professor Collins suggests that "fantasy" replace "fanchise."

Though Faulkner shifted some of the imagery in the third stanza, his most remarkable change is to translate *"paysage"* as "garden"; in doing this, he allowed himself to narrow the confines of the dramatic action in *The Marionettes* and give these puppet-like figures (*fantoches* also means puppets) less room to move in.

The Marionettes and a considerable amount of poetry directly and indirectly related to this play provide important insights into "The World and Pierrot: A Nocturne." In *The Marionettes*, Pierrot, the Shade of Pierrot, Marietta, the Grey Figure, and the Lilac Figure comment on the significance of life, the garden, and particularly about modes of perception. The two spectral figures call our attention to the dying leaves and the inevitability of death: "All things must die, and dead things are very heavy" (30). As summer moves towards fall and death, the first figure reminds us: "This garden is old, it has felt the chill of a thousand winters. But all things must grow old, we grow old alone; the earth is already old, the earth is like an aged woman gathering fagots in a barren field" (38). When Marietta reappears alone in a brilliant gown after having gone off with Pierrot, she is shocked by the autumnal appearance of the garden which contrasts with her eternal beauty. The final pen-and-ink drawing of *The Marionettes* depicts Pierrot looking at himself in an upright mirror with his hands raised in a questioning mood as he stands above the dead Marietta, a scene which recalls the conclusion of poem XVI of *A Green Bough:*

> "Ho. . . . One grows weary, posturing and grinning,
> aping a dream to a house of people shadows!
> Ah, 'twas you who stripped me bare and set me
> gibbering at mine own face in a mirror."

Marietta's narcissism leads to her own death, and thus she joins the ranks of Faulkner's *femmes perdues*. She says, "The moon will play my body when I die, and the cacophonous cries of my peacocks have blighted the ilex before the statue of Hermes" (54–55). This mention of the statue of Hermes, the lover of Aphrodite and the father of Pan, naturally links this play, and thus the third poem in *Vision in Spring**, to the problem facing the faun as he follows Pan in *The Marble Faun*.

If we consider Pierrot in *The Marionettes* as a lover seeking a beautiful woman, one he apparently loses, then he is indeed related to the faun in Faulkner's works. In a poem called "The Faun," first published in the *Double Dealer* in April 1925, Faulkner explicitly associates nature and women with the faun:

> When laggard March, a faun whose stampings ring
> And ripple the leaves with hiding: vain pursuit
> Of May's anticipated dryad, mute
> And yet unwombed of the moist flanks of spring;
>
> (*EPP*, 119)

The faun, normally portrayed with the horns and tail of a goat and subsequently with goat legs like those of a satyr, vainly seeks the nymph of May who has yet to appear from the flanks of the earth. Both this faun, and the one in "L'Apres Midi d'un Faune," Faulkner's first published poem in 1919, and the one in his book, *The Marble Faun*, which he wrote from April to June 1919, resemble Pierrot in that all are highly self-conscious figures whose narcissistic tendencies do not allow freedom of movement or growth, but lead to stasis and death, an interpretation supported by a two-page fragment by Faulkner written on the inside cover of Ralph Hodgson's book of poetry where a faun-like statue is located inside Marietta's garden.[13]

The faun's search is ill-timed; he either looks in vain or begins his quest for the beautiful woman before the time is ripe for passion. Yet he knows well his options: he can either race through the windy woods without success or wait patiently until

*See footnote 3.

13. See Judith Sensibar's "Pierrot and the Marble Faun: Another Fragment," *Mississippi Quarterly*, 32 (Summer 1979), 473–76.

May is ready to sip the "wine sweet-sunned for Jove's delight" (*EPP*, 119). As half-man, half-lusty-goat, the faun embodies the emotional feelings and thoughts of one intensely in love. The faun, personified as March, yearly seeks the nymph of May just as the winter snows are melting and the earth is about to rejuvenate itself. In addition, the faun finds Pan's music enchanting and difficult to resist. "Naiads' Song," for instance, which Faulkner published in *The Mississippian* on February 4, 1920, is composed of four stanzas of rhyming couplets each beginning with the phrase "Come ye sorrowful and keep," and stresses the loneliness and sadness of those spurned in love. Yet peace can unfold in one's heart like a rose:

> No more in waking, come and steep
> Yourself in us as does the bee
> Plunge in that rose that, singing, he
> Has opened.

> (*EPP*, 55)

The imagery and tone of this poem have the undertones of both a lament and an epithalamion since what the Naiads offer is quiet intimacy and a chance to sleep and dream to the music of Pan.

Classical authors such as Pindar, Aristophanes, Plato, Herodotus, Virgil, Ovid, Lucian, Theocritus, and Apuleius often mentioned Pan and used him as a surrogate for the poet himself. While Faulkner seems aware of this tradition, he found the faun a figure with much more potential, perhaps because it might have served as a surrogate for himself. In his "L'Apres Midi d'un Faune," the faun chases an unnamed woman until she pauses and shakes down her hair. Her eyes dart kisses to the faun's limbs, and together they go hand-in-hand until they reach a stream by silent shadows where she can sleep and dream. In this poem, derived perhaps from Mallarmé's poem published in 1876 or from Debussy's 1892 orchestral prelude, or from both, the faun leaves little doubt about his intentions:

> I have a nameless wish to go
> To some far silent midnight [noon]
> Where lonely streams whisper and flow
> And sigh on sands blanched by the moon,
> And blond limbed dancers whirling past,
> The senile worn moon staring through
> The sighing trees. . . .
>
> (*EPP*, 39–40)[14]

The scene concludes with the sound of a bell, an echo of the bell in "Vision in Spring." The faun never possesses the woman who is eventually replaced by some dancers. In the version printed in the October 29, 1919, edition of *The Mississippian*, Faulkner places greater emphasis on spring:

> It was the earth's great heart that broke
> For spring broke before the world grew old.
>
> (*EPP*, 125)

The changing seasons constantly intrude into life and bring with them the passing of time; yet they are testimony to an unchanging eternal cycle which offers ultimate consolation. Spring does follow winter; death does encourage new birth; Bayard Sartoris's death occurs simultaneously with the birth of Narcissa's baby; Lena gives birth as Joe Christmas is sacrificially murdered.

In a review of William Alexander Percy's *In April Once*, Faulkner wrote what could well be a self-indictment:

> The influence of the frank pagan worship of the past is heavily upon him, he is like a little boy closing his eyes against the dark modernity which threatens the bright simplicity and the colorful romantic pageantry of the middle ages with which his eyes are full. One can imagine him best as a violinist who became blind about the time Mozart died, it would seem that the last thing he saw with his subjective intellect was Browning standing in naive admiration before his own mediocrity. . . .
>
> (*EPP*, 72)

14. See *EPP*, 123–25 for a variant of this poem.

In writing *The Marble Faun*, Faulkner imitated the thought and feeling of Keats's "Endymion" in that this poem which he knew provided him with both a suitable landscape and the *persona* of Pan. Keats's "I stood tip-toe upon a little hill," written in the summer of 1816 just before he wrote "Endymion," which acknowledges Pan as the one being whom every faun and satyr seeks since he is the "Dread opener of the mysterious doors / leading to universal knowledge" (I, 278–79), does offer the poet rest and security:

> And when a tale is beautifully staid;
> We feel the safety of a hawthorn glade:
>
> (129–30)

In this poem, one of the tasks of the poet is to reveal how the fearful syrinx fled Arcadian Pan:

> Poor nymph,—poor Pan,—how he did weep to find,
> Naught but a lovely sighing of the wind
> Along the reedy stream; a half-heard strain,
> Full of sweet desolation—balmy pain.
>
> (159–62)

Yet the poet himself becomes transformed in his search for Endymion. As Faulkner hinted in his "Verse Old and Nascent: A Pilgrimage," the authentic question is posed by Keats in "I stood tip-toe upon a little hill": "Was there a poet born?" (241). In the "Hymn to Pan" ("Endymion" I, 232–306), Endymion, like Faulkner's faun, does not heed a maiden's sigh:

> But in the self-same fixed trance he kept,
> Like one who on earth had never stept.
> Aye, even as dead-still as a *marble man*,
> Frozen in that old tale Arabian.
>
> (1, 403–06; emphasis mine)

Though Endymion, associated with the marble man, has the companionship of Peona, he seems willing to accept his melancholic lot and admit to himself that he will pass his days alone and sad. When Peona takes up her lute and sings, Endymion learns that he can ultimately bear up against sorrow. Like Faulkner's faun, Endymion is terribly aware of his situation:

> There, when new wonders ceas'd to float before,
> And thoughts of self come on, how crude and sore
> The journey homeward to habitual self!
>
> (II, 274–76)

Towards the conclusion of the poem, Endymion synthesizes the events and phenomena he has dealt with; in many ways, this adumbrates the themes in *The Marble Faun*:

> Pan will bid
> Us live in peace, in love and peace among
> His forest wilderness. I have clung
> To nothing, lov'd a nothing, nothing seen
> Or felt but a great dream! O I have been
> Presumptuous against love, against the sky,
> Against all elements, against the tie
> Of mortals each to each, against the blooms
> Of flowers, rush of rivers, and the tombs
> Of heroes gone! Against his proper glory
> Has my own soul conspired: so my story
> Will I to children utter, and repent.
> There never liv'd a mortal man, who bent
> His appetite beyond his natural sphere,
> But starv'd and died.
>
> (IV, 634–48)

Keats's Endymion represents the poet's quest for Beauty and by means of the various transformations he undergoes in his relationship with women, he learns that the highest form of Beauty is the union of man and woman.

Faulkner's faun, however, does not reach these heights; this is not to deny, however, that he is not in the tradition of either the faun alone, or the faun as related to Pan. Horace proposed the image of *"Faune, nympharum fugientum amator"* (*Odes* III, 18) while Eusebius would rather identify Pan with God since both have a linguistic and metaphysical relationship to "All." Likewise Rabelais in his *Le quart livre* identifies Virgil's shepherd Pan with the Good Shepherd of John 10:11. In addition, it is not surprising that the Romantics and Victorians, given their enthusiasm for discussing nature and poetic inspiration, deal with Pan. Both Elizabeth Barrett Browning in her "Pan is Dead" and Robert Browning in his "The Bishop Orders His Tomb at St. Praxed's Church" provide an important link with the history of this figure. Lewis Simpson, who discusses at length Faulkner's use of Pan while relying on Patricia Merivale's *Pan The Goat-God: His Myth in Modern Times*, notes that the basic meaning of the Pan-Christ dialectic is "the restoration of the sexuality of art. Satyrs, nymphs, and fauns that range through the nineteenth-century imagination . . . belong to the impulse to rediscover through artistic vision the mythical basis of culture in the biology of male and female, and the variations thereof."[15] Browning captures this tendency and exemplifies it well in "The Bishop Orders His Tomb at St. Praxed's Church":

> Those Pans and Nymphs ye wot of, and perchance
> Some tripod, thyrsus, with a vase or so,
> The Saviour at his sermon on the mount,
> Saint Praxed in a glory, and one Pan
> Ready to twitch the Nymph's last garment off,
> And Moses with the tables. . . .
>
> (ll. 55–62)

Faulkner's religious sensibility, at this point in his life, did not appear disposed to establish this equilibrium of god and goat, of Christ and Pan, though he restores the sexual dimension of this relationship in his portrayal of Pierrot and Marietta in *The Marionettes*.

Following the English aesthetes of the late Victorian period,

---

15. Lewis Simpson, "Faulkner and the Legend of the Artist," *Faulkner: Fifty Years After the Marble Faun,* ed. George A. Wolfe (University: University of Alabama Press, 1976), 77. See also Simpson's "Faulkner and the Southern Symbolism of Pastoral," *Mississippi Quarterly,* 28 (Fall 1975), 401–15.

Faulkner presented the faun, like Pan a surrogate for the poet, as alienated from the social world where an inner landscape could be exteriorized in order to make visible the beauty they were seeking. As David Perkins and other historians of poetry have noted, Yeats, Bridges, and Housman were melancholic stylists who retreated from their contemporary society. Art was exalted, and for the decadents among them who modelled their attitudes and activities after their French counterparts, dubious subject matter could be discussed without any type of prior explanation or apology. Given this retreat, it is understandable that there be an emphasis on austerity, tragedy, and pessimism in their quest for the mythic and supernatural explanation for truth. In fact, the quest itself becomes a central motif in what Gautier calls *"l'art pour l'art,"* a sentiment acknowledged in different ways by Flaubert, Baudelaire, Pater, and Keats. Since the accent is not on the concrete specifics of everyday life, form, convention, and style become the guiding concepts. What is praised, in the final analysis, is a combination of a beautiful style and a psychological structure, which explains in large measure the French hyperdulia towards Poe. In light of this, literature has one purpose: to show that the supernatural dwells in the beauty crafted by man.

In *The Marble Faun*, which employs primarily octosyllabic couplets, Faulkner stresses the themes of isolation, mutability, heightened consciousness, the memory and tug of the past, and the struggle for identity. In this pastoral poem without a definite landscape, the immortal faun cannot find release from his animal nature, but is condemned or destined to remain locked in marble. Thus, he is free to explore an interior landscape where purity, lucidity, and universality flourish. As Stonum notes, "The prologue to *The Marble Faun* is typical of Faulkner's landscapes: slender poplars moving lightly in the breeze and overlooking a calm pool and surrounds a silver fountain. . . . Such cultivated, formalized natural beauty presents a momentary calm that evokes the poet's desire for a gently swaying of eternal stillness."[16] In contrast to the lithe poplars hovering above the hollyhocks, asters, phlox, and daisies, the faun presents a melancholic mien:

> Why am I sad? I?
> Why am I not content? The sky
> Warns me and yet I cannot break
> My marble bonds.
>
> (12)

The faun sighs "For things I know, yet cannot know, / 'Twixt sky above and earth below." Faulkner does not conceive of the faun in terms of a real-ideal dichotomy; rather the problem is to find personal freedom which seeks expression in the pursuit of an ideal woman. Unlike the powerful women in Swinburne's "Atalanta in Calydon," for example, Faulkner's faun encounters no such person, though there are intimations of a woman's presence:

> Dogwood shines through thin trees there
> Like jewels in a woman's hair.
>
> (14)

With the appearance of Pan, however, nature becomes alive and like the "quick keen snake," a reference with biblical overtones, the faun dreams that he is able to roam and peer about even though he is still marble-bound. With an echo from Housman and perhaps a direct reference to Pound's 1912 "hokku-like sentence" ("The apparition of these faces in a crowd; / Petals on a wet, black bough"), the faun's lethargy is reflected in his surroundings until that moment when he decides to follow Pan:

---

16. Gary Lee Stonum, *Faulkner's Career: An Internal Literary History* (Ithaca: Cornell University Press, 1979), 47. Also of interest are H. E. Richardson's "Maecenas and Mars: Portrait in Marble," *The Journey to Self-Discovery* (Columbia: University of Missouri Press, 1969), 38–60, and William Boozer's *William Faulkner's First Book: The Marble Faun: Fifty Years Later* (Memphis: The Pigeon Roost Press, 1974).

All the air is gray with rain
Above the shaken fields of grain,
Cherry orchards moveless drip
Listening to their blossoms slip
Quietly from wet black boughs.

(18)

Nature gives solace to the faun and the shade will protect him when he lacks strength; unfortunately, contemplation, not procreation, will be his sort.

In the sixth section, Pan's flute encourages the faun not to remain static, but to enter the realm of the supernatural:

"There is a great God who sees all
And in my throat bestows this boon:
To ripple the silence with my call
When the world sleeps and it is noon."

(23)

What the cosmos can offer is the assurance of continuity and this seems to be more important than the vagaries of a male-female relationship:

The dying days gives those who sorrow
A boon no king can give: a morrow.

(28)

Unlike the depiction of the moon in the ode to the moon in the fourth section of "Endymion," the moon in *The Marble Faun* resembles a mad, old woman. The faun senses "aching bliss unbearable" as he tries to bring to light the muted qualities in nature while knowing that it is Pan, not himself, who seeks the lovely Philomel.

As the seasons advance and change from green to purple, and as the moon, still mad, casts a spell on each rock, winter arrives and the faun reflects on the asymptotical nature of his life:

Why cannot we always be
Left steeped in this immensity

225

Of softly stirring peaceful gray
That follows on the dying day?

(46)

Pan's blessing, one of sleep, is the faun's assurance of peace and since he has become one with the landscape, he will never weep. And the faun, though eternally marble-bound, knows that he will always have a full heart:

> I would be sad with changing year,
> Instead, a sad, bound prisoner,
> For though about me seasons go,
> My heart knows only winter snow.

(51)

To a certain extent, André Bleikasten might be right in calling these particular stanzas *l'épigone appliqué et attardé des poètes de la Décadence,*[17] and thinking of them in terms of schoolboy exercises, though I think it could be argued that they offer an insight into the themes and tensions Faulkner struggled with as he tried to elucidate his poetic vision, structured more grotesquely in a poem entitled "Old Satyr":

> Her unripe shallow breast is green among
> The windy bloom of drunken apple trees,
> And seven fauns importunate as bees
> To sip the thin young honey of her tongue.
> The old satyr, leafed and hidden, dreams her kiss
> His beard amid, leaving his mouth in sight;
> Dreams her body in a moony night
> Shortening and shuddering into his;
> Then sees a faun, bolder than the rest,
> Slide his hand upon her sudden breast,
> And feels the life in him go cold, and pass
> Until the fire that kiss had brought to be

17. André Bleikasten, "Pan et Pierrot, ou les premiers masques de Faulkner," *Revue de littérature comparée,* 53 (Juillet-Septembre), 304.

226

Gutters and faints away; 'tis night, and he
Laughing wrings the bitter wanton grass.

(*AGB*, XLI)

In short, Faulkner's pastoral poetry which dealt with the faun allowed him an opportunity to struggle with ideas and feelings that remained constant throughout his poetic career; this type of poetry, however, did not provide him with a vocabulary or rhythms by which he could authentically express the nuances and subtleties of these themes.

In addition to "L'Apres Midi d'un Faune," *The Mississippian* published during 1919 three other poems by Faulkner which showed his concern for the passage of time and the relationship of man to woman: "Cathay," "Sapphics," and "After Fifty Years." "Cathay," Faulkner's version of Shelley's "Ozymandias," presents a bleak, desert landscape where Fate, Fame, and Death interact with one another. Life's struggles continue as each succeeding generation builds on and covers up past glories:

So is it: who sows
The seed of Fame, makes the grain for Death to reap.

(*EPP*, 41)

Part of the task of the poet is to reveal the good with the bad and to explain to one's peers what is before them even though they might be reluctant to see it:

They know thee not, nor will
To see thy magic empire when the Hand
Thrusts back the curtain of shifting sand,
On singing stars and lifting golden hill.

(*EPP*, 41)

"After Fifty Years," a Petrarchan sonnet, incorporates the relationship of the past to the present, this time as the husband or lover recalls the presence of a woman after a hiatus of fifty years. The first eight lines portray a woman whose house and heart are

227

empty and cold, yet who continues to attract men. Years before, legend has it, her hair and general beauty were the envy of all of young women; the man in the poem, though old, blind, and like the marble faun with "his bound heart," still feels her presence after all these years. "Sapphics," a poem whose inspiration came directly from Swinburne's poem of the same title, portrays another backward glance at a beautiful woman, this time Aphrodite. Not only did Faulkner collapse Swinburne's twenty stanzas into six, but he used the sapphic meter, three lines of hendecasyllables followed by a fourth line of five syllables. Fortunately Faulkner did not copy some of Swinburne's infelicities, such as "unclosed a feather," "necks reverted," or "awful roses of holy blossom." Aphrodite, the goddess *sans pareil*, is beyond both Swinburne's and Faulkner's reach.

> And yet though sleep comes not to me, there comes
> A vision from the full smooth brow of sleep,
> The white Aphrodite moving unbounded
>   By her own hair.
> In the purple beaks of the doves that draw her,
> Beaks straight without desire, necks bent backward
> Toward Lesbos and the flying feet of Loves
>   Weeping behind her.
>
> (*EPP*, 51)

As these lines suggest, this poem gives new meaning to what Faulkner means by a vision in Spring.

In addition to reworking Swinburne's "Sapphics" and translating Verlaine's "Clair de Lune," Faulkner also looked to Verlaine for three other poems: "Streets," "Fantoches," and "A Clymène," though it seems quite probable that he knew of Arthur Symons's translations of the last two. In "Streets," the lover proclaims the virtues of the beloved, yet when this love is not reciprocated completely, the thought in the lively refrain helps to alleviate the lover's plight since he will retain at least an image of her:

Her face will be
In my mind's infinity
She broke the coin and gave it have to me
Dance the Jig!

(EPP, 59)

The love affair is more intense in "Fantoches," in that we see
Scaramouches and Pucinella silhouetted against the night sky in
a manner reminiscent of Pierrot and Columbine; in addition we
see the daughter of the doctor of Bogona gliding from her bed to
meet her waiting lover. Though Faulkner has remained faithful
to the spirit of the original, he changed the last line and replaced
it with "La lune ne garde aucune rancune," which he borrowed
either from Laforgue's "*Complainte de cette bonne lune*" or from
Eliot's "Rhapsody on a Windy Night." Poem XXXII of A Green
Bough is related to this poem through its title: "La Lune ne
Grade [sic] Aucune Rancune":

> look, cynthia,
> how abelard evaporates
> the brow of time, and paris
> tastes his bitter thumbs—
> the worm grows fat, eviscerate,
> but not on love, o cynthia.

For Faulkner, the moon in these poems does not harbor any
resentment, nor does it facilitate the various love relationships,
and if Faulkner were thinking of the conclusion of "Rhapsody on
a Windy Night" when writing his "Fantoches," then the conclusion to "Fantoches" has a different twist since Eliot's poem concludes with a shattering thought:

> ['] Mount.
> The bed is open; the tooth-brush hangs on the wall,
> Put your shoes at the door, sleep, prepare for life.'
> The last twist of the knife.

Faulkner's translations are significant not only because they give

229

us a clue to his reading and his ability to translate, but because, as with "A Clymène" in particular, they reinforce the images found in some of his less successful poems, such as "A Poplar," "To a Co-ed," and "Alma Mater."

One poem that Faulkner wrote about the time he gave Estelle *Vision in Spring** was "On Seeing the Winged Victory for the First Time." In this poem, Faulkner was able to transfer the image of the marble-bound figure from a faun to a classical woman who is at once beautiful and marred. This poem is a direct invocation to the inner woman frozen in stone and Faulkner's concern is to relate the story of Atthis, one perhaps already perceived by scores of others who have looked at her. In particular, Faulkner highlights an eagle, which in some subliminal way we might identify with a falcon and thus with Faulkner himself, a strong masculine bird in this case riding in his ecstasy while the wind stirs up the seas into white foam. Faulkner is very much in control of the evocative imagery and language in this poem:

> o atthis
> for a moment an aeon i pause plunging
> above the narrow precipice of thy breast
> what before thy white precipice the eagle
> sharp in the sunlight and cleaving
> his long blue ecstasy and what
> wind on hilltops blond with the wings of the morning
> what wind o atthis sweeping the april to lesbos
> whitening the seas
>
> (*AGB*, XVII)

Above all, what this poem indicates is that Faulkner could well have used the plural, since in fact, he had several visions in spring.

Thus, we have seen that Faulkner's third poem in *Vision in Spring**, "The World and Pierrot: A Nocturne," unlocks many of

*See footnote 3.

230

the relationships between and among *The Marionettes, The Marble Faun,* and a sizable number of the poems in *A Green Bough* and *Early Prose and Poetry.* Yet in this third poem, we see a Pierrot different from the one in *The Marionettes* in that we have no Marietta to serve as a genuine foil to Pierrot; he is presented as a solitary figure. When he is told that he must die a romantic death in which he himself will be the silver arrow "tipped with jade desire" (17), he retreats to the top of a frosty mountain and cries in anguish to the stars. As star-pilgrims appear, Pierrot becomes more and more despondent:

> Pierrot shivers, his soul is a paper lantern
> Hung sadly in a garden of dead trees.
>
> (23)

Finally he assumes an attitude and posture that the faun did in *The Marble Faun* and as Pierrot seems to do at the end of *The Marionettes:*

> Shall I stay alone,
> Shall I stay alone to watch a dead man pass,
> Gibbering at the moon and twisting a paper
>   rose petal by petal apart,—
> Or do I see my own face in a glass?
>
> (26)

Ultimately there is resignation:

> I am bound with chains of blue and green;
> I am alone in a forest of sound around me
> Woven with all beauty that I have felt and seen.
>
> (29)

Pierrot's final act is to wake into a dream and though everything has vanished, he does perceive some shadows, lights, and faces which give him slim satisfaction.

If this performance of Pierrot had been a stage show, then the subsequent poem, "After the Concert," is appropriate for it pro-

231

vides a comment on both *The Marble Faun* and *The Marionettes*. As the lights go up in a theatre, a young couple walks out
trying to recall what they have just witnessed:

> So we walk, and dimly raise our eyes,
> Arm in arm in intimate talk;
> In a haze of trivialities
> We walk, and pause, and walk.
>
> **********
>
> Weave, your luminous flowers, weave
> A gold devise upon dark's lowered shield.
> We rise, to a hidden music, out of night,
> We laugh and weep, and then to night we yield.
>
> (32)

What are the couple discussing? A movie? Yes. Of Pierrot, or
Pan or the faun? Though they never talk directly about what
they have witnessed, it would seem logical that it might have
something to do with the previous poem. Whatever, it is with
this fourth poem that Faulkner becomes a modern, using a realistic situation and couching it in everyday speech. In silhouet-
ting this couple as they walk along a shadowed street, in contrast
to Pierrot and Columbine in one version of "Nocturne," the
woman leans her breast against the man and he responds sym-
pathetically by saying that she still has a good deal to learn:

> You are so young. And frankly you believe
> This world, this darkened street, this shadowed wall
> Are bright with beauty you passionately know
> Cannot fade nor cool nor die at all.
>
> (34)

As laughter breaks the rhythm of their feet, Faulkner has succeeded in presenting a couple that is both physically and intellectually attractive.

Two subsequent poems (VI and VII), both begin with similar
phrases, thus suggesting that Faulkner is dealing with variations
of a musical theme:

Poem VI: "The dark ascends
                 Lightly on pale wings of falling light."
Poem VII: "The dark ascends
                 On golden wings of violins."

In poem VI, the male character from poems IV and V continues speaking, this time imitating almost to the point of parody the strains of Eliot's "Love Song of J. Alfred Prufrock," a poem that Faulkner paraphrased in much of the middle poems of this booklet:

> Let us go then; you and I, while evening grows
> And a delicate violet thins [sic] the rose
> That stains the sky;
> We will go alone there, you and I,
> And watch the trees step naked from the shadow
> Like women shrugging upward from their gowns.
>
> (38)

The musicality of this poem is made more explicit in poem VII, entitled "A Symphony" perhaps by Estelle, and underscores Pater's belief that all poetry is essentially music. The man knows, as he listens to the bells and rain outside, that "Life is not passing: it is an endless repeating" (48).

As a preparation for poem IX, entitled "Love Song," Faulkner in the eighth poem portrays this man as alone by the sea who ponders how strange it is that nothing is accomplished in life. We live with past experiences that never cease to inundate us:

> We cannot know, we only grope and stare
> At restless lights reflected in the sea.
>
> (54)

Like Pierrot and the faun, this man must accept incredible loneliness:

> Shall I walk, then, through a corridor of profundities
> Carefully erect (I am taller that [sic] I look)
> To a certain door—and shall I dare

233

To open it? I smoothe my mental hair
With an oft changed phrase that I revise again
Until I have forgotten what it was at first;
Settle my tie with; I have brought a book,
Then seat myself with: We have passed the worst.

Then I shall sit among careful cups of tea,
Aware of a slight perspiring as to brow,
(The smell of scented cigarettes will always trouble me);
I shall sit, so patiently at ease,
Stiffly erect, decorous as to knees
Among toy balloons of dignity on threads of talk.

And do I dare
(I once more stroke my hand across my hair)
But the window of my mind flies shut, I am in a room
Of surcharged conversation, and of jewelled hands;
Here one slowly strips a flower stalk.
It is too close in here, I rise and walk.
Firmly take my self-possession by the hand.

Now, do I dare,
Who sees the light gleam on her intricate hair?
Shall I assume a studied pose, or shall I stand—
Oh, Mr. . . . ? You are so kind. . . .
Again the door slams inward on my mind.
Not at all. . . .

      Replace a cup,
Return and pick a napkin up.

(55–57)

In portraying this man whose only solace is to walk the streets at
night, the poet has touched the depths insofar as the protagonist
has accepted inner diminishment and solitude even when in the
presence of another. Poem X, "The Dancer," restates the inability of the other to appease the lover; in fact, she has flown like
music from his mind, though some residual image and feeling
remain.

While poems XI and XII of *A Green Bough* do present a
happy view of marriage, poem XI of *Vision in Spring**, entitled

*See footnote 3.

"Marriage," shows the isolated male of the previous poems in this booklet, but this time watching reflectively the firelight dance on the walls and the ceiling as his wife plays the piano. The references of music and light repeat in a different key the Pierrot/Columbine/Marietta scenario. Like Pierrot, the husband's brain whirls as he encourages his wife to change the piano pieces she is playing, until finally he explodes as he pictures himself subduing his wife, much like the swan with Leda or the stallion and mare in poem XXXVI of *A Green Bough*, reminiscent in its own way of Jewel's inarticulate attachment to his horse where they are described as "two figures carved for a tableau savage in the sun." Uncharacteristically, Faulkner gives us this scene from her perspective too:

> This she saw, beyond all empty gesturings,
> Beyond the cryptic remnants that remain
> To her, of a shattered spring that, softly playing,
> She sought to build into a whole again.
> This she saw, and heard, and played;
> While beyond there ghostly springs in which she strayed
> She saw again, with pain dark eyes, a face
> Now purged of hunger, quiet with time and space.
>
> (73)

The husband's vision repeats itself as he mounts the stairs after her. Poem XXIX of *A Green Bough*, entitled "Pregnancy," builds on the implied sexuality here while relying on the musical motif:

> Her hands moaned on her breast in blind and supple fire,
> Made light within her cave: she saw her harried
> Body wrung to a strange and bitter lyre
> Whose music once was pure strings simply married.
>   **********
> Three stars in her heart when she awakes
> As winter's sleep breaks greening in soft rain,
> And in the caverned earth spring's rumor shakes
> As in her loins, the tilled and quickened grain.

235

The seduction in "Marriage" and its completion in "Pregnancy" constitute what might well be the primary vision in spring, the moment of ecstatic and romantic love, the descent into her cave, the moment of bliss that cannot be sustained precisely because sexual fulfillment emerges from a genuine knowledge of the other and not from lustful daydreaming. Ironically, poem XLIII of *A Green Bough* even goes so far as imagining a conversation between a fiancé and his future mother-in-law as he lasciviously thinks about his fiancée.

At this point, the vision vanishes; the woman is lost; the romance terminated. Yet the poet does not give up since he tries to recover this woman whom the faun, Pierrot, and the husband in *Vision in Spring** have tried so desperately to seek and win. Poem XII of *Vision in Spring**, appropriately entitled "Opheus," a variant of poem XX in *A Green Bough*, reveals the struggle Faulkner as poet felt in bringing up from the recesses of his imagination not only the woman he had lost, but perhaps as well, life's feminine principle. In the version of "Orpheus" in *Vision in Spring**, Faulkner added over six stanzas, each of which emphasizes the dilemma of the man:

> I am he who, ringed about with faces,
> Stared on a spectral darkness stiff with eyes.
> I raise my hand in a darkness stagnant with faces,
> I break thin violin threads of cries
> As softly I go where together we walked and dreamed.
>
> (78)

In this poem, Faulkner presents the image of a man who is somewhere, but nowhere, who like Orpheus must come up from the nether world himself, and through his song and poetry, bring into the light of day his Eurydice. The poet stands alone between gray walls that seem to reach up to great heights:

> Here he stands, while eternal evening falls
> And it is like a dream between gray walls
> Slowly falling, slowly falling

*See footnote 3.

Between two walls of gray and topless stone,
Between two walls with silence on them grown.
The twilight is severed with waters always falling
And heavy with budded flowers that never die,
And a voice that is forever calling
Sweetly and soberly.

(*AGB*, XX)

As in poem XIX of *A Green Bough*, there is the illusion that he is under water, a sort of Eliotic death by drowning, yet the rest of the poem suggests that he is above ground. The world that envelopes him is eternal and never seems to change or fade. While the woman calls to him, Orpheus cannot help but think that he should penetrate the gate in front of him, just as Faulkner had to penetrate the white sheet of paper in front of him as he wrote his poetry and novels, just as Thomas Sutpen and Sarty Snopes had to penetrate in one way or another the white doors of the mansions, just as the lover must penetrate the hymeno-membrane of the beloved.

On June 20, 1923, Faulkner proposed to The Four Seas Company that they consider publishing his manuscript entitled "Orpheus and Other Poems." While we have no way of knowing what Faulkner had read about Orpheus, Rainer Maria Rilke's *Sonnets to Orpheus* obviously come to mind, particularly as they concern the experience of death which feeds the creative spirit while attempting to make a correlation between desire and loss. Orpheus, often syncretistically fused with the the cult of Dionysius, and later with the resurrecting Christ, reveals and brings to light the secrets of the earth; he gives the world knowledge as he leads forth Eurydice through music.[18] Tragically, Orpheus cannot contemplate Eurydice directly without losing her. One approaches the other to form a unity, but the consummation can never take place unless Orpheus accepts the radical dissolution

18. I am grateful to Professor Monique Pruvot of the University of Paris III for sharing her ideas concerning Faulkner's use of Orpheus with me.

of the relationship. Faulkner's most significant treatment of the Orpheus/Eurydice theme, subtly foreshadowed in this poem, is when he leads the dead Addie Bundren back to life so that she can share her thoughts on love, language, and experience.

Faulkner's personal quest for his Eurydice is intimately linked with his career as a poet. Though Estelle Oldham wore Faulkner's gold ring in January 1918, she was in the process at that time of planning her wedding to Cornell Franklin, a man seven years her senior who had recently been commissioned Judge Advocate General of the Hawaiian Territorial Forces. That April, Faulkner gave Estelle a small booklet of three poems made from a folded single white sheet of paper. On the back in pen-and-ink, he had sketched a nymph standing with her head raised in an ecstatic swoon while seated next to her is a faun with hairy legs, cloven feet, and a reed pipe. Looking down from above is the head of a masked devil with pointed ears and a pointed beard, not unlike the sketch Faulkner drew of himself in a letter to his mother in early September 1925. Clearly the rapture of the nymph is caused by the unheard music; thus Faulkner in this sketch has fused the character of Orpheus with a faun, later associated with Pan. One of these poems, "A Song," is definitely Orphic in character:

> It is all vain to implore me,
>   To let not her image beguile,
> For her face is ever before me—
>   And her smile.
> Even though she chose to ignore me,
>   And all love of me deny,
> There is nought then behind or before me—
>   I can die.[19]

Although the song is really a romantic lament, the poet surrounded by images of the beloved chooses to die because he

19. *Faulkner: A Biography*, I, 195.

sees and accepts her decision. Poem XIII of *Vision in Spring**
reinforces this sentiment as one negative image leads to another
in the quest for the "shortening-breasted nymph":

> Here the sunset paints its wheeling gold
> Where there is no breast to still in strife
> Of joy or sadness, nor does any life
> Flame these hills and vales grown sharp and cold
>> And bare of sound.
>
> (AGB, V)

The inevitable has arrived and little can be done except to look
forward and think about death.

The final poem in *Vision in Spring**, seasonally entitled
"April," and reprinted in the February 1, 1932, issue of *Contempo,* presents a quiet scene as the energy and intense love felt
by the protagonist is absorbed by the pool and the poplars;
Faulkner is not denying the love experience, he is sublimating it
and making it ethereal:

> Somewhere a slender voiceless breeze will go,
> Unlinking the poplars' hands
> And ruffling the pool's face quietly below
> Where each clump of hazel stands,
> Clad in its own simply parted hair;
> And mirrored half in sleep and half awake
> And casting slender white hands on
> The pool's breast, dreaming there to slake
> The thirsty alders pausing in the dawn.
>
> (86)

Love continues "somewhere," perhaps in myth and legend and
poetry; the final image is one of the wind and sky kissing ever-
so-gently the epicene poplar:

> In dim-lit ways
> A sighing wind shakes in its grasp
> A straight resilient poplar in the mist,
> Until its reaching hands unclasp

*See footnote 3.

And then the wind and sky bend down, and kiss
Its simple, cool whitely breathless face.

(88)

With this, Faulkner has resolved the dilemma facing the lover
searching for the beloved. His conclusion is not harsh, nor is the
separation of the man and woman violent. Yet a number of
published and unpublished poems deal with the consequences
of this final separation. Faulkner questions the nature of the
vision:

> Was this the dream?
> Thus: It seemed I lay
> Upon a beach where sand and water kiss
> With endless kissing in a dying fall.

(*AGB*, XXV)

Both Faulkner's poem, "After Eros," poem XXVI of *A Green
Bough*, and "A Raven bleak and Philomel," poem XXVII of *A
Green Bough*, show the poet not only trying to distance himself
from the love experience, but even, echoing Eliot's "The Waste
Land" and "Sweeney Among the Nightingales," attempting to
portray in a decadent manner the degeneration of the love relationship. Music and nature are now vividly depicted in terms of
cacophony and excrement:

> The Raven bleak and Philomel
> Amid the bleeding trees were fixed.
> His hoarse cry and hers were mixed
> And through the dark their droppings fell
> **********
> On rose and peach their droppings bled;
> Love a sacrifice has lain,
> Beneath his hand his mouth is slain,
> Beneath his hand his mouth is dead.
> Then the Raven, bleak and blent
> With all the slow despair of time,

240

> Lets Philomel about him chime
> Until her quiring voice is spent.

Such bleakness, I suspect, cannot be sustained except by poets who are severely depressed, since bleakness is usually portrayed as a reaction to a far more positive sentiment.

Unable to retrieve Eurydice, the poet is willing to take the next logical step. In "Cleopatra," also published as "The Races Splendor" in the April 12, 1933, issue of the *New Republic*, Faulkner buries what could well be considered the archetypcal woman (identified as Cleopatra in the version in the Alderman Library):

> Lilith she is dead and safely tombed
> And man may plant and prune with naught to bruit
> His heired and ancient lot to which he's doomed,
> For quiet drowse the flocks when wolf is mute—
> Ay, Lilith she is dead, and she is wombed,
> And breaks his vine, and slowly eats the fruit.

Likewise, Faulkner celebrates the death of a courtesan and believes that another will replace her, a deep-seated wish perhaps since the replacement is never named. What comes through clearly, however, is that death is not to be considered an abrupt cessation of life.

> The courtesan is dead, for all her subtle ways,
> Her bonds are loosed in brittle and bitter leaves;
> Her last long backward's look to see who grieves
> The imminent night of her reverted gaze.
>
> **********
>
> Thus the world, turning to cold and death
> When swallows empty the blue and drowsy days
> And lean rain scatters the ghost of summer's breath—
> The courtesan that's dead, for all her subtle ways—
> Spring will come! rejoice! But still is there
> An old sorrow sharp as woodsmoke on the air.

> (*AGB*, XXXV)

This sense of renewal after death is most poignantly articulated in a poem that again questions the significance of love:

> Did I know love once? Was it love or grief,
> This grave body by where I had lain,
> And my heart, a single stubborn leaf
> That will not die, though root and branch be slain?
>
> Though warm in dark between the breasts of Death
> That other breast forgot where I did lie,
> And from the tree are stripped the leaves of breath,
> There's still one stubborn leaf that will not die
>
> But restless in the sad and bitter earth,
> Gains with each dawn a death, with dusk a birth.
>
> (*AGB*, XXXIII)

Likewise in poem XXVIII of *A Green Bough*, the death knell signals the coming of November, cold moons, and the retreat of wild geese, reminiscent of the images in poem XLVIII of *A Shropshire Lad*. For Faulkner the earth is home and there is nothing really fearful about it as the plowmen in poems VIII and IX of *A Green Bough* demonstrate. In fact, there is a joyous dimension in dying, one that Faulkner expresses as he contemplates the cyclic pattern of nature:

> And bonny earth and bonny sky
> And bonny'll be the rain
> And sun among the apple trees
> When I've long slept again.
>
> (*AGB*, XV)

In the Alderman Library version of "I will not weep for youth . . . ", the emphasis on "one" and "simple" suggests both a harmony and beauty in the process of being reconciled to eternity:

> I will not weep for youth in after years
> Nor will there haunt me, when I am old,
> The world's face in its springtime, blurred with tears
> That healed to dust harsh pageantries of gold.

242

Nor will dulled brain, nor ears at a sound scarce heard
Trouble old bones asleep from a sun to a sun
With a dream forgot, a scent on a senseless bird,
That now with earth and silence are brethren: one.

****

Death and I'll amicably wrangle, face to face,
Mouthing dried crumbs of pains and ecstacies,
Regarding without alarm cold seas of space—
Eternity is simple where sunlight is.

All that remains is the epitaph and Faulkner thought of that, too. In looking back over the world of nature, of green woods and blue hills, he is conscious of his place in the order of nature. Death does not blot out life, nor is life diminished by death:

If there be grief, then let it be but rain,
And this but silver grief for grieving's sake,
If these green woods be dreaming here to wake
Within my heart, if I should rouse again.

But I shall sleep, for where is any death
While in these blue hills slumbrous overhead
I'm rooted like a tree? Though I be dead
This earth that holds me fast will find me breath.

(*AGB*, XLIV)

There is a neatness to such a conclusion and a sense that there is not much more that can be said in poetry and verse; the cycle has been completed and the rest is silence.

Compared with the poetry of Robert Frost, Wallace Stevens, and William Carlos Williams, Faulkner's poetry is of a paler hue. While I have suggested that his poetry concerns the returning soldier, the quest and subsequent loss of a young woman, and the final acceptance of solitude and death, Faulkner's poetry is always more complex and more varied than any groupings we try to discover and establish. "The Lilacs," "Marriage," "Orpheus," "Did I know love once," and "Mississippi Hills: My Epitaph" are indeed fine poems and well worth our

243

critical attention. Though Faulkner felt pressure from Swinburne, Shakespeare, Keats, and Eliot, his better poems echo *A
Shropshire Lad* and give us a far deeper understanding of what
he means by enduring and prevailing. Housman taught him that
the lyrical and pastoral modes spring naturally from a sense of
place, and that one does not achieve an authentic poetic voice
until after one has explored and cultivated one's native ground.
The landscapes of Mallarmé and Verlaine, of Virgil and
Wordsworth will always be foreign; France, Italy, and England
are not the United States, nor the South. In addition, Faulkner's
visions, his interior and exterior rhythms and patterns of speech
were too expansive, needing too many qualifications; in face of
such expanding density, lyric and pastoral poetry can only limp,
or falter, or burst. To some extent, Faulkner's poetry served as a
rehearsal or paradigm for his fiction. Perhaps this is why he took
the final stanza of poem XXX of *A Green Bough*, entitled at
various times "November 11," "Gray the Day," and "Soldier" as
his epigraph for *Soldiers' Pay:*

> The hushèd plaint of wind in stricken trees
> Shivers the grass in path and lane
> And Grief and Time are tideless golden seas—
> Hush, hush. He's home again.

Faulkner did indeed land in luck the first time as pilot and poet.
With his second landing as pilot and novelist, I think he had
greater confidence and knew far better the land that was receiving him: "Hush, hush. He's home again."

"Truths More Intense than Knowledge": Notes on Faulkner and Creativity

DAVID MINTER

Behind this paper lie two assumptions that I want directly to acknowledge, particularly since my subject, "creativity," or more precisely, what Faulkner's fiction can tell us about the nature of "creativity," is fraught with difficulties—one being that creativity is hard enough to recognize and harder still to define, describe, or account for, and another being that Faulkner's fiction obviously does not constitute any direct address to what artistic creativity consists of or how we can propose to recognize and understand it. These difficulties, together with others implicit in them, in fact relate in a curious way to my assumptions—the first being that the emergence of any writer of Faulkner's stature, at any time and in any culture, is inherently and inexhaustibly problematic, which means that such emergence defies sufficient explanation even as it calls for such explanation; the second being that in Faulkner's particular case the problem of emergence is compounded in at least two important ways, one having to do with his relation to the flowering of Modernist literature that occurred in the years following the Great War, the other having to do with his relation to the flowering of Southern writing that began in the middle to late twenties and continued into the thirties. As the careers of John Crowe Ransom, Allen Tate, and Robert Penn Warren show, these two developments were clearly interrelated. Among the many things they share, one is their slightly unusual relationship to William Faulkner, who, though he looms large in both developments, was never very active in either.

It is important, of course, not to exaggerate Faulkner's isolation. His own statements on the subject—his declarations that he knew nothing about ideas, was made uncomfortable by literary talk, and was not a literary person—must be dealt with cautiously. Faulkner in fact found several ways of nourishing relations with the new literature that was emerging in Europe, England, and America as well as the South. Still, if we think of other central figures of his time—if we think of Eliot, Mann, Pound, and Joyce; if we think of Frost, Fitzgerald, and Hemingway: if we think of William Carlos Williams, who maintained an active professional career while also being a poet with wide literary acquaintances, or even Wallace Stevens, who like Williams maintained a professional career and unlike Williams limited his literary exchanges largely to correspondence; if we think of Ransom, Tate, and Warren—the contrast is clear, and with it the point: that Faulkner looms larger by far as a maker of Modernist literature and as an instance of the literary renascence of the South than as a participant in either development. Whether one chooses to stress the "European roots" of Faulkner's "narrative poetics," as Arthur Kinney does in tying Faulkner to Symbolist and Impressionist art, or decides to stress what Kinney sees as mere distraction, Faulkner's tie to "Southern regionalism, folktale, and myth," the problem of Faulkner's "genius" persists.[1] And it does so not only because, as I have noted, originality and creativity are always problematic but also because Faulkner's ties to the literary and historical contexts in

1. Arthur Kinney, *Faulkner's Narrative Poetics: Style As Vision* (Amherst: University of Massachusetts Press, 1978), 246–48.

which he wrote, and in relation to which we cannot help seeing his work, were tenuous.

Two contrary tendencies run through Faulkner's great work, and though they tend, on one side, to complicate any effort to understand, even provisionally, his emergence and his achievement as an artist, they provide, on the other, a way of getting at several crucial issues. To borrow metaphors more frequently encountered in political arenas, we may say that Faulkner's imagination was in one of its aspects "conservative" and that it was in another "radical." Although Faulkner's fiction is rarely sentimental or nostalgic about the past, it always engages the past and often engages it concertedly. Even if we insist on qualifying David Wyatt's recent assertion that "the burden of the past" is Faulkner's "true subject" and that he always keeps it "directly in view," we recognize the ground from which such an assertion springs. "Maybe nothing ever happens once and is finished," Quentin says in *Absalom, Absalom!*[2]

History enters Faulkner's fiction in at least two distinguishable modes and on at least four different levels. In one mode history comes as past experience, as lived time, as actual events and actual people; in another mode it comes as remembered experience, as recollected or recorded time, as shadows of events and shades of people. Although the second of these must always follow the first chronologically, and is therefore from one perspective derivative, it always lives, or comes to live, a life of its own in Faulkner's fiction; and though the first eludes even our best efforts to recapture it, although it never directly presents itself to us in Faulkner's fiction, it is always with us as shaping force. The great complexity of novels like *Absalom, Absalom!* and *Go Down, Moses* derives in part from the dual

---

2. David Wyatt, *Prodigal Sons: A Study in Authorship and Authority* (Baltimore and London: Johns Hopkins University Press, 1980), xvii and chap. 4. *Absalom, Absalom!* [1936], (New York: Random House, 1972), 261. All subsequent references to *Absalom, Absalom!* are to this edition; where consistent with clarity, they appear parenthetically in the text.

presence of history—its force as actual event, as actions and reactions within a long continuum of actions and reactions "all mixed up with" one another; and its force as recorded events, as letters and ledgers, or as remembered events, as "shade[s] who in life had acted and reacted."[3] In both of these modes, moreover, as event and as myth, as rippling pebble and as resonating word, history shapes four interrelated stories—the story of man, the story of region, the story of family, and the story of self. The various references to historical and mythical figures and events that dot Faulkner's fiction—they come primarily from Judaic-Christian traditions and Greek traditions, as well as more recent literature of the West, though Buddha, for example, also puts in appearances—are rarely esoteric or ornamental; they evoke other lives, other battles, other stories that add yet another level to the three levels on which Faulkner's stories always more or less overtly move—the regional, the familial, and the individual. In *Absalom, Absalom!* and *Go Down, Moses* these various levels are so tightly interlaced that one work becomes a medley of voices, the other a medley of episodes. But even in *The Sound and the Fury* and *As I Lay Dying*, where felt isolation haunts the individual voices we hear, we find that the story of an individual is always the story of a family, and the story of a family, always the story of a region.

The most striking feature of Faulkner's "conservative" imagination, or more neutrally perhaps, his conserving or preserving imagination, however, is not finally the double presence of history so much as the various activities that in one sense account for the presence of history and in another sense are justified by the force of history. Much of the action of Faulkner's novels—*Absalom, Absalom!* is again an obvious though not a singular example—consists of remembering that becomes talking and listening that in turn becomes remembering and talking. In this

3. *Absalom, Absalom!*, 127 and 280.

way old tales are evoked, preserved, transmitted, and with them *a sense* of what happened, *a sense* of what might have happened (this being the pang of fear), and *a sense* of what should have happened (this being the pang of hope). Built into recalling, recounting, listening, and repeating, however, are two commitments that tend further to *emphasize* the conservative bent of Faulkner's imagination, one being a commitment to, at times even a felt reverence for, one's données, one's givens, one's inherited stories, or more broadly, perhaps, one's traditions; the other being a commitment to the principle of repetition.

Faulkner's commitment to his region—its history and its traditions, its victories and defeats, its customs, folkways, and mores, its sights and sounds, or as Camus once put it, its dust and heat—requires little elaboration. One part of the complex desire that moved Faulkner to write was the desire to evoke both the lost world of the South's past and the fading world of the South's present. He wanted to take "the essence of his special world" and create an "evocative skeleton" of it.[4] To Ike McCaslin, Sam Fathers is an evocative figure and becomes an evocative voice. Through Sam's guidance, Ike becomes a participant in the rituals of Sam's world. Following Sam's voice, he comes so fully to share the sense of Sam's world that his own existence is revised.

> And as he talked about those old times and those dead and vanished men of another race from either that the boy knew, gradually to the boy those old times would cease to be old times and would become a part of the boy's present, not only as if they had happened yesterday but as if they were still happening, the men who walked through them actually walking in breath and air and casting an actual shadow

---

4. The quoted phrases are from a manuscript fragment in Beinecke Rare Book and Manuscript Library, Yale University. For a published version of it, see Joseph Blotner, "William Faulkner's Essay on the Composition of *Sartoris*," *Yale University Library Gazette*, 47 (January 1973), 121–24. See also David Minter, *William Faulkner: His Life and Work* (Baltimore: Johns Hopkins University Press, 1980), 77–78.

on the earth they had not quitted. And more: as if some of them had
not happened yet but would occur tomorrow, until at last it would
seem to the boy that he himself had not come into existence yet.[5]

Commenting on the difficulty of communication, Faulkner once
remarked, "But man keeps on trying endlessly . . . to make
contact with other human beings."[6] In serving the cause of evo-
cation, the human voice also serves the cause of contact, and in
Go Down, Moses it serves both causes in several different ways
simultaneoulsy. On one side, Faulkner insists on stressing the
provisional nature of Sam's achievement, by structuring the passage quoted above in terms of contrasts between past and present, actualities and simulations, and by repeating "as if" three
times; on the other, he stresses the force of Sam's achievement.
For Ike, both Sam's talking and "the ledgers in their scarred
cracked leather bindings," his other source of contact and evoca-
tion, become almost sacred, like some holy word presented
"upon some apocryphal Bench or even Altar . . . for a last
perusal and contemplation and refreshment" (261).

The depth of Faulkner's life-long loyalty to the memories,
scenes, and turns of speech he inherited is attested to, then,
both within the stories he wrote and through the stories he
wrote in the elaborate analogue they comprise. His works are
both historically grounded and culturally specific. The close relations, the remarkable reciprocities that exist between the
world he inherited, on one side, and the world he created, the
world he sang, and singing, made, on the other, are clear
enough in our predicament: that most of us cannot see Oxford,
changed and changing though it is, without remembering Jeffer-

5. *Go Down, Moses* (New York: Random House, 1942), 171. Subsequent references
to this novel are to this edition; where consistent with clarity, they appear parenthetically in the text.
6. Faulkner to Loïc Bouvard, in James B. Meriwether and Michael Millgate, eds.,
Lion in the Garden: Interviews with William Faulkner, 1926–1962 (New York: Random
House, 1968), 70–71.

son, or read about Yoknapatawpha without experiencing Lafayette.

Still, though the most obvious sign of Faulkner's commitment to his region resides in the rich texture of his fiction, another sign, perhaps more remarkable and certainly less expected, is to be found in the structure of his fiction. More than any other major writer of our time, with the possible exception of Ezra Pound in the *Cantos,* Faulkner plays with the recalling and recounting of old stories, and more than any other writer, including Pound, he plays with repeating what he has already evoked, recalled, or recounted. At first glance, Faulkner's use of repetition as a structural principle might seem to derive from and give expression to his conserving bent, for it is closely allied with ritual and sacrament and thus with affiliation and celebration.[7] But Faulkner's use of repetition soon brings us to the other side of his genius—the radical (or at least radically innovative) imagination that is perhaps implicit in my evoking Pound and the *Cantos* and is certainly implicit in my stressing Faulkner's preeminence in using repetition.

Faulkner has been chided at least as often for his prodigality and his transgressions as for his obsessions with the past and with fading traditions. At one time or another he has been accused of breaking almost every known rule, not only of grammar, syntax, and diction, but of decency, logic, and comprehensibility. In a recent review, Sean O'Faolain repeats old complaints: that Faulkner's fiction frequently fails to entertain or instruct us and occasionally fails to make even minimal sense to us.[8] Those more sympathetic or understanding have, of course, described the strangeness of Faulkner's fiction, and the variety of its strangeness, in very different terms. In this regard, Faulk-

---

7. See Eric Sundquist, *Home as Found: Authority and Genealogy in Nineteenth-Century American Literature* (Baltimore: Johns Hopkins University Press, 1979), 81–88.

8. Sean O'Faolain, "Hate, Greed, Lust and Doom," *London Review of Books* (April 16, 1981), 16.

ner's perhaps unfair assessment of Hemingway's caution—that Hemingway found "a method which he could control" and repeated it[9]—is instructive. For, though Faulkner's characters sometimes seem to repeat themselves endlessly, and though his works frequently overlap one another, he was clearly not the kind of writer who found a formula and kept repeating it. Indeed, it is of crucial significance that the very overlapping of his works—the ways in which they tend to extend and revise as well as repeat one another—should figure prominently in our sense of his originality.

A recent reassessment of the central thrust of modern fiction by Robbe-Grillet can help us, I think, to get a line on the radically adventuresome quality of Faulkner's imagination and on why it chose not simply to reconcile itself to repetition but to manifest itself in repetition. "What constitutes the novelist's strength," Robbe-Grillet remarks, "is precisely that he invents, that he invents without a model." In this formulation, Robbe-Grillet reiterates a point made several years ago by Ian Watt in *The Rise of the Novel* when he noted that of all literary modes the novel places the highest premium on novelty. By adding the phrase, "without a model," however, Robbe-Grillet wants to extend Watt's point, as we see clearly when he goes on to assert that "the remarkable thing about modern fiction is that it asserts" its inventiveness "quite deliberately, to such a degree that invention and imagination become at the limit, the very subject of the book."[10] In brief, we now have novels whose subject is, or becomes, their fictive status as novels just as we have poems ("The Idea of Order at Key West," for example) whose subject is their status as poems, or movies (8½ and *Blowup*, for example) whose subject is their status as movies. Certainly in Faulkner's

9. Frederick L. Gwynn and Joseph Blotner, *Faulkner in the University* (Charlottesville: University Press of Virginia, 1959), 143–44.

10. Alain Robbe-Grillet, "On Several Obsolete Notions," *For a New Novel: Essays on Fiction*, trans. Richard Howard (New York: Grove, 1965), 32.

fiction, deliberate engagement with invention and imagination takes many forms. Sooner or later, in one way or another, imaginative play touches the lives not only of young college students like Quentin and Shreve and old poetess laureates like Miss Rosa Coldfield but of a wide variety of men, women, and children. Mid-way through *Mosquitoes*, Dawson Fairchild suggests that words, despite "a kind of sterility," can under proper force be "brought into a happy conjunction" and so "produce something that lives."[11] Early in *Flags in the Dust*, we read about a story Virginia Du Pre, now an old woman, has told "many times," mixing memory and desire. Although the core of the story has remained as evocative skeleton, "the tale itself" has grown "richer and richer" as the years have passed and tellings have multiplied. A little earlier in *Flags in the Dust*, we see "old man Falls" bring the long dead "John Sartoris into the room with him," freeing Sartoris from time and endowing him with presence.[12] In *The Hamlet* tale-swapping is both the principal entertainment within Frenchman's Bend and our principal means of entering Frenchman's Bend. In *The Sound and the Fury* we watch three boys as they talk "about what they would do" if they had twenty-five dollars: talking all "at once, their voices insistent and contradictory and impatient," they make "of unreality a possibility, then a probability, then an incontrovertible fact, as people will when their desires become words."[13]

Behind Robbe-Grillet's assertions, however, lie two crucial assumptions—one allying imagination not so much with desire as with the unconscious, the other allying it with madness and against society—that tend, contrary to Faulkner's spreading it around, to remove imagination from the realm of the ordinary. In a book called *The Death of Tragedy*, George Steiner uses the formulations, "truths more intense than knowledge," to describe

11. *Mosquitoes* [1927] (New York: Liveright, 1955), 210.
12. *Flags in the Dust* (New York: Random House, 1973), 13–14, 5–6.
13. *The Sound and the Fury* [1929] (New York: Vintage Books, 1963), 145.

the forces that drive Greek heroes to their fates.[14] With this
formulation, Steiner links the action of tragedy to the irrational,
which is of course "the unconscious [that] poets have always
known—that aspect of human nature which, from Plato's dark
horse to [Delmore] Schwartz's 'heavy bear that goes with me,'
has been seen as our other [darker] self."[15] In much modern
thought, the irrational that Steiner sees shaping the action of
classical tragedy is also regarded as the source of creativity, a
notion which, like so many others, goes back to the beginning.
"No one without a touch of the muses' madness will enter the
Temple of Art," Socrates says. "One must harbor chaos within to
give birth to a dancing star," Nietzsche says. For the politicized
Arthur Koestler, art represents a triumph of the individual over
society, of internality over externality, of need and desire over
habit and requirement. For the conservative Wallace Stevens,
poetry is an unofficial view of being. For Roland Barthes, story-
telling is both "a way of searching for one's origin" and a way of
seeking mastery over one's origin—of "speaking one's conflicts
with the Law, entering into the dialectic of tenderness and
hatred." But for each of these varied writers, art is the self's
imposition of itself on its world, and for each of them art involves
ignoring boundaries and breaking rules.[16] Ordinary men accept
the fate of living official lives and harboring official thoughts, and
so forfeit the chance of losing anything worth losing or winning
anything worth winning, while the artist charts his solitary way
to heaven or plots the theft of fire.

In such a context, we might be inclined to think of Faulkner's
creativity solely in terms of his transgressions and innovations,
in which case we would view his conservative bent—his readi-

14. George Steiner, *The Death of Tragedy* (New York: Knopf, 1961), 7. See
Meredith Skura, *The Literary Use of the Psychoanalytic Process* (New Haven: Yale
University Press, 1981), 34–35.
15. Skura, *Literary Use of the Psychoanalytic Process*, 34–38.
16. See the discussion in Meredith Skura, "Creativity: Transgressing the Limits of
Consciousness," *Daedalus*, 109 (Spring 1980), 128–30.

ness frequently to follow traditions and actualities and his willingness to try occasionally even directly to copy them—as allied with the enemy: that bland official world of sanity and habit that poets are presumed to hate and are thought of as being put here to overcome. Mindful of certain facts, moreover—of Faulkner's description of *The Sound and the Fury*, his first great experimental novel, as a "dark story of madness and hatred"; of his use of "Twilight" as an early title of *The Sound and the Fury*, and of "Dark House" as an early title, first, of *Light in August* and, then, of *Absalom, Absalom!*; to say nothing of his repeated depictions of bizarre psychic derangements—it is easy enough to locate the shaping presence of the irrational in Faulkner's art. For Faulkner as for Foucault, fiction is what it is in part by virtue of "the madness which interrupts it," opening a void, creating a silence, provoking a breach that calls all things into question.[17] In fact, however, those of Faulkner's novels in which invention and imagination directly enter rather than merely infuse the action tell a far more complicated story than simply locating the source of imaginative creativity in the irrational and allying it with transgressions and innovations would suggest.

Absalom, Absalom! begins with a scene in which, by remembering-talking-listening, characters commence to gather old tales and talking from the air; it continues through scenes in which these tales are passed on, here condensed and there expanded; and it culminates in scenes in which Quentin and Shreve take "the rag-tag and bob-ends" given them and begin not only to piece them together once again, but to create out of them people and actions, conversations and motives (303). Still, there is a crucial sense in which we end not where but as we begin. For the most striking feature of Quentin's and Shreve's creative enterprise—in which regard it bears a striking resem-

17. Michel Foucault, *The Archaeology of Knowledge*, trans. A. M. Sheridan-Smith (New York: Pantheon Books, 1972), 76.

blance to Faulkner's own—is this: that it involves embracing rather than shunning models. In one sense, to be sure, Quentin and Shreve put their predecessors, Miss Rosa and Mr. Compson, General Compson and Thomas Sutpen, behind them. One part of Quentin and Shreve wants to assert their independence—for Quentin, independence of fathers and grandfathers and neighbors, for Shreve, at least, independence of an aunt of sorts, and for both independence of a prodigious progenitor. They are determined to avoid mere passive acceptance, just as they are determined to meet the needs they feel, needs that inspire them more fully to evoke figures—Henry Sutpen, Charles Bon, and Judith Sutpen—who are closer to them not only in age but presumably in desire. Probably it would not be too much to say that Shreve in milder ways and Quentin in many ways enjoy dispensing predecessors. Quentin feels, as a burden he carries within him, too many echoing "sonorous names" (12); which is to say that he feels more than he can say about the anxiety of influence, the anxiety of subordination, the sad fate of being an inheritor. Still, no one familiar with *Absalom, Absalom!* can describe Quentin and Shreve as creating without models. Just as the fragments that they inherit enter the fabric of the story they create, the very voices that presented those fragments, imposing them as burdens and bequeathing them as gifts, remain with Quentin and Shreve, as putative presences in the cold room in which they talk, and as echoes in every word they utter. Furthermore, though Quentin often feels restless, resentful, burdened, even imprisoned—"But why tell me about it?"; "Am I going to have to have to hear it all again?"; ". . . I am going to have to hear it all over again . . . I shall have to never listen to anything else but this again forever . . ." (12, 277)—still he never ceases to be moved by the fragments and voices that are his inheritance, never ceases to love as well as resist them, to follow as well as revise them. Finally, it is precisely because he retains his models, as sources and as examples, that he and

Shreve are able to create something that strikes us as both new
and appropriate. Quentin's need of Shreve, not only as audience
but as collaborator, derives from the fact that he is held too
closely by the past, is too little capable of independence. We can
see in Quentin, then, the dangers of loyalty. "There is a time in
every man's education," Emerson writes in "Self-Reliance,"
"when he arrives at the conviction . . . that imitation is suicide
. . ."[18] Quentin needs to move on, to feel more free in his play
than alone he can ever feel, this being a part of what the action of
The Sound and the Fury may surely be said to show. For a few
moments, though, Shreve's greater distance and detachment, or
put another way, his greater commitment to the principle and
possibilities of revision, of seeing and making things new, bal-
ances Quentin's greater proximity and involvement, his commitment to the principles of repetition and loyalty, and so enables
them together to enter the realm of creation. Even in that
realm, however, both living and imagining turn out to be a
matter of following, copying, and repeating as well as playing,
improvising, and inventing. Quentin and Shreve condense and
abbreviate, elaborate and amplify, substitute and rearrange. But
nothing they do involves them in betrayal or repudiation, nor
can anything they do be defined as creation *ab ovo*, which is why
we see what they create as both new and appropriate:[19] For
them the search for origins becomes the path to originality, just
as for their creator going back always became a new beginning.

If *The Sound and the Fury* and *Absalom, Absalom!* may be
said to assume repetition as a structural principle and then to
show not only that one telling necessarily leads to another but
also that no telling is ever the same as another, they may also be
said to show that repetition is in one sense inevitable and in
another impossible. Put another way, they show that repetition,

18. Ralph Waldo Emerson, "Self-Reliance," in Brooks Atkinson, ed., *The Selected
Writings of Ralph Waldo Emerson* (New York: Modern Library, 1950), 146.
19. Skura, "Creativity," 128.

itself permitted, invited, and required, always, simultaneously, permits, invites, and requires play. *The Sound and the Fury*, as Faulkner was fond of noting, is a single story several times told, which means that it is also a story in which crucial events are seen and reseen, and even, as readers know, read and reread. Yet, just as retelling turns one story into several stories, reseeing turns one event into several events. On neither of these levels, moreover, are we able to say that this is *the* story of which others are mere variations, or this *the* scene of which others are lesser versions. Tentative, provisional stories, partial and filtered scenes are all we have, and it is in the end their notable inadequacies that account for, that justify and inspire, Faulkner's remarkable proliferations. In *Absalom, Absalom!* we move from teller to teller, following a complex story through a web of remembering-talking-listening. Like *The Sound and the Fury, Absalom, Absalom!* is several times told, and like it, it is always provisionally told. Unlike *The Sound and the Fury*, which renders and enacts repetition, *Absalom, Absalom!* begins first to dramatize it and then overtly to explore its implications. *Play*, the term Shreve hits upon to describe the kind of creation to which he leads Quentin, takes us beyond repetition, beyond extension, elaboration, and rearrangement, to the creation of characters, scenes, and motives we would not otherwise have. But even as Shreve advocates and engages in "play," Faulkner discloses to us the work of the human imagination as both conservative and radical, as both derivative and creative.

Faulkner's insistence on holding to everything that had been given him and his insistence on going beyond it came from the same ground. His reponse both to the lost world of the Old South and the already fading world of the New South was shaped of course by familiar ambivalences—fascination and repugnance, love and hate; as was his version of what we now, rather euphemistically, refer to as "the family romance," with its fatal rivalries, especially between sons and fathers, and its forbidden affiliations, especially between sons and mothers or sisters. But there was in Faulkner another doubleness—almost certainly related, perhaps even as deep. Rooted in memory, this doubleness committed him, on one side, to loyalty and, on the other, to play; and it manifested itself in his sense that both of his worlds and all of his rivalries and romances permitted, even invited, perhaps even required, concerted play as well as abiding loyalty.

Listening was for Faulkner a crucial human act precisely because it was a way of (as well as a metaphor for) absorbing his world. Listening never stands alone in his world, however, its primary alliances being on one side with remembering and on the other with talking. At first glance talking, both as activity and as metaphor, not only for writing but for all expression raised to an active pitch, might seem to move in a single direction, away from the relative passivity of listening beyond repetition toward play and invention, just as remembering might seem to move in the opposite direction, toward passivity and regression, toward recalling and recounting the old. In fact, however, both activities are double in Faulkner's art. Talking serves the cause of moving latent needs into expressive form as well as the cause of making contact with other human beings, dead and alive, and the cause of evoking lost and fading worlds. Aside from being the repository of old stories and old experiences, however, memory is the home of that sense of the world that always seemed to Faulkner earliest and best. It takes Faulkner's characters back to a world that is more pre-conscious than conscious—a world where fantasies and perceptions, feelings and thoughts mingle. Here things are "absorbed . . . without the medium of speech somehow" simply by virtue of being;[20] here the familiar is always strange, the strange always familiar, and here all demarcations and distinctions tend to dissolve: things

20. *Absalom, Absalom!*, 212–13.

get done before they are planned and live after they are dead; things are even known before they are seen, remembered before they are recalled: "Memory believes before knowing remembers. Believes longer than recollects, longer than knowing even wonders."[21]

Like Faulkner himself, several of his characters are able (in some cases one might better say doomed) to keep in touch for virtually the whole of their lives not only with the scenes and experiences of their childhood but also with their child's sense of the world as simultaneously dark and beautiful, sinister and blessed. In Faulkner's art, therefore, memory always has as much to do with process as with content, and as much to do with form as with either. The complexity of Quentin's section of *The Sound and the Fury* owes a great deal to his willingness to let his fantasies revise his sense of his world, and his sense of his world revise his fantasies. Similarly, since talking not only shapes and reshapes, adding here and taking there, but always turns up memories as it goes, uncovering fears and expectations, conserving and preserving as well as revising, it too is double. Like memory it both serves and betrays the cause of loyalty, betrays and serves the cause of independence. In *Absalom, Absalom!* we must make do with conversations recalled, recounted, revised; in *The Sound and the Fury* we must make do with monologues. In *The Sound and the Fury* we move from voices that strike us as subjective and even private toward voices that seem to us more familiar, public, accessible. As *Absalom, Absalom!* unfolds, we hear more and more of the relatively detached voice of Shreve. But in neither work do reverberations between past and present slow; in neither do relations among remembering, listening, and talking simplify; and in neither does Faulkner take us toward a voice whose authority displaces the authority of

21. *Light in August* (New York: Harrison Smith, 1932), 111.

other voices. Both works withhold as well as bequeath, and one of the things they withhold is certitude.

In a sentence that bears clearly on several of Faulkner's greatest works, Eugene Goodheart describes "the fate of modernist literature" as "a 'decentering' of the imagination and intelligence—a deliberate loss of poise amidst the variety of experience, so that no point of view, no position is privileged."[22] Behind this statement, as behind Robbe-Grillet's sense that the imagination has been the implicit center of the novel and has recently become its explicit center, lies André Malraux's sense of our era as that "twilight of the absolute" where painting and sculpture, and by implication, literature, too, have become autotelic.[23] What both Robbe-Grillet and Goodheart sense, moreover, is that, having become their own ends, the arts were destined as well to become their own means: that they are now self-involved as well as autotelic. For Goodheart a self-centered literature means nothing so much as a "decentered" literature, a development that seems to him about as appealing as the sight of a decentered universe seemed to W. B. Yeats in "The Second Coming." Both "decentered" art and "deconstructive" criticism strike Goodheart as inseparable from the loss of "a secure conviction about different and opposed realms of values," and with it the loss of "the moral sense of contrast" that makes both irony and evaluation possible. As a result, he says, our art and criticism tend ambiguously to preserve everything and to make "everything the object of suspicion. Nothing disappears, but nothing is stable."[24]

The Sound and the Fury is probably as clear an example as we can find of the world Yeats foresaw, where "the best lack all

22. Eugene Goodheart, *The Failure of Criticism* (Cambridge: Harvard University Press, 1978), 2–5.
23. André Malraux, *The Twilight of the Absolute* [*The Psychology of Art*, Vol. III], trans. Stuart Gilbert (New York: Pantheon Books, 1950), 117–34.
24. Goodheart, 2–5.

conviction" and the "worst are full of passionate intensity."[25] If, moreover, we think of Dilsey as transcending the moral confusion of her world, we do so mindful that she is allied with an older, fading world, and mindful, too, that her life bespeaks resignation as well as commitment. The moral complexity of *The Sound and the Fury* is matched, then, by moral confusion within it, both of these being tied to its strikingly decentered form. Its art is not only an art of discontinuities, of breaks and interruptions, of jumps and shifts; it is also an art of shifting, proliferating perspectives that force us to see many things several times, yet never permit us directly to see Caddy, the novel's central figure. Other novels by Faulkner—*The Wild Palms* and *Go Down, Moses*, for example—may well strike us as clearer, more aggressive experiments in "decentered" art. Even the seemingly more conventional *Light in August* is a story of three distinct strands in which the female protagonist and the male protagonist essentially cannot meet. In *As I Lay Dying*, as tellers proliferate, the story continues to shift, due in part to proliferating perspectives, but due also to the virtual absence of the novel's center, Addie, whose only direct appearance is brief and posthumous. Like Addie, Thomas Sutpen is the shaping center of his world, the one it takes to make all the rest; like Addie, he is "somehow a thousand times more potent and alive" in death than in life (280); unlike her, he makes no direct appearance—the very words he utters come to us second or third or fourth hand. Even more than these novels, however, *The Sound and the Fury* is Faulkner's great experiment in "decentering." Of all Faulkner's heroines, Caddy is the most compelling, the most haunting, and the most elusive. She impinges on the consciousness of each of her brothers, in love, in obsession, in hatred; what they feel for her becomes the crucial sign of everything that they feel for their worlds—of all their needs, desires, and fears; and the cru-

25. See the discussion in Minter, *William Faulkner*, 98–99.

cial sign, too, of everything that we come to feel for them. But Faulkner practices an art of concealment as well as an art of disclosure in *The Sound and the Fury,* and where Caddy is concerned, he practices it more. In *The Sound and the Fury* he abandons familiar procedures to order to face radical variety and fluidity. Separations and losses account for most of what we see. Like each beginning, each ending is tentative, provisional. The first two versions of the story are replete with false starts and hesitations, with repetitions and regressions; but even the last two, though more familiar and accessible, provide only a sense of beginnings, a sense of harmonies, a sense of endings. Not even the last provides a point of view sufficiently privileged to overcome the loss of poise that the novel displays amidst the variety and confusion of experience.

The Sound and the Fury runs counter, then, to our efforts to insist on formal perfection.[26] As each section of the novel unfolds, it creates a new sense of synthesis and wholeness, but as each gives way to the next, and by implication, to the other three or four, depending on how we treat the Appendix, it calls into question the very possibility of the synthesis and wholeness that it labors to create. To compensate for this double activity, of creating and questioning formal wholeness, *The Sound and the Fury* calls attention both to its own elaborate experiments and to its own intricate processes. To a certain extent, the satisfactions of process replace the satisfactions of form. In fact, however, no proliferation of activities or processes can compensate for genuine attenuation of form; and unlike some recent critics, and perhaps a few recent artists, Faulkner never pretended that it could. Just as he held to the importance of repetition as well as play, held even to the interplay in which each of these becomes a version of the other, he also held both to the possibility of

26. See Frank Kermode, "The Structure of Fiction," *Modern Language Notes,* 84 (1969), 891–95.

achieving formal perfection and to the sufficiency of achieving mere approximations of it, held even to that interplay in which each of these becomes a reminder of the other. His great novels are provisional and tentative in the extreme; they withhold certitude and forego closure; but, they do not take us into a world where "the moral sense of contrast" disappears, and with it the possibility of evaluation and meaning.[27] We move slowly in them, knowing that the worlds we explore lie before us without known origins, known boundaries, or known ends; knowing too that language as medium is too responsive to be responsible, that its irreducible figurativeness matches in more ways than one the radical fluidity of its world. Yet we move, caught as it were between Judith Sutpen's sense that "it cant matter" and her balancing sense that "it must matter" (127), knowing that all judgments and points of view, though partial and provisional, are not equally valuable or equally valid. Although Faulkner's art always leaves some things out and always leaves everything unfinished, and so yields no "explanatory systems," it does yield stories that suffice by being "probably true enough," a part of their sufficiency being that they enable us to make "meaningful assertions" about them.[28]

Radical articulation, Roland Barthes remarks, forces us to see "not man endowed with meanings, but man fabricating meanings."[29] To this as to Robbe-Grillet's stress on creation without models, Faulkner's art poses big problems, not by running contrary but by forcing revisions. Creativity appears in Faulkner's works neither in the repetitions we associate primarily with Quentin nor in the play we associate primarily with Shreve but in the happy conjunction of the two. And it manifests itself in the creation of meaning that is human in the fullest sense of that

27. Goodheart, 3.
28. Wesley Morris, *Friday's Footprint: Structuralism and the Articulated Text* (Columbus: Ohio State University Press, 1979), 61–62, 3.
29. Quoted in *ibid.*, 50.

term: it is created by man out of his own traditions to meet his own needs; and however tentative it may be, it represents man's highest achievement precisely because it brings the only tools he has, remembering and talking, to bear on the only problems that fully engage him, not only his origin and his destiny but his heart in conflict with itself.[30]

William Faulkner's strength as an artist lay, then, as William Shakespeare's had, in his willingness to follow models, believing that he could go beyond them. And his wisdom lay, deeper than knowledge, in sensing that a writer not endowed at least with tentative, provisional meanings had no chance of fabricating them. This wisdom he shared not only with Eliot, Pound, and Joyce but with the primary makers of the Southern Renaissance. As much as any writer of his time, he found his imaginative task in internal division; in addition he found the courage to entertain and explore rather than resolve that division. It was *in* going back and forth that he discovered his art and *by* going back and forth that he made it. There are times, to be sure, when he seems to commit himself wholeheartedly in one direction or the other—here to copying, following, and repeating, there to strange visionary or revisionary flights; here to form and meaning as endowed or given, there to form and meaning as arbitrary or impossible, as sheer fabrication or mere illusion. But in his great art, he maintains his poise, forcing the various pressures he felt to meet and measure one another, and so gives us works that bring the problem of creation and the problem of meaning into conjunction, under the aspect of things inherited and bequeathed and under the aspect of things fabricated and invented.

30. See Robert Penn Warren, Introduction, Joseph Conrad, *Nostromo* (New York: Modern Library, 1951), xxii–xxiii.

Faulkner's
Ultimate Values

CLEANTH BROOKS

In the last twenty-five years I have often been asked: what did Faulkner really believe about man and his relation to the universe in which he finds himself? What were Faulkner's ultimate values? What did he think of Christianity? These are perfectly proper questions and I have often asked them of myself. But they are not easy to answer—at least if a rather specific answer is demanded. What makes the problem more difficult is that the answers that Faulkner gave, during the last thirty-odd years of his life, to the various people who interviewed him are usually vague, highly subjective, and frequently contradict each other. In preparing this lecture, I have reviewed every scrap of such evidence that I could find. This morning there just isn't time for me to discuss each of Faulkner's various comments on the subject, I shall have to ask you to bear with my own generalizations and interpretations of the pronouncements that Faulkner has, at various times, left us.

Thus, Faulkner said that he believed in God but had some problems with accepting Christianity. Yet at another time he will remark that Christianity provides the supreme example of compassion and self-sacrifice—two virtues that Faulkner held in the highest esteem. Furthermore, at various times Faulkner did call himself a Christian, though he wanted to define the word in his own terms. The best book that I know on this general subject

266

is by John Hunt. It is entitled *William Faulkner: Art in Theological Tension*. Hunt's conclusion is that though Faulkner veered toward stoicism, he remained, on the whole, rather close to the Christian revelation. I cheerfully accept this estimate. Though Hunt is a layman, he has had solid theological training and he has a detailed acquaintance with Faulkner's work. Faulkner's stoicism comes out rather clearly in his stress on endurance. More than one of the characters in his fiction discovers that a man sometimes finds that he can endure almost anything, and Faulkner compels some of his characters to endure a great deal. Think, for instance, of the Tall Convict adrift on the raging flood waters of the Mississippi. The stoic bias in Faulkner comes out also in his little concern for God's grace—either as a concept or as an experience that is vouchsafed to any of his fictional characters. But Faulkner's own early nurture in Christianity was indeed powerful, and I agree with Hunt in finding a great deal of residual Christianity in his writings—even though that Christianity is rarely, if ever, presented in precise theological terms.

Yet since Faulkner was not versed in theology, and since very few of us are—I certainly make no such pretence for myself—I think that my best method of procedure is to make no further references to what Faulkner at one time or another declared to be his beliefs, but to try to discover his beliefs as they are presented, in dramatic terms, in his fiction. After all, his great accomplishment was in his fiction. There we will find him speaking most truthfully—and least ambiguously—about the values that make meaningful the lives of men and women.

One of Faulkner's most interesting quasi-theological discussions occurs in *Go Down, Moses*.[1] Isaac McCaslin is engaged in a debate with his elder cousin, McCaslin Edmonds. Their general topic is the nature of man and mankind's characteristic virtues and vices. Isaac asserts that God "had seen in individual cases

1. Quotations from Faulkner's novels are from the first editions.

(that men) were capable of anything any height or depth" (282). And surely young Isaac is correct. Man can rise to heights far above those of any of his fellow creatures, but then again he can also sink to depths below those of any beast. That is to say, unless a human being is better than a mere animal, he or she is bound to be worse than any animal.

Isaac goes on to say that God knew all about men's capacities for both good and evil because He "had created them and knew them capable of all things because He had shaped them out of the primal Absolute which contained all . . ." (292). This version is not precisely the orthodox Christian account of a good creation in complete harmony with its maker God, a relation to the Creator which Man broke through his own perverse will. Nevertheless, Faulkner is careful to shy away from any notion that man is naturally good, and he avoids the Gnostic heresy which blames the Creator of the universe for placing mankind in an evil world. In sum, Faulkner insists on man's responsibility for his actions. Elsewhere he will stress that point in saying that man must strive to be just a little better than one would normally expect him to be. In short, man's better nature must strive against his worse, and Faulkner clearly believes that there is a better and a worse. It is not sufficient that man should simply do what comes naturally, for man is not naturally good. He is created with a potentiality for good, but he must achieve it—and Faulkner seems to imply that it must be largely through his own efforts.

Later still, Faulkner was to say in his Nobel Prize speech that the great theme of literature is that "of the human heart in conflict with itself." Faulkner's characteristic saints and heroes are those who come out of this conflict as victors over themselves.

Now that I have completed this perhaps over-lengthy preamble, let me ask what are the virtues that Faulkner stresses in his fiction? One can find a convenient, though not necessarily exhaustive, list of them in *Go Down, Moses*. I have already mentioned the long debate between Isaac and his elder cousin. There McCaslin Edmonds tries to define truth for the younger man. Truth—by which of course, he means the truth that governs or ought to govern all human actions—"Truth covers all things that touch the heart—honor and pride and pity and justice and courage and love" (297). All the virtues listed come in for great emphasis in Faulkner's fiction, a fact that any reader of his novels can easily corroborate. In what is to follow I mean to give some examples and illustrations from specific passages of the stories and novels. These will tell you much more precisely than any abstract definitions can what Faulkner meant by pride or honor.

Let me begin, then, with courage. For Faulkner, it was apparently the prime virtue. It is indeed a basic, though not necessarily the highest, virtue, for courage undergirds all the other virtues. Let me illustrate. In the New Testament we are told that, when someone smites you on the cheek, you should turn the other cheek. Yet if you turn the other cheek simply because you are afraid not to, then you have exercised no virtue at all— mere cowardice. To turn the other cheek is only virtuous if you do it not out of fear but, although you have the courage to strike back, because you refuse to do so.

One of the clearest examples of courage in Faulkner's novels occurs in *Go Down, Moses*. Isaac McCaslin is being taught the lore of the wilderness under the tutelage of Sam Fathers, an old man who is part white, part black, and part Indian. Sam has taught Isaac how to find and follow the paw prints of Old Ben, an enormous bear that the hunters, year after year, have failed to bring to bay. On one of their encounters with Old Ben, Isaac has with him a little fyce dog—as most of you know a fyce is a little yappy mongrel terrier—feisty by name and feisty by nature. The fyce, not much "bigger than a rat" (211), rushes at the bear, and the boy Isaac has to rush after it and pick it up in the very shadow of Old Ben to save it from instant annihilation. But Old Ben exhibits his own sense of chivalry by not attacking either the dog or the boy. He simple slips back into the wilderness. After this incident, Sam addresses the little dog as he strokes it: "You's almost the one we wants. . . . You just aint big enough. We aint got that one yet. He will need to be a little bigger than smart, and a little braver than either" (212). Bravery is bravery, however, and is not to be measured by one's size or strength. Indeed, the little fyce's size proves his bravery to be proportionally all the greater.

On another occasion, one of the young hounds chasing Old Ben dashes in so close to the bear as to have her head raked by the great animal's claws. Later, Sam treats her wounds and muses that the young hound took the risk because she just had to do so in order to prove that she was worthy of being called a hunting dog. Thus, in Faulkner, courage is often, and indeed usually, involved with pride. A man and, as Sam imagines it, even a dog, fears the danger less than he fears to be thought a coward. One's pride in being a man or a dog is at stake.

I have used animals to illustrate Faulkner's belief in the importance of courage, for Sam Fathers is obviously projecting human qualities onto the animals he loves. But, of course, Faulkner sees moral courage as something far more important than mere animal courage. I shall provide some examples a little later, but I shall postpone them until I have first examined instances of honor and pride.

Honor is a quality that in our day is often misunderstood and even actually frowned upon. The consequence is that many readers simply do not know what Faulkner is talking about when he refers to honor. That, at least, has been my experience in teaching Faulkner to college students. This is my excuse for taking time here for a definition and clarification of the term. Faulkner, if I understand him, means by honor something very close to self-respect—an unwillingness to stoop to certain ac-

270

tions that a man believes are degrading and contemptible. An honorable man will not lie, for instance, even if his lie could pass undetected or if a lie would gain him an advantage. Moreover, in Faulkner's world, an honorable man will not allow himself to be treated in a fashion that he regards as undermining due respect for himself. Thus, he will not allow himself to be called a liar or accused of some shameful action.

When we demand a certain treatment from others, we, of course, begin to touch upon the more old-fashioned masculine code of honor which insists that one's own self-respect demands that other men accord one a corresponding respect. Thus, a man would not let another accuse him of ungentlemanly conduct, let alone of an actual crime, and if such insults were offered, he would insist on a formal apology, or if that were not forthcoming, on meeting his traducer on the field of honor. With this last situation, we come to the code duello, which lasted longer in the South than elsewhere in the nation. But in the earlier decades, we must remember, it was general in the country at large. For example, one of our founding fathers, Alexander Hamilton, was killed in a duel in New York, and one of our early presidents, Andrew Jackson, had killed his man in a duel.

A remnant of this older and more violent code makes its appearance in Faulkner's fiction. A little later I will indicate how Faulkner deals with it, but let me first comment on his treatment of the simpler cases: those in which one's own self-respect will not allow him to do certain things, even to an enemy. A telling illustration occurs in Faulkner's magnificent novel, *Light in August*. Byron Bunch is a homely and awkward little man, quite lacking in the social graces, who earns his living working with his hands at the local planing mill. Nevertheless, Byron is a man of honor as well as of compassion. He takes pity on Lena Grove, a young woman who arrives at the mill, heavily pregnant, who tells him that she is looking for her husband, though it soon becomes apparent that the girl is not married to the scamp who has fathered her child. Byron Bunch at once proceeds to protect her and befriend her, and sees her through her accouchement. He even sees to it that the father of the newborn child is brought by a deputy sheriff to the cabin in which Lena is staying. But Brown, the wretched man in question, proves to be utterly irresponsible and completely lacking in a sense of honor. After making a few lame and awkward apologies to Lena, he notices that a window at the back of the room is open; and, realizing that the deputy sheriff will not be able to see him if he climbs out this back window, he suddenly jumps out and bolts.

Byron has been hiding in some bushes toward the back of the house, for he means to see his mission through to the end. When he sees Lena's paramour leap out the window and flee the scene, Byron prepares to intercept him. This is what he says to himself: " 'You're bigger than me. . . . But I dont care. You've had every other advantage of me. And I dont care about that neither. You've done throwed away twice inside of nine months what I aint had in thirtyfive years. And now I'm going to get the hell beat out of me and I dont care about that, neither' " (415). Byron, who scorns to take even this contemptible man by surprise, confronts him directly, and true to his own prediction, does have the hell beaten out of him. But after Brown has left him on the ground and has continued in his flight away from his responsibilities to Lena and his child, Byron lies "bleeding and quiet" but with the satisfaction that he has done what every right-minded man would feel that he had to do.

One of Faulkner's most powerful illustrations of bravery—and of very special moral as well as sheer physical bravery—is to be found in the last episode of his novel *The Unvanquished*. This episode also constitutes Faulkner's most brilliant account of what he calls in his Nobel Prize speech the proper subject matter for great literature: the "problems of the human heart in conflict with itself." Here the conflict is in the heart of young Bayard Sartoris. Bayard learns that his father has just been shot

272

down by a former business partner, but now bitter enemy, Ben Redmond. Bayard knows that the whole community expects him to call Redmond to account. At this time the code of reprisal and vengeance was still powerful in the South and nowhere more powerful than in the relatively new country of North Mississippi. The time of the story is the mid-1870s. The region has not really recovered from the effects of the Civil War and the Reconstruction Era. Nearly every person close to Bayard certainly expects him to avenge his father: the members of the Colonel's old Civil War troop led by George Wyatt; Bayard's young stepmother; Ringo, the young black man who had been Bayard's childhood companion; and even the kindly old Professor Wilkins, under whose tutelage Bayard has been reading law.

But Bayard has his qualms against killing. He takes very seriously the sixth Commandment: "Thous shalt do no murder." Though he loved his father, he cannot hide from himself that his father has become a ruthless man, bemused with his dream of creating a little Sartoris empire. Even George Wyatt admits that the Colonel had pushed Redmond too hard. Most of all, Bayard has already once before killed a man. During the closing days of the war, in which there was no law to which one could appeal, Bayard and Ringo, boys of sixteen, had hunted down the bushwhacker who had coldbloodedly killed Bayard's grandmother. The effect of this experience on the boy has evidently been traumatic, for when Ringo brings Bayard news that the Colonel has been shot down, Bayard has apparently already resolved never to kill again. Yet he respects the community's standards. He does not want to be thought of as a coward.

Jenny Du Pre, Bayard's aunt, begs him not to go into town the next morning, but hers is the only sane and moderate voice that he hears during this evening. She begs her nephew not to insist on living up to the expectations of his father's old cavalry troop or to heed the pleas of his stepmother, Drusilla, whom she calls a "poor hysterical young woman" (276). Aunt Jenny knows that

273

he is no coward. Bayard, however, tells her that he must confront Redmond. "You see," he tells her, "I want to be well
thought of" (280). And Aunt Jenny evidently understands that as
a man he must do what his honor dictates. So next morning
Bayard rides into town and finds George Wyatt and some of the
other members of his father's old Civil War cavalry troop already
standing by the stairs that lead up to Redmond's law office.
Bayard mounts the stairs and enters Redmond's office. He faces
there a man freshly shaven and carefully dressed, a man who is
"holding a pistol flat on the desk before him, loose beneath his
hand" (286). As Bayard walks steadily toward Redmond, Redmond raises the pistol, but Bayard can see that it is pointed away
from him. Redmond fires twice. He then walks out of the office,
down the stairs, and strides unmolested right through the clump
of Wyatt's companions. Evidently he accomplishes it by sheer
force of presence and bearing. He goes straight on to the railroad station and leaves town by the train that has just pulled in.
He is never seen in Jefferson again.

As for Bayard, he sits down in the office, stunned by the turn
of events and emotionally drained until Wyatt and his companions enter. Wyatt says to him: "'My God!'. . . You took the pistol
away from him and then missed him *twice?* Then he answered
himself—that same rapport for violence which Drusilla had and
which in George's case was actual character judgment. 'No;
wait. You walked in here without even a pocket knife and let
him miss you twice. My God in heaven.' He turned, shouting:
'Get to hell out of here! You, White, ride out to Sartoris and tell
his folks it's all over and he's all right. Ride!'" (288).

Even the implacable George Wyatt is won over by Bayard's act,
and Drusilla herself comes to acknowledge Bayard's courage, for
later, much later, when he enters his bedroom back home, Bayard smells the odor of verbena and finds that Drusilla has left a
sprig of verbena on his pillow. It is Drusilla's way of saying "You

274

were brave," for she always asserted that verbena was the only flower the odor of which could be smelled above the smell of horses. Horses, for Drusilla, were always the steeds of the warrior.

My students often say to me that Bayard repudiated the code of his forebears, and I have to correct them by saying that he does not repudiate but rather transcends the code: that is, he takes all the risks that the code of honor demands even though he refuses such protection as firing at his opponent might give him.

If Bayard's action exemplifies the way in which bravery and honor were tied together in Faulkner's mind, I ask you to note that Bayard's opponent also exemplifies the union of honor and bravery and to the same degree. He has satisfied the claims of honor by giving Bayard full opportunity to execute vengeance on him. If Redmond felt justified in killing Colonel Sartoris, he had evidently resolved not to kill the son. His careful attention to his appearance on the crucial morning makes it plain that he never expected to leave his office alive. Neither, of course, had Bayard. Indeed, we see in the incident the meeting of *two* brave and honorable men.

I have spent a good deal of time in developing the theme of bravery and honor, but of course these were not the only, or even the chief values that Faulkner cherished. Pity and love probably stand even higher on his list.

Byron Bunch's compassion for Lena Grove and his concern for her happiness, I have already mentioned. Another Faulkner character of the yeoman white class, V. K. Ratliff, the itinerant sewing-machine agent of Faulkner's *The Hamlet,* is also a man of honor and of compassion. The plight of the idiot Ike Snopes moves him to sympathy and he gives a sum of money to make life somewhat happier for him. A number of Faulkner's women, black as well as white, exemplify pity and maternal concern, and not just for their own children. One of the most signal instances of devoted love and a deeper compassion is to be found in Faulkner's masterpiece, the novel *Absalom, Absalom!*

Judith Sutpen is the daughter of a powerful and ruthless man. By his own efforts, her father acquires a hundred square miles of land and builds on it an enormous house, which he means to make a kind of baronial hall. Judith is brought up with all the protective care that one would expect to be given to a girl who is destined to be the chatelaine of a great estate. Soon, however, she meets hardship and even disaster. The handsome young man from New Orleans with whom, after a brief courtship, she had fallen in love, is shot to death just outside the gates of the Sutpen estate, and shot down by Judith's own brother. The two young men had appeared to be the closest of friends and they had served together throughout the four years of the Civil War. Yet now her brother Henry had killed his best friend, Charles Bon, and had done so just before his intended marriage to Judith. Henry does not explain to his sister; he simply flees the country.

A little later, Colonel Sutpen, Judith's father, returns from the war to a ruined plantation. Gone now is any pretense to baronial splendor. Sutpen ekes out a living by setting up a little country general store and Judith is the dutiful daughter who cares for her father until his death. One would not have thought the pair were ever close to each other, but Judith has inherited much of her father's iron will and resolution. She has known that her father had opposed her marriage to Bon, though he has never given her a reason. But her love for Bon has not wavered, and now that Bon is dead, she continues to hold him dear, even after discovering on Bon's dead body a picture of another woman enclosed in the locket that she had supposed contained her own picture.

Later, Judith seeks out Bon's former mistress. She finally locates her in New Orleans and invites her to visit Sutpen's

Hundred so that she may see Bon's grave. The woman, a beautiful creature whom Bon had met at the Quadroon Ballroom in New Orleans, does come, and brings with her the child that Bon had fathered. It is a generous act. One might have expected Judith to feel jealousy and a sense of betrayal, for Bon had paid his court to her without ever hinting that he had ties with another woman who had borne him a son.

A still more generous act is to follow. Judith, later on, sensing somehow that something is amiss, sends her mulatto half-sister, Clytie, to New Orleans to bring back with her Bon's little son, for the mother has indeed recently died. Clytie and Judith undertake to rear the child. On the ruined plantation the two women manage to eke out only a bare living. Judith takes on the heaviest farm work and holds steady the handles of the plow as she plods behind the mule that pulls it.

As he grows up, Bon's son comes to suspect that he is of mixed blood. In his anguish, he repudiates the whole white community and takes as his wife the darkest-hued woman he can find. Judith begs him to go away—to go North, where no one can know his background, where he can make a new life of his own. If he will only do this, Judith promises to look after his wife and son. Though in matters of caste and race Judith is the daughter of her own time and comes quite naturally by its views of the yawning chasm between the black and the white races, she is willing to abrogate the color line.

Judith, however, is unable to persuade the young man to go North and find a new life. Shortly thereafter, he contracts yellow fever. Judith nurses him until his death and then herself succumbs. Judith, as Faulkner conceives her, is a heroic woman—compassionate, loving, possessing a fidelity that triumphs over what would seem to most women a betrayal by her lover. But Judith also powerfully exemplifies another virtue that stands high on Faulkner's list of virtues—the ability to endure all of Fate's buffettings.

In this matter of endurance, we must place beside Judith the black woman Dilsey, of *The Sound and the Fury*. Dilsey is the faithful servant in the Compson household who tries to hold together that crumbling family. It was for Dilsey and her kind that Faulkner penned the resonant epitaph: "They endured" (427). Judith Sutpen and her mulatto half-sister Clytie are also worthy of the same salute to their steadfastness.

Thus far I have talked about the virtues that Faulkner so often stresses in the characters that inhabit his fiction. Yet it occurs to me that something is to be gained by mentioning the negative cases—Faulkner's villains as well as his heroes and heroines. With regard to a writer's spiritual values, one may learn almost as much from what the writer despises as from what he celebrates.

Faulkner has provided us with a God's plenty—or rather, I should say, a devil's plenty—of villains from which to choose. In fact, most of Faulkner's characters have flaws. There are among them no plaster saints. Contrariwise, some of his worst offenders have a few noble traits. Judith Sutpen's father provides a notable example of such a mixture: though he is a hard, ruthless, and self-centered man, he is also courageous and apparently able to endure anything. There are, however, a couple of Faulknerian characters of almost unmitigated depravity: Jason Compson and Flem Snopes. Jason is the wicked presence of *The Sound and the Fury*. One senses that he positively enjoys hurting other people. He is an almost congenital liar; he steals money from his sister; he delights in torturing his young niece who suffers the fate of being brought up in the poisonous atmosphere of the Compson household. Jason's worst trait is this streak of sadism.

Yet, though Jason is perhaps Faulkner's most detestable and sadistic character, I choose to award first place in sheer meanness to Flem Snopes, for Flem, to my mind, represents almost the nadir of human virtue—an abstract zero of the human spirit. Therefore, though Flem seems to be more properly an instance of negativity than of positive malignity, he may best suit my purpose here—which, in brief, is simply to mark the bottom line on Faulkner's scale of human virtues. Thus, Flem comes close to being simply inhuman; yet, just because he is, he can help us see more clearly Faulkner's conception of the human enterprise.

Flem is a sharecropper's son who means to rise from rags to riches. From the very beginning, his only goal is to acquire financial power. Nothing can cause him to deviate. His whole personality streamlines him for efficient movement toward that goal. Flem is a man almost without appetites. He does not drink or smoke, and he is sexually impotent. The ordinary temptations of the senses have no hold on him—neither vices nor innocent pleasures. If Flem ever enjoys a good dinner or a pleasant ride in the country, that fact is never made apparent. Thus, there is nothing to distract him from his pursuit of wealth.

Flem does get married, having been offered a sufficient consideration to marry a wealthy man's daughter who has become pregnant by another man. His marriage is thus simply another matter of business. Since Flem seems to lack all human sympathies, compassion does not deter him from making money wherever the opportunity offers. No widow is too poor, no orphan too helpless, to escape him. Nor are the takings ever too small: every ill-got penny counts. Flem's money-making proclivities are his whole life: that is what the good life means to him—gathering in the dollars or even just the quarters and dimes.

V. K. Ratliff, who knows Flem well and who is a first-rate raconteur in the folk idiom, contrives a very amusing narrative in which he treats Flem as a kind of Faustus, a man who has sold his soul to the Devil in return for his almost magical skill in turning a pretty penny. But as Ratliff sees it, Flem is too shrewd a businessman to have *sold* his soul. He has simply borrowed on it, leaving his soul for security in the Devil's safety-deposit box. Finally, Flem goes down to the infernal regions to pay off the loan and recover his security—that is, his soul. When the soul cannot be immediately produced, one of the junior executives of hell tries to put him off, but Flem stands on his legal rights and demands to have an interview with one of the head devils. This is what ensues—as Ratliff tells it, the junior devils are here speaking to the Prince of Hell:

> "He says a bargain is a bargain. That he swapped in good faith and honor, and now he has come to redeem it, like the law says. And we cant find it," they says. "We done looked everywhere. It wasn't no big one to begin with nohow, and we was specially careful in handling it. We sealed it up in a asbestos matchbox and put the box in a separate compartment to itself. But when we opened the compartment, it was gone. The matchbox was there and the seal wasn't broke. But there wasn't nothing in the matchbox but a little kind of dried-up smear under one edge. And now he has come to redeem it. But how can we redeem him into eternal torment without his soul?"
>
> "Damn it," the Prince hollers. "Give him one of the extra ones. Aint there souls turning up here every day, banging at the door and raising all kinds of hell to get in here, even bringing letters from Congressmen, that we never even heard of? Give him one of them."
>
> "We tried that," they says. He wont do it. He says he dont want no more and no less than his legal interest according to what the banking and the civil laws states in black and white is hisn. He says he has come prepared to meet his bargain and signature, and he sholy expects you of all folks to meet yourn."
>
> "Tell him he can go then. Tell him he had the wrong address. That there aint nothing on the books here against him. Tell him his note was lost—if there ever was one. Tell him we had a flood, even a freeze." (149–50)

Time does not permit me to quote in its entirety the rest of Flem's interview with the Prince of Hell. It will have to suffice to say that Flem's logic and cold-blooded legality overpower Satan himself, and the episode ends with Flem triumphant, seated on the very throne of hell. As Ratcliff imagines the final scene, the Prince is leaning forward:

> And now he feels that ere hot floor under his knees and he can feel

his-self grabbing and hauling at his throat to get the words out like he was digging potatoes outen hard ground. "Who are you?" he says, choking and gasping and his eyes a-popping up at him setting there with that straw suitcase on the throne among the bright, crown-shaped flames. "Take Paradise!" the Prince screams. "Take it! take it!" And the wind roars up and the dark roars down and the Prince scrabbling across the floor, clawing and scrabbling at that locked door, screaming . . . (153)

This story seems to me very funny. But it is serious too. Ratliff (and through him, Faulkner) has found an elaborate way of saying that Flem has no soul, and in saying so, to indicate that s soulless person like Flem, lacking pity, compassion, concern for others, and all the other ties that link one with the brotherhood of man, is not human at all—a thing as conscienceless as a natural force such as an earthquake or a freezing north wind. In a sense, even vicious Jason Compson, who is worse than Flem, is more nearly human, for he at least feels some things, if they are only jealousy, anger, and hate.

Faulkner's conception of the human being is thus right in the mainstream of the great classical-Judaic-Christian tradition. To become incapable of love and pity is to read oneself right out of the human race.

Contributors

ALEXANDER BLACKBURN founded *Writers Forum* and has edited seven volumes of that literary annual. Among his publications are *The Myth of the Picaro: Continuity and Transformation of the Picaresque Novel, 1554–1954* and a novel, *The Cold War of Kitty Pentecost*. He is Associate Professor of English and Director of Creative Writing at the University of Colorado at Colorado Springs.

CLEANTH BROOKS is co-author with Robert Penn Warren of the epoch-making *Understanding Poetry* and its successors *Understanding Fiction* and *Modern Rhetoric*. He is the author of other celebrated works, including *Modern Poetry and the Tradition, The Well-Wrought Urn, William Faulkner: The Yoknapatawpha Country*, and *William Faulkner: Toward Yoknapatawpha and Beyond*. A founding editor of *The Southern Review* at Louisiana State University and Gray Professor of Rhetoric Emeritus at Yale University, he has taught and lectured at colleges and universities in America and abroad.

RICHARD H. KING, who received a master's degree in American Studies from Yale University and a Ph.D. degree in history from the University of Virginia, is Professor of Philosophy at the University of the District of Columbia. His teaching interests are philosophy and methods of history, American thought and culture, and the history and literature of the South. Among his publications are *The Party of Eros: Radical Social Thought and the Realm of Freedom* and *A Southern Renaissance: The Cul-*

tural Awakening of the American South, 1930–1955. The latter was described in *The New Republic* as "a book that henceforth every serious student of southern literature and southern history will have to take into account."

DAVID MINTER, Professor of English at Emory University and Dean of Emory College, is the author of *William Faulkner: His Life and Work.* This literary biography, published by The Johns Hopkins University Press in 1980, explores "the reciprocities between Faulkner's great art and his flawed life." Professor Minter has also published *Twentieth-Century Interpretations of "Light in August," The Interpreted Design as a Structural Principle in American Prose,* and a number of essays on English and American literature.

LOUIS D. RUBIN, JR., has taught at Johns Hopkins, Louisiana State University, the University of California at Santa Barbara, Harvard, and Hollins College. Among his numerous publications are *Thomas Wolfe: The Weather of His Youth, The Curious Death of the Novel, The Faraway Country: Writers of the Modern South, William Elliott Shoots a Bear: Essays on the Southern Literary Imagination,* and two novels, *The Golden Weather* and *Surfaces of a Diamond.* He is University Distinguished Professor of English at the University of North Carolina at Chapel Hill.

PATRICK SAMWAY, S.J., received a Ph.L. in philosophy, an M.Div. in theology, and a Ph.D. in English. In 1975–76 he was a Fulbright Lecturer at the University of Nantes, and again in 1979–80 at the University of Paris where he co-sponsored the First International Colloquium on Faulkner. In February 1980 Father Samway lectured on Faulkner at various universities in five Francophone African countries at the invitation of the American Embassy in Paris. He has written *Faulkner's "In-*

truder in the Dust": A Critical Study of the Typescripts and has co-edited with Ben Forkner *Stories of the Modern South*. He is Associate Professor of English at LeMoyne College, Syracuse, New York.

ELIZABETH SPENCER published her first novel, *Fire in the Morning*, while she was on the English faculty at the University of Mississippi. Since the publication of that work in 1948, she has written numerous novels, including *This Crooked Way, The Voice at the Back Door, The Light in the Piazza, No Place for an Angel,* and *The Snare*. She has also published a novella, *Knights and Dragons,* and two collections of short fiction, *Ship Island and Other Stories* and *The Stories of Elizabeth Spencer*. Among the numerous awards she has received for her work are a Guggenheim Fellowship in 1953, the Rosenthal Foundation Award in 1956, the *Kenyon Review* Fellowship in Fiction in 1957, and the first McGraw-Hill Fiction Award in 1960. A native Mississippian, she now lives in Montreal, Quebec, where she is writer-in-residence at Concordia University.

FLOYD C. WATKINS is author of *Thomas Wolfe's Characters, The Death of Art, The Flesh and the Word: Eliot, Hemingway, and Faulkner,* and *In Time and Place: Some Origins of American Fiction* and co-editor of *The Literature of the South,* a popular anthology, and *Old Times in the Faulkner Country,* based on oral interviews with John Cullen. Chandler Professor of American Literature at Emory University, he has received the Thomas Jefferson Award, the Thomas Wolfe Memorial Trophy, the Georgia Writers' Association's Award for Literary Achievement, and a Guggenheim Fellowship.